"For ages, in-laws have been the butt of jokes, the source of anguish at couples counseling sessions, and, in some happy cases, the wellspring of much joy and peace. In *I Married My Mother-in-Law*, an anthology of true tales by seventeen writers, the jokes are blessedly few; the stereotypes all but nonexistent; and the poignancy, affection, and strain that can accompany family expansions are penned with insight and grace. The strongest offerings mine the complexity of human relations, going for neither a simply warmhearted response nor a vindictive, angry tirade. Exploring the good, the bad, and the ugly when it comes to in-laws ... the work reflects how we learn about ourselves and the ones we love by navigating the thorny, dubious waters of in-law-hood, and live (one hopes) to tell the tale."
　　　　　　　　　　　　　　　　　　　　　—Los Angeles Times

"For every gleeful in-law basher (Ayelet Waldman, acknowledging what a bad mother-in-law she intends to be, and Amy Bloom, cheerfully explaining why she hates her partner's parents), there's a strong representation of in-law lovers. There's Martha McPhee, who wishes hers hadn't died before she'd known them; Peter Richmond, who came to know his wife better by knowing her mother; and Barbara Jones, who realized her tyrannical father-in-law regretted his poor parenting and was actually a devoted grandfather. For many, having in-laws from another culture ... is unexpectedly rewarding. ... [And] while there's a lot of death in this collection—people seem to experience in-laws mostly in their passing—there's wit, wisdom, and great writing, too."
　　　　　　　　　　　　　　　　　　　　　—Publishers Weekly

continued . . .

I Married My Mother-in-law

AND OTHER TALES OF IN-LAWS
WE CAN'T LIVE WITH—
and
CAN'T LIVE WITHOUT

Edited by

Ilena Silverman

RIVERHEAD BOOKS

NEW YORK

THE BERKLEY PUBLISHING GROUP
Published by the Penguin Group
Penguin Group (USA) Inc.
375 Hudson Street, New York, New York 10014, USA
Penguin Group (Canada), 90 Eglinton Avenue East, Suite 700, Toronto, Ontario M4P 2Y3, Canada
(a division of Pearson Penguin Canada Inc.)
Penguin Books Ltd., 80 Strand, London WC2R 0RL, England
Penguin Group Ireland, 25 St. Stephen's Green, Dublin 2, Ireland (a division of Penguin Books Ltd.)
Penguin Group (Australia), 250 Camberwell Road, Camberwell, Victoria 3124, Australia
(a division of Pearson Australia Group Pty. Ltd.)
Penguin Books India Pvt. Ltd., 11 Community Centre, Panchsheel Park, New Delhi—110 017, India
Penguin Group (NZ), cnr Airborne and Rosedale Roads, Albany, Auckland 1310, New Zealand
(a division of Pearson New Zealand Ltd.)
Penguin Books (South Africa) (Pty.) Ltd., 24 Sturdee Avenue, Rosebank, Johannesburg 2196, South Africa

Penguin Books Ltd., Registered Offices: 80 Strand, London WC2R 0RL, England

While the author has made every effort to provide accurate telephone numbers and Internet addresses at the time of publication, neither the publisher nor the author assumes any responsibility for errors, or for changes that occur after publication. Further, the publisher does not have any control over and does not assume any responsibility for author or third-party websites or their content.

First Riverhead hardcover edition: January 2006
First Riverhead trade paperback edition: January 2007
Riverhead trade paperback ISBN: 978-1-59448-233-5

The Library of Congress has catalogued the Riverhead hardcover edition as follows:

I married my mother-in-law : and other tales of in-laws we can't live with—and can't live without / edited by Ilena Silverman.
    p.   cm.
1. In-laws—Anecdotes. I. Silverman, Ilena.
HQ759.8.I63   2006   2005044939
306.87—dc22

PRINTED IN THE UNITED STATES OF AMERICA
10   9   8   7   6   5   4   3   2   1

Contents

● ● ●

I Married
My
Mother-in-law

INTRODUCTION

The People We Inherit

ILENA SILVERMAN

● ● ●

When I first started contacting writers to ask them whether they'd be interested in contributing to a collection of essays on in-laws, they often responded in two ways, usually in the same breath, and summed up nicely by the one who said, "Arrggg, my in-laws, they're driving me crazy. Insane, really. But I couldn't possibly write about *that*."

In conversation after conversation, these writers had stories to tell, almost blurt, as if they'd been harboring pressing thoughts for a long time. Most agreed that the in-law relationship was complex, even tangled, deeply personal and yet at the same time universal. Many said they'd love to read a book about in-laws, they just couldn't write about their own. Their relationship with them was fraught enough; who wanted to ratchet things up by taking it public?

Eventually, I was able to encourage, persuade, or cajole a group of writers to commit their particular in-law dynamics to paper. Of course, the intensity of those dynamics is nothing new, but the nature of the entanglement has changed over the years. As Stephanie Coontz, the author of *Marriage, a History: From Obedience to Intimacy or How Love Conquered Marriage,* explains, for thousands of years, the primary reason for marrying was to acquire in-laws. Some anthropologists speculate that even in Paleolithic times marriage existed not for companionship, not even to protect women and children, but to connect families. For most of history, who you were related to was everything.

With the stakes so high, parents were extremely involved with their child's married life, beginning with their choice of spouse. Indeed, for thousands of years parents all but controlled their child's marital decisions—with little concern about how the child felt about the potential mate. By the early sixteenth century, both the Catholic and Protestant churches had begun to put more emphasis on encouraging a harmonious relationship between husband and wife, but theological and secular thinkers disapproved of young people marrying mainly for love. Parents were supposed to help their child find someone who the family thought was suitable and whom the child could learn to love. While the Protestant churches did believe that parents shouldn't force a child into a marriage against his or her will, they also held that parents had the last word, especially if they thought the union wasn't in the family's best interest. Indeed, Protestant authorities often dissolved marriages made without parental consent. (The Catholic Church could be a bit looser. Though church officials usually strongly urged a lovestruck couple to capitulate to their parents' wishes to break off marriage, the officials did concede that if the couple successfully resisted those entreaties, they should be able to stay together.)

All of this began to change in the West at the end of the eighteenth and the beginning of the nineteenth centuries. Enlightenment thinkers, committed to the idea that each individual is a rational being with free will, argued that people should be able to make their own choices, including whom to wed. Around the same time, the economies became increasingly nationalized. Getting a job or, say, a loan, was no longer wholly contingent on local and familial connections. By the end of the nineteenth century as people were increasingly judged on their own merits, acquiring the right kind of in-laws became less vital.

But it wasn't until the 1950s, especially in the United States, that a true shift in the role of in-laws took place. With the explosion of suburban single-family housing, marriage counselors, social workers, and some domestic commentators started discussing the merits of *not* involving your in-laws in family life, promoting for the first time the concept of a more independent nuclear family. Yet even as young people were encouraged to be more self-reliant, and even as they embraced that freedom, breaking away was not so easy, nor always entirely desirable. Since then, we've all been struggling with the role of in-laws in our lives.

In this anthology, a broad range of writers—novelists, essayists, journalists—with a broad range of in-law experiences, make their way through this swampy terrain. One issue that comes up again and again involves boundaries. Today, although many of us strive for autonomy from our parents and in-laws, we often come to realize that that inclination conflicts with another: being autonomous from our children. After all, who other than those in-laws or parents will take our children on short notice, for a weekend (or even a week) while we take off on vacation? As Barbara Jones explores in her essay, sometimes having your in-laws involved in your kids' life is worth the price of having them overly involved in your own—even when it means enduring the jolt of finding your father-in-law puttering around your kitchen at seven-thirty on a Saturday morning. Jonathan Goldstein, who lived in an apartment with his girlfriend two floors above her father, isn't sure anything is worth the price. He had to sneak in and out of their building to avoid the possibility of being placed in a headlock by a man nearly three times his age.

Although the nuclear family is now the American model, we still marry into extended families and have ideas about the kind we find attractive. Money can play a role, certainly—as Martha McPhee writes in her essay, some in-laws come with lovely vacation homes and college funds for their grandchildren. So can cultural aspiration. Having grown up a bookish working-class Catholic boy, Anthony Giardina dreamed of falling for Lionel Trilling's daughter, or some equivalent, a Jewish woman endowed with a sort of cultural dowry—intellectual parents who could smooth his entry into the New York literary circles he longed to be part of. He did end up marrying a Jewish woman, but as these things often go, her parents couldn't have been further from what he had envisioned.

There can be emotional benefits as well. When Kathryn Harrison married her husband she also got his father—a great bonus given her troubled ties to her own father. Michael Chabon was also thrilled to have gotten his first wife's father in the bargain, though it meant that one of the painful things about later divorcing was losing his father-in-law, too. And Peter Richmond decided to marry his wife when he met his mother-in-law, believing that she'd step into the role of (distant) superego, eliminating the need for the inevitable spousal nagging, and allowing his marriage to hold its romance forever (you can imagine how successful that was).

While many people are drawn to those who come from similar backgrounds, for others, marriage is an opportunity to step out of their own world and into another. The extent to which you embrace your new family seems connected to the extent to which you found your old family oppressive. Sarah Jenkins was immediately taken with her in-laws, who were far less sophisticated, moneyed, and uptight than her own parents, all of which she found liberating—until the in-laws turned on her as her marriage collapsed. Tom Junod grew up in a loud, chaotic, impractical family with parents who refused to think about the future. He found himself disconcerted but drawn to the steely pragmatism of his in-laws—even while they were dying. And in the case of Dani Shapiro, choosing to get married at all meant rejecting her mother's harsh and narrow view of family life (your immediate family is everything; in-laws are the enemy) and coming to terms with an unfamiliar, inclusive philosophy of family.

Marrying across cultures of all kinds is as old as Romeo and Juliet and yet the tensions those marriages create are forever intriguing: Susan Straight had to prove herself in ways she could hardly have imagined before she was accepted into her husband's African-American family. And Matt Bai had to fall back on his skills as a reporter in order to get his Japanese-American in-laws to tell him anything about their troubling past.

Of course, sometimes in-laws are just an unanticipated burden that nevertheless comes with the territory. Marriage vows speak of sticking it out in sickness and in health, but don't mention anything about the sickness or health of your in-laws. Colin Harrison was confronted with this when, a year into his marriage, his wife's grandmother fell ill. Before he knew it he was scrutinizing the nasal cavities of a ninety-year-old woman, carrying her up and down the stairs, and trying to calm her middle-of-the-night screaming jags.

Then there are the psychic burdens that in-laws inflict on their children and the ways those burdens reverberate through marriages. Darcey Steinke fell in love with her husband because of his rebellious nature and because he tried to reject his parents' life, especially his critical father. But as she eventually and painfully discovered, her father-in-law's malevolence had seeped into his son, too. Amy Bloom hates her in-laws for their inept, mean-spirited parenting. For Ta-Nehisi Coates, even an absent in-law can leave a scar. His partner's father left when she was a baby. Coates has struggled with his partner's resulting distrust of him—and her mother's. And psychic burdens can also work in reverse: Though she tried to tamp them down, Ayelet Waldman was awash in aggressive competitive feelings toward her husband's mother. When her mother-in-law was around, Waldman couldn't help but flaunt the fact that she alone was number one in her husband's heart.

Historically, in-laws meant one set of things: money, connections, status. Today, things are messier, and the essays in this book plumb those messy issues—religion, race, class, boundaries, obligation, envy—that we all wrestle with. For some, in-laws represent a refuge, a great escape from some sort of hardship—economic, cultural, or emotional. For others, they are nothing but trouble, further complicating our already complicated lives. In any case, the ways that our own lives become entwined with the lives of our in-laws provide delicious narratives, and a window onto twenty-first-century family life.

PETER RICHMOND

I Married My Mother-in-Law

● ● ●

I don't remember my mother-in-law's exact words to me
the day I met her for the first time on the beach, nearly
a quarter of a century ago. I do remember that I wasn't
the least bit concerned about having arrived several hours
later than I'd promised I would. What could be the big deal
about showing up late on a Memorial Day weekend anyway?
Wasn't I the best thing that had ever happened to her daughter? I was Choate! Yale! I was a copy editor at *The Washington
Post*! Hadn't Melissa advertised her mother as Philadelphia
Main Line all the way, with a master's in history from Bryn

Mawr, who in her spare time wrote Regency romance novels under a pseudonym? Surely my Ivy-lit pedigree would outweigh what I generously referred to as my personal eccentricities, such as generally giving less than a damn about anyone else.

So on the day in question I'd slept in after my late shift and leisurely made my way from D.C. to Cape May, the resort town at the bottom of the Jersey Shore. It was midafternoon by the time I ambled across the sand and extended a hand in greeting to the woman sitting in the beach chair by Melissa's side. She was deeply tanned, long-legged, slim and fit, silver hair gathered into a neat, aristocratic-looking French twist. No makeup. At fifty-seven, patrician Patricia Davis was an imperiously handsome woman.

Like I said, I'm not certain what her exact words were, but they were probably something along the lines of, "*So glad you could make it.*" I am certain that whatever they were, she delivered them with only a trace of sarcasm, since anything more would have been superfluous, given the expression that accompanied them. It was not a glare. How could a face set in stone express something as overt as a glare? No. It was as if the light in her eyes had blinked out entirely. As if she saw no one in the spot where I stood. The disdain was fairly Rushmored into her finely planed features.

It was a look all too familiar to me by then, an expression I'd seen on the faces of countless deans, headmasters, professors, and editors for years: exasperation, anger, vast wells of disappointment in all the possibility I was squandering.

To which, invariably, my own expression had always been a variation on, "Well, screw you, too."

But this time, I had an entirely different reaction to Patricia Davis's frosted response. I liked it. I liked it a lot.

This is where I should probably mention a few things about Melissa, the woman whom I was actually courting, and why I was doing so. It wasn't just for her looks—striking enough for a sizable number of *Post* reporters and editors to be as interested in her as I was: both pretty and handsome, but nothing too glam. Or the understated and perfectly proportioned and splendidly fit physique. Or the wild sense of humor that made a smile her most natural expression.

No. I was mostly courting Melissa because she was strong and confident and decisive, but soft about it, opinionated without being caustic. She had no fear, and she brooked none in anyone else. On one of our first dates, at my apartment, after we'd finished our late copyediting shifts—she in financial, me in sports—I was moaning about my fear of my boss, a guy named George Solomon, at which point, holding a tumbler of gin with a plum crushed into it (my larder being bachelorly bare), Melissa pronounced, with a surety that stunned me, "Fuck George Solomon."

This was clearly a woman who demanded of the world: put up or shut up. I liked that. At least in theory. In practice, well, that might be another matter. Especially if, over the course of decades, it was me she was demanding it of.

Anyway, back on the beach I found myself apologizing to Pat profusely as Melissa, none too pleased herself, stammered something in my defense. Pat clearly enjoyed my groveling. Then, her point having been sufficiently made, she lightened up, and we instantly set off on a discussion of the book on her lap. I don't remember its title. I am safe in guessing that it was a weighty biography of someone English, at least one century removed.

Was this the moment I decided I would one day propose to her daughter? No. Was this the moment I began to seriously entertain the possibility? Absolutely. For one thing, if this was what Melissa was going to look like thirty years hence, I could definitely live with it. But something else was at work that day. My response to Pat represented one of the first smart impulses I'd ever had. Maybe the first.

For it was about that time in my life that I had begun to pick up distant warning signals from everyone around me, through the thick fog of my prolonged adolescence: that at twenty-seven years old, my irresponsible puppy-dog act was wearing thin on the world at large. The signs were fairly obvious: I was about to be fired from my job. I was developing more than a routine fondness for cannabis and the grape. I was setting my sights on a singular goal of a lifetime of foundering, lazing, and general wastrelness. In short, I was in need of discipline, and on some level I knew it. Somewhere inside most men—usually buried fairly deep—there's enough self-knowledge to admit that they need to have their worst urges restrained. But no man in his right mind would actually seek out a bride to whip him into shape and save him from himself.

But what if the woman came with a mother who could do the job? A surrogate superego as attractive and stylish and classy as her daughter? Who could effect the behavior modification from afar without the man losing face? We all need a conscience. Had I found mine in my prospective mother-in-law?

I must have met Melissa's dad for the first time that night, at dinner at their house, but I don't remember any details. And I should. He was B. Dale Davis, Silver-Haired Newspaper Legend. The kind of guy who lived for the smell of blood-thick newspaper ink and the thunder of a printing press. Dale had arisen from an Appalachian Ohio city to Ohio State University to city editor at the *Detroit Free Press* to eventually take over the whole show as editor-in-chief at *The Philadelphia Bulletin,* which at that time had the largest circulation of any afternoon newspaper in the country. He was a distant, sternly handsome man with a jutting jaw who worshiped at the altar of the Sanctity of the Power and Rightness of the Press. Sometimes he even came home.

But I can't remember a thing about meeting him that night when he showed up at the summer house in Cape May. I do remember one thing about that first evening with the Davises. After dinner, as I scanned their wall-to-wall bookshelves, I came across a history of the Pennsylvania Railroad. Being a railroad freak of serious order, I immediately pulled it down. The author was Patricia Davis. "Yeah, she wrote that," Melissa said. "She doesn't just write the Regency romances. But check this one out." Melissa pulled out a small, thin, leather-bound volume. It was a history of the railroad air brake. By the same author.

Was this the moment I decided I would one day propose to her daughter? Probably not. Was this the moment it became distinctly possible? Absolutely. For, as any railroad-obsessive male can tell you, the invention of the air brake was to railroading what the invention of barbed wire was to the settlement of the West. Clearly this woman's writing had to be taken seriously. So I started scanning the Regency-era romances (*A Scandalous Journey; A Rake's Portrait*) and soon discovered that they were thick with historic detail about England in 1821. Pat loved Great Britain. She didn't approve of its tradition of wanting to rule the world, but she heartily endorsed its undying desire to lather the globe in Britannic customs. Her novels reveled in the minutiae of the period: the height of the candelabra on the lord's table, the texture of the heroine's dress ("a warm cherry cashmere trimmed in lace"). Her books were full of words like "widgeon" and "cosset."

I was not only intrigued by Pat's unabashed reverence for All Things Anglo, but the restraint her WASPness implied, too; she seemed to need no obvious sensory pleasures. She hardly ever ate. (It was that first weekend when Dale told me about the shopping list he'd once left for Pat, magneted to the refrigerator. It read, "Food. Any kind.") She had a few close friends, but she didn't care if she was in touch with them. Between the books she wrote and the books she read, between her annual month in London and her annual month in Antigua (the British Caribbean), she had all that she needed.

To Pat's publisher's dismay, her tales were short on bodice-ripping, but this only suggested to me that her sexuality was one step removed, relegated to a discreet place—a state which—ah, youth!—wasn't the case at all with her daughter. In their other appetites, though, Melissa and her mother were quite alike. Melissa didn't eat more than was nutritionally necessary. Both smoked cigarettes. Melissa enjoyed good wine, and while Pat was a recovered alcoholic—nearly thirty years sober when I met her—she fully understood the place of a good drink in an otherwise well-lived life.

Over the course of the next several months, as I spent more time in Melissa's apartment, one thing more than any other drove home how much the two had in common intellectually and emotionally: their Sunday *New York Times* crossword competitions. Immediately upon arising every Sunday, Melissa would procure a *Times* from Schwartz's drugstore on Connecticut Avenue, flounce down on her couch, discard the actual paper, and attack the crossword. Up on the Main Line, Pat was procuring her paper from the pharmacy down by the train station in Haverford. Somewhere between ten and eleven in the morning, Melissa would let out a cry of triumph and grab the phone (unless Pat had called first, to declare her own victory). But instead of saying "I finished," or "I won" (she never uttered those words, as I assume Pat never did; it would have been too crass), Melissa would say something like, "I thought it was easy—didn't you?"—a not-so-subtle but good-spirited dig, because obviously, if Pat hadn't finished yet, she hadn't found the thing easy at all. On the surface, these were hotly contested contests of wills and wits, where Pat would triumph if the big clue involved an obscure quote from a John Marquand novel or a working knowledge of monarchical lineage. Melissa would prevail if the puzzle were anchored, say, in modern fiction, or a familiarity with Tears for Fears and the B-52s. Their competition was admirably civil, too; the winner would give the loser help in the clues she hadn't gotten, and the loser would gladly accept it. At first, I thought this was odd: in any contest, I couldn't imagine myself or any of my male friends asking for help after we'd been defeated. But quickly I came to understand that the puzzle was just a front: a ritual that gave Melissa and her mother a weekly forum to exchange notes on life. Overhearing one end of their conversation during this weekly dialogue, I was able to fill in the other end of the conversation and intuit many of their shared views—not only about people and places and authors and eras, but about character and integrity and the relationship between the sexes.

This latter category could pretty much be whittled down to a handful of Pat Davis truisms, most of which involved a single tenet, one that her daughter had obviously embraced: that while a woman was not only every man's equal but in most ways his superior and could certainly take her rightful place in any workplace, she was also entitled to marry—should marry—a GP: a Good Provider. Said GP was expected to ensure financial and emotional solvency for the length of the relationship—which, in the Davis household, had to be a term that lasted for the rest of time. This was a given: there were to be no divorces in Davisland, and the onus for that lay entirely in the lap of the male, who, being severely flawed by nature, was always going to work harder at keeping the couple together.

All of this seemed reasonable enough to me. I expected to earn my fair share of the bread. I liked the idea of sharing it with an equal. But by now it was fast becoming clear that my assumption that I'd be able to easily convince Melissa to marry me—when I was ready, on my own terms—was a fragile one. Clearly, I now knew, if I was going to marry a Davis I was going to need not only Pat's approval, but her wholehearted endorsement. And Pat was constantly chiding me about all the loose ends in my bachelor life—the insurance forms left unfilled-out, the expired car registration, the un-pressed dress shirts, my general obliviousness to and disre-gard for anything that didn't directly involve the fulfillment of my own needs. If Pat gave me grief about something, I tended to respond. And while I welcomed this editing of my life from afar, a troubling thought began to occur to me: the more Pat got to know the real me, the less likely it might be she'd rubber-stamp my proposal, if and when it came.

That autumn, I escaped from *The Washington Post* one step ahead of the guillotine and landed a plum sportswriting job at *The San Diego Union:* my kind of paper, where reporters called it a day at six o'clock to go home to light the coals and a joint, off the same match, even if their story for the next day's paper was unfinished. In San Diego in the early '80s, where a photograph of the day's sunset led the eleven-o'clock news, news could wait, but beach volleyball couldn't. Melissa, for some reason, had thus far refused to consider chucking her promising career as an editor at a real newspaper to come live with me in eternal, brain-dead sunshine.

It was a couple days before Christmas, and I was on a plane flying back east for a weekend with Melissa and Pat and Dale at their house in Haverford, Pennsylvania, when I noticed that the guy in the seat in front of me was huge with muscle. He had to be a football player. He had to be a San Diego Charger. So he had to be a story.

I had two choices: enjoy my vodka and tonics for six hours, or be an enterprising reporter. Was it with Pat in mind that I literally climbed over my seat and dropped into the empty seat next to the big guy? I'd been right: he was a Charger, a little-used substitute lineman, with—if memory serves—a sad season behind him, anxious to get back to his family. It was a good story for the newspaper. And it made for an even better story for me: after arriving at the Davises's rambling clapboard, I breathlessly asked if they had a quiet room so I could work.

It was Pat who flew into action. Dinner could wait. She sat me down in a corner of the kitchen, provided me an electrical outlet, a phone line, coffee, and silence. I wrote my story and filed it in time to make the front of the sports page the next morning. As soon as I finished, I could tell that I'd just climbed about eight notches in Pat's estimation. I remember Pat beaming at my enterprise. I even remember my beaming at my enterprise. It was one thing to meet your deadline writing a sidebar to a baseball game for a last-place baseball team in an empty stadium. It was another to ferret out a narrative, weave an uplifting Christmas tale, and make the front page of the section—without even being asked to—and then sit down to your well-earned reward: a game bird, some great wine, the respect of the table in a family whose newspapering standards were high.

W as that the night I decided that my instincts about the Davis women were good? That a partnership with a woman whose mother, by playing the role of absent disciplinarian, might even lighten the psychic load on the marriage, and free Melissa and me to concentrate on the romance? Apparently so. My next flight east came a few months later, so I could accompany Melissa to a party honoring the promotion of a *Post* editor. The event was held in a lovely, comfortable, fireplace-blazing home. Maybe it was the surroundings. Maybe it was the superb cabernet. I sure hadn't given it much forethought. But when the time came for the speeches, I hauled Melissa into the next room, planted her in a chair, got down on my knee, and proposed. After several excruciating seconds of silence, designed and brilliantly executed to torture me, she accepted.

So now I had a woman for life. Well, I had two.

A few months after we married in a small civil ceremony, *The Philadelphia Bulletin* folded beneath the weight of obsolescence. Shortly after, Dale called it a career, and he and Pat retired to Cape May to live full-time. My own career had done a one-eighty. I'd become an enterprising enough writer to be hired away from San Diego by *The Miami Herald* as their national sportswriter, where, over the next several years, I covered World Series and Super Bowls and title fights and Olympics, first out of Miami, then out of the paper's New York City bureau.

Melissa's and my first decade together went pretty much as I'd envisioned it, only a little better. Surprised and delighted that we might have actually made the right choice, we not only got along increasingly well as partners, we discovered that we were really good friends, too. We produced a matched set of children, one boy and one girl. Both had red hair, though neither of us did, and this somehow confirmed the charmed nature of the quest on which we'd embarked.

I traveled extensively for my job, and I looked forward to my trips. With two small kids at home, who wouldn't relish the chance to regularly check out and leave the day-to-day responsibilities behind? Especially when my sojourns were all justified in the name of being a GP? ("Honey, it's not my fault the All-Star game is in Kansas City this year.") I came to anticipate my visits to anonymous chain motel/hotel rooms in various midwestern downtowns, at endless highway intersections. The rooms collectively grew on me like a cocoon from which I never hoped to hatch. They were silent. They had sports on the TV. In elevators, at breakfast, I was surrounded by nameless men with whom I had to exchange few, if any, words: the ideal notion of male friendship.

We'd visit the Shore on occasion, but hardly frequently. Pat had never been the kind of woman who enjoyed being around kids, and while she had six grandchildren by now, counting Melissa's four nieces and nephews, she would never in a million years have described herself as a grandparent—not because of the age it implied (she had no fear of growing old), but because such a label would convey too passive an identity for her. While Pat made it clear we could visit if we wanted, she never encouraged it. Dale liked the idea of being a grandfather in theory, but in practice, he was sort of clueless when it came to small children.

As we began our second decade of marriage, I landed a staff writing job at a major magazine. We settled into a drafty, asbestos-shingled old farmhouse on ten sweet acres in the outback of upstate New York, where Melissa, having put her career on hold to raise the kids, took to rural life and its manual-labor rigors with a true passion. She found an unforeseen calling in gardening, and in the winters, she single-handedly renovated just about every room in our house.

Soon after we'd moved in, a cancer that Dale had beaten back years earlier returned; this time its invasion was persistent. One day, Pat called to ask me to telephone Dale's oncologist in Philadelphia to get a bottom line on his chances.

She didn't want to make the call herself. Despite the circumstances, I remember feeling a guilty pleasure that I'd been chosen for such a grave task.

It wasn't good, the doctor told me. It would be fatal, and it wouldn't take too long. I relayed the news to Pat, who had expected it, and took it well. If nothing else, she could now prepare. I suspected her apparent stoicism was a solid defense mechanism, another example of the Davis women's innate strength.

Within a year, Dale died. I began to visit Pat regularly, driving down to Cape May from upstate New York in the middle of the week in the dead of winter to keep her company. These trips struck Melissa and her sisters as generous. I never disabused them of the notion, but it wasn't entirely accurate. My regular visits to the Shore were islands of sanity for me. Because somewhere along the line, things had shifted in our marriage: where once I'd counted on Pat to be my superego, freeing up space so that Melissa and I could be in love, in our second decade, the friendship that had formed the core of our marriage had started to erode. It was apparent that having Pat as a critic from afar hadn't done anything to temper the same instinct in her daughter. By now, Melissa's support of me was everything I'd expected it to be, and less: that is, entirely equivocal. She tolerated no whining, no self-indulgence. My complaints about the inequities of life, of the successes of my peers, of the increasing difficulty of writing, fell on her deaf ears. She was fair. She was tough. Sometimes her reprovals were just about what I wanted to hear. Mostly they weren't.

I began to feel increasingly nagged, and underappreciated. My stories were chosen for Major Anthologies! I'd published two books! I got fan mail from strangers! What could my mundane domestic failures—not washing the bottom of the dinner plates; not paying the electric bill; forgetting where I put her hammer, or the kids' Christmas presents, or my wallet, or my paycheck—matter in the grand scheme of things? I could be sitting in a distant wing of our rambling house and feel Melissa's heat-seeking darts of disapproval, issued from another floor. That this was (almost entirely) delusional on my part didn't lessen my growing sense that I deserved more fawning at home. Melissa, of course, was growing increasingly tired of raising three kids— the two real kids, and me.

During this time, paradoxically, my emotional refuge turned out to be with Pat. Down at the Shore, she would always have a good bottle of wine waiting for me as soon as I arrived, and vicariously delighted in my enjoyment of it. I'd show up armed with a trunkload of firewood I had split at home, and I'd light a fire in the big fireplace that Dale had always loved.

Over my glass of wine and Pat's Perrier—where did she get Perrier in a bottle the size of a flashlight battery?—she would ask about my career, my triumphs, my mess-ups. In a way, it was as if I were checking in with an old professor. A mentor. But in retrospect, there was a sort of romantic quality to it, too. Pat and I would talk about news, and movies, and history. Well, she'd talk. I'd listen. Having surrendered most of my schooling years to various narcotic influences, I was making up for lost time, happy to absorb her lessons. I delighted in being her only student. Increasingly, we'd debate politics. The older Pat grew, the more conservative and intractable she became, but she never lost her sense of humor about it.

She still kept me in line—if she didn't like a story I'd written, she let me know. If she thought I was being unreliable with money or the other mundane responsibilities that other husbands seemed to cope with instinctively but baffled me entirely, she'd let me know about it.

But she was also fulsome in her praise, when I deserved it. By now, I knew that she was taking more satisfaction in my victories than in my setbacks. I could count on her to be disapproving in predictable ways, but her disapproval was easy for me to take, far easier than it would have been if I heard it from her daughter. Which, of course, I did. Interestingly, Melissa didn't seem to mind my visits down to the Shore. She would never admit it, but I knew that she delighted in my attention to her mother. Not only did it represent the affirmation of my love for Melissa (she was most definitely her mother's daughter), but also it got me out of the house, and gave us space, without any scratches, dents, or scars in our marriage.

On most of my visits, Pat and I would go out for lobster, at the restaurant on the Cape May dock, where the waitresses dressed in old-style white uniforms, the kind of place that's unashamed to serve a lot of melted butter. Sometimes we'd have the huge dining room almost to ourselves: me, the disheveled New York writer in his forties, she, the reed-thin woman in her seventies wearing a Chanel suit, her gray hair piled elegantly on her head, a beacon in the dead of winter in a tacky beach town. She'd have us in and out of there in fifty-nine minutes, tops, and afterward, back at her house, she'd watch TV while I pulled books down from those shelves.

The next morning I'd drive into town to get the newspapers—the *Times,* the *Inquirer*—and bring them into her bedroom, and sit in the large easy chair at the foot of her bed while she did the Jumble and the crossword and I read the sports section. It was the only time I ever saw her with that great hair down, spilling over the back of her ankle-length nightgown, like some Englishwoman from a Merchant-Ivory film.

For a brief time, I'd found a sort of netherworld: I could spend time with a woman who was very much like the woman I loved back home, without any of the stupid day-to-day friction that inevitably accumulates over so many years. On top of which, in a weird way, my relationship with Pat helped guarantee my relationship with Melissa. It helped ensure I wouldn't pull a midlife about-face, the way some guys did. Like any sane man who'd spent twenty years being told by the same person to pick up his towels, I often entertained thoughts of independence, of the freedom to watch three football games on a single Sunday, to play old Clash CDs at the volume they were intended to be heard, and to meet Kate Winslet at a hotel bar in Topeka one night when neither of us had anything better to do. But spending time with Pat always helped bring me to my senses. It reminded me that if I left, I'd probably miss her nearly as much as I would miss Melissa. Also, there's no way I could have survived Pat's wrath. Remember Melissa's heat-seeking darts? Pat would have used nuclear missiles. If I'd ever flown the coop, Pat's sheer force of will would have hunted me down wherever I was and vaporized me.

I don't get down to the Shore much anymore. Pat doesn't need the company; over the last few years, she's acquired a close-knit group of friends, including some younger couples in their sixties. She continues to travel to England each autumn.

But we did all get down to Cape May for a recent Thanksgiving. Pat hadn't seen the kids in a while. My daughter Hillary, a ninth-grader in an all-girls boarding school, instantly met with Pat's approval. But Pat didn't try to hide her disdain for my son Max, a state-university college-freshman Holden Caulfield who possessed the self-initiative of a slug on Quaaludes. His thick red hair spilled, unwashed, to the middle of his back; his red beard was scruffy. On a good day, he looks like Charles Manson playing the lead in a passion play. On any day, for most of his life, he has paid little to no attention to my attempts to discipline him. I consider this normal, if hard to take day-to-day.

Five minutes into the meal, Pat was on Max's case: his grades, his surface carapace of grumbly attitude, his looks. And he was taking it, good-naturedly. He was listening to her. Then, as is his wont, Max steered the conversation into politics, and the Great Debate began. As far to the right as Pat's beliefs have become, Max's are even further left. And with each reactionary generality Pat threw out, Max answered—not only countering her ideology, but producing statistics. Then, halfway through the turkey, Max abruptly rose to leave the table, with no explanation. I feared the worst until, seconds later, he returned with a sheet of condemnatory facts about the Bush administration he'd downloaded from his grandmother's computer, and handed it to her.

Pat read the pages, nodded, conceded a few of his points, and parried back. Max conceded a few of her points, but pressed on. As the two of them hurled words back and forth, I took in the scene: an imperious woman in her eighties dressed in an elegant pumpkin-colored suit and a nineteen-year-old kid wearing a T-shirt imprinted with the Moscow subway system—the two of them locked in verbal and intellectual combat, and each of them clearly enjoying it.

I felt two overwhelming emotions: jealousy that Max had Pat now, as a surrogate superego; and a sense that the mantle had been rightly passed on. Max definitely needs Pat. Me? Not anymore. Not in that way. Now well into decade number three of marriage to her daughter, I can see that many of Pat's lessons have taken hold. I no longer need Pat to be anything more than a grandmother to my children, a weekly crossword contestant for my wife, and a host for beach visits during summer holidays. Our kids are more or less fully baked; we've given them our best shot, for better or worse, and how their lives turn out is mostly up to them, which means that Melissa and I have the psychic space and time to be friends again. As we both pass fifty it's as if we've cleared the rapids on a whitewater plummet and reached the calm waters; we can drift with each other again.

Melissa is now just four years younger than Pat was when I first met her over Labor Day a quarter century ago, and sure enough, there's more than enough of the old Pat-on-the-beach in Melissa now, to go along with all her Melissa-ness. My wife is my best friend, my lover, my companion, and my superego all rolled into one. By now it's a given: One lifetime, one marriage. I have abided by the No-Divorce statute in Davisland. This pleases Pat immensely, of course, and it pleases me, too.

AYELET WALDMAN

Dividing the Man
from His Mother

●●●

When my son Zeke was in preschool he came home every day and headed straight for the couch. He pulled me down next to him and cleaved his plump body to my own less adorably rotund one. He pressed his soft lips to my neck, nuzzling under my chin, breathing deep as if he wanted to inhale every molecule of the fragrance he had missed in the four hours of our separation. He placed his palms on my cheeks and kissed me on the lips, languidly yet gravely, like a very small, round-cheeked lover.

I can't say that while he was gone I missed him as much as he missed me; after all, I did not prove my devotion by spending our time apart dripping tears onto the sand table and rocking in misery on the cushions of the book nook. I was too busy reveling in my time alone, getting my work done, going for solitary walks, reintroducing myself to my husband. But when Zeke returned I leapt onto the couch with as much eagerness as he. Holding his fleshy, silky body was the most satisfying tactile experience I have ever had in my life. The flawlessness of an infant's skin is a trite metaphor, but his baby skin was even more buttery than most. And I'm not a child-aggrandizing mother blinded by love. I have four children, and this boy's skin was different. It felt like the freshest heavy cream tastes: smooth and round, fat and thick on the tongue. His body, too, was different. It's a wonder how what can inspire such disgust on an adult can be so delectable on an infant. Zeke is seven years old now, as thin and wiry as a half-starved whippet, but when I close my eyes, I can still feel the give of his plump baby flesh under my fingers.

Once, a few years ago, while we were driving over the hill leading to our house, we passed the bright purple house that had always been his older sister's favorite.

"That's where we'll live when I grow up," Zeke said.

"Who? You and the person you marry?" Note that I didn't say wife. Those of us who raise our families in Berkeley would never make assumptions about our children's sexual orientation.

"No. You and me."

"Aren't you going to get married and have children?" I asked, hearing to my horror a hint of the whine of my fore-mothers. You can take the babushka off the Jewish mother and dress her up in a pair of 7 jeans and Marc Jacobs sling-backs, but she's still going to expect a passel of grandkids.

"My wife will sleep on the first floor with daddy. You and I will live on the top floor. Together."

It's possible that a psychologically sound mother, a mother whose role model isn't the floating maternal head in Woody Allen's *Oedipus Wrecks*, would not have been quite so pleased. Certainly a better mother would not have congratu-lated her son on such a fine plan and offered to cover half the mortgage.

Even now, although Zeke's pride does not allow him to linger in my arms for much longer than a minute or so, he still calls for me to lie with him at night, he still gives me "movie kisses"—kisses that last for a little longer than usual and involve a lot of twisting of the head and moaning. He still cuddles up to me, pressing his needle-chin and knobby knees into me before spinning off to pick up his skateboard or go to the computer. And he still plans to exile his wife to the far reaches of the lower floors of the purple house.

I do not envy this phantom daughter-in-law of mine. I pity the young woman who will attempt to insinuate herself between my mama's boy and me. I sympathize with the monumental nature of her task. It will take a crowbar, two bulldozers, and half a dozen Molotov cocktails to pry my Oedipus and me loose from one another. She'd be better off turning her attention to decorating that downstairs in-law unit.

I sympathize with how much work she faces, but not with *her*. In fact, the very thought of this person, imaginary though she is, sends me into paroxysms of a kind of envy that is uncomfortable to admit. I make jokes about how I hope Zeke is gay so that he will bring home a lovely young man, rather than a nubile young girl who will cast a disparaging and dismissive eye on my crow's-feet and thick waist. This young man would be my friend. My ally even. In the more likely but far less appealing scenario, Zeke and his wife will screen their calls and roll their eyes as I leave increasingly frantic voice-mail messages. She will perfect an impression of me, complete with nasal whine and pinched lips, while he winces at the droll accuracy and drags her off to the bedroom while my forlorn voice begs to the empty air, "Please, darling, give your mother a call, just so that I know you're all right."

You'd think that my experience with my own son would give me sympathy for my mother-in-law. My mother-in-law and I are, in many ways, perfectly matched. Like me she is an attorney. Like her I am an eclectic and voracious reader. Both my mother-in-law and I are far too attracted to stories of personal and medical misfortune, and we enjoy recounting them with exquisite detail. We share the rather unattractive qualities of being both nosy and snoopy. These are not identical traits—the first indicates that we're interested in other people's doings and the second that we are not above making inquiries, subtle or not. A nosy person listens closely to a friend's confidences about her husband's sexual dysfunction, and maybe asks a prying question or two. A snoopy person combs through a friend's medicine cabinet looking for Viagra.

We should have gotten along famously, from the very first moment. And in a sense, we did. We could kill an hour with relative ease. My husband's eyes would glaze over early on in the conversation, but I was always willing to egg her on.

"Was it more like an orange or a grapefruit? Did they get it all?"

"Can't he get his wages garnished for that?"

"How did she even know to get herself tested for chlamydia?"

We share these similarities and I should have had empathy for her. After all, she had experienced what I knew I would eventually: being the first love of your son and then watching helplessly as that devotion shifts.

But I found myself without compassion for her. On the contrary, I couldn't help but feel that my job was to step between her and her son. I cannot trace my attitude to any flaw in my mother-in-law. She is not domineering or overbearing, nor does she treat my husband as a prince around whom she flutters in constant and obsequious attendance. She is a calm and pleasant woman, unassuming and benign.

Our first meeting augured well. We spent an entire weekend in a small hotel suite. My husband, then my boyfriend, brought me to Washington, D.C., where his mother was spending a month working, so that I could meet her. We slept on a pullout sofa, separated from her by the tissue-

paper-thin walls of the suite-hotel. We had not been together very long, my husband and I, only a couple of
months, and we were in the throes of that first hysteria of
sexual infatuation where your body is attuned to your lover's
every breath, and passing a night without proving that to
each other is impossible to imagine.

My mother-in-law gamely ignored us. At meals, she kept
her eyes on her menu while we snuggled on the other side of
the table. She accompanied us on our visits to friends, walks
through the city, nostalgic forays to the neighborhood where
she had raised her son, the man I knew even then that I
would marry, and never once behaved as I would have, if it
had been Zeke canoodling with his girlfriend in the backseat
of the car while I tried to point out how big the trees had
grown in the yard of our old house. My mother-in-law not
only tolerated what can only have been highly irritating behavior, but she actually seemed to enjoy our company.

Despite her fondness for gossip, my husband's mother is a
reserved, quiet woman, the polar opposite to me in this regard.
If, as my husband is fond of saying, my autobiography would
be entitled *Me and My Big Mouth,* hers would be called *Quiet, I'm
Reading.* She is as restrained physically as she is verbally.

The next time we saw each other, at her house, she put
her hand on my shoulder while placing a bowl of broccoli
on the table. That instant of contact had my husband wax-
ing rhapsodic for hours.

"She's never just spontaneously embraced one of my
girlfriends like that," he said, his voice hushed with awe.

"Embraced?" I replied, genuinely confused. "When did she embrace me?"

"At the table. She hugged you at the table."

"You mean that time she sort of bumped into me?"

She's a little looser nowadays, and we hug and kiss easily when we meet after an absence, but she is by no means physically effusive. I have never seen her bump into someone she does not know very well. What felt to me like cool friendliness at the time was warmth to her; what felt to me like an accidental brush of her arm was to her a sign of something special.

None of which explains why, not long after that meal, when my then fiancé and I moved to within half an hour's drive of my mother-in-law, I began to feel an intense sense of competition. The idea to move to San Francisco was mine, I had a new job that took us there, but something about the proximity made me anxious. It brought forth a jealousy that might otherwise have simmered barely noticed, under the surface. I fear that I generated this, entirely within my own head. My mother-in-law had, after all, been through this once before; I am my husband's second wife, and the last in a long line of girlfriends. She must have been resigned to her fate as perennially second in his heart.

From early on, I felt deeply territorial about my husband and approached our relationship with a kind of ravenous intensity. When we first met, my husband and I told each other about our previous relationships. We traded details, laughed over them, shared inside jokes with one another. I think I felt that only if I could insert myself into his history, consume it, if you will, could I assert the primacy of our relationship over all those prior ones. If I knew as much as he did about those women, especially his ex-wife, I could be secure.

My husband also told me about his childhood, as much as he remembered. I think much of my jealousy of my mother-in-law sprang from my belief that there were long years of his life that belonged exclusively to her, that lived only in her own memory. Those were years, I imagined, when she was the sun around which his little-boy self revolved. I could never own those years the way I tried to own the other epochs and loves in his history.

In thinking about my husband's relationship with his mother, I wonder if the very thing that should have given me the most peace of mind was what caused me the most consternation. There was none of the *Sturm und Drang* I was used to from my own family. They seemed genuinely to enjoy each other's company, but not to be overly involved with one another. There was no bickering, no unrealistic demands, no slammed phones, no waves of passion and rage. They were *easy* with one another—mild even. They were the very opposite of Woody Allen and his mother's floating head. I was confused by it. It was so unlike anything I understood a maternal-child bond to be. I, who called my mother three times a day, just didn't *get* that my husband and his mother could love each other without being overly entangled.

At the same time, I failed to be comforted by the fact that he made a deliberate choice to be with a woman whose temperament, unlike his mother's placidity, runs to extremes of passion and mood. You'd think these very differences would have made me more confident in my primary place in my husband's heart. You'd be wrong.

This tug-of-war between a mother and her daughter-in-law over a man is an age-old phenomenon, the stuff of sit-com jokes and Greek tragedy. Two women, decades apart, vying over the favors of a man who most often doesn't even know a battle is being fought. It's easy to imagine why women who define themselves through the status of the men in their lives and the attention those men pay to them would end up in competition. But neither my mother-in-law nor I is a woman like that. We are both women who pride ourselves on our independence, our careers. Even in the absence of an overbearing and territorial counterpart, I slipped into the combative role easily, as if it was an inevitable part of being a woman marrying a man. It was as though the need to be the one, the *only*, in his life overcame even the most common of sense.

My campaign was subtle, and at the time I didn't even realize I was waging war. I insinuated myself between them delicately but decisively. I began complaining to my husband about my mother-in-law, and my primary target was her reserve. "How can you stand such diffidence?" I kept asking.

"Doesn't it drive you crazy?" Through cues as understated as holding his hand when we were with her, I tried to make my primacy known. My husband and I were planning and paying for our own wedding, and we limited the guest list to our families and our own friends, effectively making my mother-in-law—and, by necessity of fairness, my own parents—mere invited guests at their own children's wedding.

When my husband and I spent time with my mother-in-law, I found myself using the first-person plural, an exclusionary tense if ever there was one. "We loved that movie," I would say. Or, "That's our very favorite restaurant, we'll take you next time we go." All this by way of showing her that he and I were a unit, a couple. *The* couple.

I even resented the weekly lunch date my husband and his mother shared. I had the grace to be ashamed of this resentment and tried to hide it, but I must have failed dismally, because over the course of our first few months together those lunches gradually ceased. Then I thought she barely noticed that they no longer lunched together, or didn't care, but in retrospect I think she just kept her feelings to herself.

My mother-in-law's style is much more subtle than my own. Because of her natural reserve she would never have mentioned our rivalry, and it's even possible that she didn't feel it. Or at least wouldn't acknowledge the feeling. But it was there, lurking under the surface of even our most positive of interactions.

My husband, like husbands in so many of this most stereotypical of domestic dramas, did his best to keep everyone happy, but I think the primary emotion he experienced was confusion. After all, it was clear to him I was his beloved. She was his mother. Two relationships entirely different one from the other.

I think he probably wished I'd just give it a rest.

And so this undercurrent of tension remained, with me grudging the time we spent with my mother-in-law, suggesting, for example, that he and I have a private Thanksgiving dinner in a beautiful lodge in the mountains, instead of with his family.

Then we had children, and something began to change. It was a gradual shift, one that it took me a while to notice. But when I became a mother I began, almost imperceptibly at first, to relax. Suddenly there could be no question that *we*, my children and I, were the primary family unit in my husband's life. It was as if once it became obvious that the competition was over, I could take my mother-in-law into my heart with all the grace of a good winner. Somehow, effortlessly, all the antagonism of our relationship began to evaporate. Once I was absolutely sure of my ascension and her usurpation, I could give in and become her friend.

A couple of years ago I invited my mother-in-law on our yearly family vacation. The invitation was a selfish one. With four children, the hotel would not allow us to cram into a single bungalow, and if we didn't bring a third adult, my husband and I would be forced to spend our vacation in separate rooms. I invited her as a glorified nanny. Within hours it became clear that she was much more than a third pair of hands.

Travel with four small children had always been gratifying in its way, but so too it had been a special kind of misery, with anxiety, squabbling, and lots of vomit. This time, while one child threw up in my lap, another ran down the airplane aisle to the bathroom, and two more catapulted out of their seats in a shrieking wrestling match, my mother-in-law kept her cool. She always keeps her cool. That's who she is. She can sometimes be stern, but she never loses control. What was miraculous was that when she was there, neither did I.

I went from resenting my mother-in-law to accepting her, finally to appreciating her. What appeared when I was first married to be her diffidence, I now value as serenity. The capacity for extravagant emotion that my husband finds so attractive in me can be exhausting, especially to a child. My moods are mercurial, and this can be terrifying. I know, because I was a daughter of a mother with a changeable temperament. My mother-in-law's mood is always consistent. She is the opposite of capricious. She is the most reliably steady person I have ever known.

Once, I chafed at any hour my husband spent with his mother, somehow viewing it as time stolen from me. Now they take our oldest daughter to musicals, an entertainment I find tedious in the extreme, or my husband takes all four of the kids to his mother's house for dinner when I am out of town. But my mother-in-law and I are far more likely to go out just the two of us. We go shopping, we go to the movies.

I enjoy spending time with her. She's a good companion, part friend, part mother. When my husband is out of town, she comes over for dinner, and having her in the house eases all of us.

Last February, in Hawaii, we sat side by side under a tree on matching lounge chairs. My husband was in the water with the older children and the babies were playing in the sand next to us. We had each just finished the novel we were reading and had swapped, something I can rarely do with my husband, because he is a slow and methodical reader and because he is most often immersed in something like a 1,300-page annotated volume of Sherlock Holmes short stories or Gnome Press's *The Porcelain Magician* by Frank Owen. My mother-in-law can be relied upon to have the new Philip Roth or Lorrie Moore. I remember looking out at my husband diving smoothly under the waves, and at the sun-kissed faces of my two youngest towheads as they dumped sand on their grandmother's feet. In the moment of quiet before the baby walloped his older sister on the head with his shovel and she kicked him over in the sand, I thought to myself, "This is nice." Then pandemonium broke out, and there were tears to dry and egos to soothe.

After we had finally managed to calm things down, my mother-in-law held my young daughter on her lap, and I held my infant son. He snuggled against me, his velvet cheek rubbing my chest. He smelled deliciously of coconut sunscreen and the strawberries he'd eaten for breakfast. He was just under a year old and had only two words reliably in his vocabulary, but one of them was "Mama." When he said my name I kissed him, rubbing my lips against his soft, rubbery mouth and tickling his sun-warmed belly. I looked over at my mother-in-law. She returned my gaze with a complicated one of her own. I could tell that the sight of her baby grand-son lolling on his mother's lap under a palm tree in the dappled Hawaiian shade pleased her. I wonder, though, if something else wasn't giving her just the tiniest bit of satis-faction. The prospect that one day I was going to do battle with this boy's wife, just as I had done battle with her. And I was going to lose.

MARTHA McPHEE

Longing for In-laws

●●●

I first met my husband at a New Year's Eve party in New
York City, a cold snowy night in 1992. He was in a room
filled with men, all of whom were drinking Scotch or cham-
pagne, smoking cigars. My husband stood among them, tall
and strikingly good-looking with his blue eyes sparkling as
he laughed at something someone had said. I watched him
from the doorway. It took only a moment for me to fall in
love. I loved the intensity of his eyes, how they caused him
to appear remote and mysterious, perhaps a little sad. I
wanted to know who he was, what made him sad, fancied I

could save him from whatever it was. But this desire made me shy.

As it happened, I was at the party with my sister Jenny and her husband, Luca. I brought her to the room of men and I said to her, "There is one man here that I find attractive." She gave the men a quick scan and made a beeline for the one who would become my husband. She wanted to help out her little sister. She began flirting with him, cocking her pretty smile, laughing at everything he said. She discovered that he was a poet, teaching in New York though he wanted desperately to return to Seattle. He had two much older brothers. His parents were dead. He knew no one at this party. Around eleven, ignited by the ease with which Jenny spoke to him, I joined the flirting. We flirted so relentlessly with this handsome man that you can hardly blame him for having a fantasy about a pair of sisters, though he was a bit confused by the presence of Luca. At midnight I claimed Mark, kissing him beneath the mistletoe.

Thus began the overwhelming gravitational pull of my family, which sucked Mark in immediately and entirely. In the first months of our love affair he visited both my childhood homes, flipped through countless photo albums chronicling my past, met all four of my sisters, my mother, my father, my stepmother, my stepfather, my five stepbrothers and four stepsisters. In my Upper West Side neighborhood, three sisters, one stepbrother, and one cousin lived within a six-block radius of my apartment. "The McPhee ghetto," Mark soon began to call it.

Just when it seemed there could be no one else to meet, my grandmother arrived for a weeklong visit.

"What is your surname, son?" she asked Mark upon first meeting him. You can tell a lot from a name, she had always said. A white-haired lady with a strong jaw and piercing green eyes, she sat in an armchair upholstered with brocade silk in yellow gold—à Victorian side chair from the late nineteenth century. She told Mark the chair had belonged to her husband's family, the Browns of the Buster Brown shoe company. My grandfather had been the model for the boy in all the ads. They were "blue bloods" from Boston—it did not matter that they had lost all their money. "Eleven generations Lynn," my grandmother was fond of saying, referring to the once upscale Boston suburb. The Battle of Bunker Hill had been fought in their pasture, Breed's Pasture. My grandmother had made it her business to know everything there was to know about her in-laws. For her they represented an arrival of sorts, her quest from childhood to better her lot. She had grown up with a divorced mother, impoverished in Montana. Paper bags served as shoes, even in snowstorms. As a small girl she had dreamed of heading east to a refined life in New York, of marrying a gentleman. She had many dreams, including a narrative for her own biography that related her to royal Stewarts from Nairn and advisers to Bismarck and heirs to the Dole Pineapple Empire and somehow to James Fenimore Cooper. Colorful stories, stories of Indian massacres and a little old woman who lived to be a hundred and six and a woman who escaped the

Confederates during the Civil War by hiking across the Alleghenies with her seven children in tow. With these stories (real or imagined, it made no difference), she and her family had a clear spot on the crowded slate of the past. She knew where she came from and where she was headed, and by George if this tall dark man sitting in front of her was going to be involved with her granddaughter, he had better have something to offer.

"Svenvold," Mark answered. My grandmother and her stories amused Mark. He had never had a grandmother. They had both died when he was quite young. Indeed, if her stories could fill a thousand pages, his could fill only a few, and the number of relatives to whom he was close could easily fit into a small room.

"Norwegian," Grammy declared. She eyed him, studying him, dissecting him. "Royalty?" she mused, though it was a question that she seemed to be trying to answer simply by studying him. "The dark-haired ones have the royal blood." She wanted something for her granddaughter even if he invented it.

"Wheat farmers," Mark said with false apology. His story was simple, honest, and short. His grandfather came to Montana at the turn of last century and settled a two-thousand-acre farm. Mark's father, Harold, left the farm during the Depression, hitching rides on freight trains to places where he could work as an itinerant apple-picker. He helped build dams with the Civilian Conservation Corps. Eventually he earned a master's in business administration and fell in love with a woman named Marian from Cody, Wyoming. He met her at a dance somewhere. Mark doesn't know where. "We didn't talk about that stuff," he says of the stories that describe his past. He does not know, for example, if he was ever baptized. After marrying Marian, Harold joined the Air Force and rose to the rank of lieutenant colonel. They had two sons and then, years later, by accident, Mark. A military family, they lived in the Philippines, Texas, Japan, and New Cumberland, Pennsylvania. Harold retired and the family moved to Seattle so that he could take a job at Boeing. In 1988 he died and soon thereafter Marian followed. Mark's two brothers, now in their mid-to-late fifties, live in Renton, Washington. The older, Steve, is a fireman; Lee drives a forklift night shift. Neither brother finished college. This, more or less, is the extent of my knowledge of my in-laws.

Mark, essentially, was alone in the world. I, on the other hand, seemed to have a family that seemed to propagate people. I was part of a circus, a crowd made bigger by the penchant my grandmother had, and that all of us have, to remember and record. We know who and when and where our parents met, that we were baptized, I even know that the priest who baptized me, on the island of Colonsay in Scotland, did not want to because my parents were not practicing Christians. We love story; it is like gossip; it is our way of knowing each other by how we respond, by the emotions we elicit.

Mark's family was not like this. In part because he did not come from storytellers, in part because he was a military child who changed homes and countries every few years, each move erasing the one that came before, erasing friends

and houses and schools and even the clutter of life: childhood drawings and photos and birth and baptismal certificates and other memorabilia, thrown out or lost with the
chaos of the move. The past was something to be forgotten
simply because there was no continuity and there was definitely no going back. The two people who would have been
able to tell me the stories that Mark could not remember or
did not know were dead. Four years would pass before I
would meet Mark's brothers. He was so distanced from
them I thought there was a rift. A family that loved but that
did not talk was anathema to my way of thinking. "Cold
Norwegian love" is how Mark described it. His father only
told him once or twice that he loved him. "I knew that he
loved me," Mark said. "He did not need to say it."

Who were these people? Who was Mark? If Mark had
been sucked into the gut of my family, I felt orphaned by his.

I have been told that I am lucky I have no in-laws. I have
been told to count my blessings. It is easier this way: no
negotiating over where to go for the holidays, a short Christmas list, birthdays that do not need to be remembered,
fewer people to understand and appease, no avoiding the
overbearing mother-in-law. My maternal grandmother had
been an overbearing mother-in-law. My father blames my
grandmother, in part, for his divorce. On their first date
while my father waited for my mother to finish dressing, my
grandmother sat him down in their parlor and told him that
her daughter would never be able to have children. "She has

a split vertebra and it has rendered my daughter incapable of bearing a child." Later, after my father proposed to my mother, my grandmother hired a private investigator to spy on my father. She was suspicious of him because he aspired to be a writer. Once the children were born, she said to my mother, "Now that you've got the babies you can get rid of him."

Notwithstanding my "luck," I have come to long for my in-laws. At holidays I am jealous of my sisters who all have somewhere else to go. My sister Jenny married an Italian and flies off to Florence for Christmas. They go skiing in the Dolomites and the Alps. Laura disappears to Lake George in the summers, Scottsdale in the winters. For Thanksgiving Sarah would always go to the Berkshires and her in-laws would host an enormous game of charades. Her father-in-law was a journalist, so the people collected were New York literary types. To hear Sarah describe the evening, the food, the people, the conversation (politics and *The New York Review of Books*), the game (all these intellectuals trying to act out *E.T., The Exorcist, A Fish Called Wanda*) was like listening to Mary McCarthy describe one of her famous dinners.

These in-laws, they came to visit, they took my sisters shopping, they babysat, they spoiled my sisters with help and good food and evenings out. Someday they might even help them pay for their children's education. Sarah's mother-in-law loved to buy her shoes; her father-in-law affectionately referred to her as being just like him in her fierce intensity, like "a fishmonger from Odessa." These in-laws teased my sisters, listened to them, encouraged them, were proud of them. They added drama and sadness and intrigue. Their lives gave my sisters alternative lives, other stories, more people to love and to be loved by.

Of course there were disagreements and difficulties and of course the in-laws were annoying, but so is everyone you are close to. With their in-laws my sisters had something I did not: they each had a world that had nothing to do with me and the experience of our family, worlds that enriched their lives with a whole cast of other characters, that shaped and explained for them who their husbands were, where they came from, and where they were going.

In late August 1996, I met Mark's brother Steve, the fireman, for the first time. He came to New York because Mark had been diagnosed with a rare form of T-cell lymphoma. I picked Steve up at La Guardia Airport. He was slightly overweight, with a big belly spilling over jeans. His face was jolly and round, his eyes blue, his head balding. Mark was in Sloan-Kettering, getting a second opinion, which involved major surgery to remove a lymph node in the center of his chest. This operation would break a rib, collapse a lung, and leave an eight-inch scar in the shape of a boomerang on his back. He had been diagnosed at another hospital and they were ready to begin treatment, though their prognosis was not good. My sister Sarah forced us to go outside the health insurance network for another opinion before beginning chemotherapy, and thus we found ourselves at Sloan-Kettering. In the midst of all this we wanted to do something upbeat and decided to marry.

At the airport, Steve gave me a big hug, squeezing me so hard it was almost impossible to breathe, a fireman's hug, like the fireman's carry, that takes all of you. The hug said, I love you little sister, and I'm going to take care of you, so you don't need to worry. The hug said, Mark's family is here now in me—every single one of us. I can't remember what he said or how he did it, but within minutes he was making me laugh. He made me laugh all the way from the airport to the hospital, laugh in a way I hadn't since Mark had been diagnosed.

After we parked the car, Steve became serious and asked if I had had experience with illness. I said I had no experience and then I began to cry. Steve held me again and he stroked my hair and he assured me that whatever the outcome I'd be all right. I cried more. I cried uncontrollably. Our odyssey into Mark's illness had begun over six weeks before. My family had, in its wonderful way, swooped down upon us with all its size and force, trying to support us and help us and guide us. Even so, something absolute had been missing. Until I was there crying into Steve's soft shoulder I had not understood how I longed for Mark's family, for it to be more than a few facts and statistics: *parents died of cancer,* filled in on all those medical forms, somehow lending reason to the unreasonable. So I cried, Steve patting my back gently, this man I didn't know holding me. We were parked on the street, somewhere on York Avenue, New York City traffic whizzing by outside the windows.

As it turned out, Mark had been misdiagnosed and did not have cancer at all. I on the other hand had, finally, an in-law. I took him all over New York. I took him to meet my parents, my sisters, my friends. I was so proud to have him. After a while I started asking questions about his parents. He could see what I was after, that I wanted him to resurrect his parents, his family with stories so that I could know them. He tried. Boy did he try. With an earnestness and a deep appreciation for my curiosity. He told me stories about the vast farm in Montana, about his grandfather Rasmus who came to America and made his gold. He went back to Norway on the *Lusitania* to an area south of Stavanger known as the Sveinovol, where everyone is a Svenvold. He came with presents and stories that made America loom large. His return made a huge impression on those he had left behind. After a short while he returned to his farm, sailing again on the *Lusitania*. On its next trip back across the Atlantic it was sunk by a German U-boat.

Steve told other stories, stories of being in the navy in Vietnam, of returning while in the Pacific to Tachikawa Air Force Base and to his high school alma mater, with the hope of recovering some of his own past. He told me that his father golfed and fished and that with his mother, Marian, they vacationed in a camper in the Arizona deserts. He told me that Marian was the creative one, that she played the ukulele and taught all her boys to sing, that Mark was the most like her, that his drive to be a poet came from her. "It did?" I asked. "How so?" I had known from Mark that Marian had been somewhat depressed, that she had had mixed feelings about his accidental conception, about raising another child in her mid-forties. I wondered back to the night I first met Mark, his slightly sad eyes, how I had wanted to know what made those eyes sad. I wanted Steve to add this all up for me. I wanted him to go deep, extricate guts and soul, stories that make you know unequivocally the answers. "Why was she depressed?" I asked boldly.

"She wasn't depressed," Steve answered, "just creative." And then he carried on with funny stories about Mark as a boy, Mark ratting on his older brothers and the like. He told about his father's slow death from leukemia and his mother's fast death from lung cancer. I listened, trying to tease out the seeds that might lead to depth so that I could know Marian and Harold a little better, so they could become more than a military couple, very much of their historic time—she making pink junket in the kitchen, he reading the evening paper in his armchair. After all the stories, however, they were still opaque.

Sometimes lying in bed at night, the room very dark, I'll ask Mark questions about his family. It's like picking a lobster clean, getting into every crevice. I've asked Mark every imaginable question, but I come up with new ways of posing them and he doesn't mind. I want to know how his parents would have treated me. I want to know what we would have done at the holidays had they still been alive. I want to know what it was about them that shaped Mark and his brothers. I want to know how deeply his mother was depressed. I want to know how she tried to hide it from Mark. I want to know why Mark went to college and the other two did not. Why did Mark become a poet? I want to know.

When Harold and Marian died in the late 1980s, Mark inherited, along with a little money, a green Volvo. It was a lime green sedan, stick shift, no power steering. It was new in 1976. They drove it for a good ten years before it became Mark's. The seats were covered in lamb's wool, the glove compartment still had a few relics belonging to my mother-in-law: a map of downtown Seattle; a pair of leather gloves (were they driving gloves?); a snapshot of her garden; a lipstick; a metal tin of Sucrets; a pair of sunglasses; matches and a handkerchief. This car and this glove compartment told me more about my in-laws in a way than anything else I had heard so far. Sitting in this car was tactile, the closest I'd ever come to touching them. The car, given its color, was not bought for aesthetic reasons. It was bought for a good price at an end-of-the-season sale, bought because it was a tank, thus safe, and would go a long distance. (We still have that car. Ten years ago the odometer broke. Already by that time the car had driven the distance to the moon.) It was bought by a man who valued safety and practicality and who also had a good sense of humor—the color. The seats were made comfortable and warm by a gentle caring woman, who wore a fair shade of pink lipstick, just enough color to brighten her lips but not draw attention to them. She liked to drive into Seattle to go to cultural events (a ticket stub to the museum was also found) but didn't know her way around that well, implying it wasn't often that she got into the city. Mostly she loved her garden, which she made riotous with color and flower. When she did drive she wore her sunglasses and her gloves. The gloves aren't for warmth because they are not lined and the glasses are black and curl slightly up at the eyes, catlike. They are stylish, a little flair for a woman who dressed simply in slacks and a shirt and who had her hair done at a local salon.

Mark and I were living part-time in Pennsylvania when I learned that I was pregnant with my first child. On a gorgeous, bright June day, not long after learning this news, I took the green Volvo out for a spin. I knew exactly what I was doing. From the glove compartment I took out the lipstick and used the rearview mirror to put it on—the closest I would ever come to kissing my mother-in-law. I put on the gloves and the glasses. I popped a Sucret in my mouth though I do not like them. I drove and drove and drove over those endless rolling Pennsylvania hills, gentle hills that had once, many millions of years ago, been higher than the Himalayas. I imagined what it would be like to be Marian— a girl from Cody who met a boy at a dance a long long time ago, what it would be like to raise three boys and have one blossom into a poet and marry a girl with an insatiable imagination living in New York City driving around in Pennsylvania pretending to be her mother-in-law. I looked at myself in the rearview mirror and seeing her glasses staring back at me it was as if I were seeing her face staring at me, the grandmother of my child. And I knew for the first time why I so desperately wanted to know who she and Harold were.

"She'd have been flattered," Mark said when I told him how I spent the day. "She'd have wondered why you were so curious about her. She wouldn't have believed there was all that much about her that one would find curious."

"Why is it," I asked, "that you're a poet, that you finished college and graduate school and your brothers didn't?"

"You mean why is one a fireman and the other the driver of a forklift?" I could sense he sensed condescension in my question. "Are you afraid the zygote will drive a forklift?" he asked.

When our daughter Livia was born, the first person I saw upon her tiny face was Steve, and I cried. Steve's pudgy middle-aged face and balding head was not my fantasy for my daughter's beauty. Of course, it wasn't simply the physical appearance, it was the sudden and overwhelming responsibility of being the caretaker of this tiny foreign soul who looked nothing like me, who seemed to belong to a world I only had a vague notion of. I was afraid. All the fears swirled around in my head. If Mark couldn't tell me where he came from (in depth and completely) then how could I tell Livia her whole story, the way my grandmother had done for us? The way the physical presence of my parents and all my siblings had done for Mark. ("You're just like your father," Mark has said after a fight in which I'm particularly impatient. "That's not fair," I always respond. I don't know which parent of his to blame his faults on.) I felt gypped, this time on a large scale. Lying in the hospital bed late at night I thought of all the questions I would have asked Harold and Marian. I would have asked all the questions Mark never did. I would know why Harold was in Wyoming and why he was at that dance. I'd know if theirs was a love-at-first-sight love. I'd know what it was like for Marian to leave Wyoming for the world, to live in Japan, to have three little boys, to be an officer's wife. I'd know her dreams and Harold's dreams. I'd know their favorite foods and their favorite pastimes and I'd know what Marian's father did and where he came from and what brought him to Wyoming and I'd know if Marian ever longed to go back, if Wyoming were in her blood the way a place can be. I'd know if Mark were baptized. I'd know what they smelled like, spoke like, looked like when animated with life. I'd know what a kiss from them would feel like upon my cheek. I'd observe them and interact with them, get caught up in their dramas, have the leisure to find them annoying. Mostly through all this I'd know my husband just a little more completely and I'd know the other half of my daughter's story. I'd know one hundred percent who she is.

After my son Jasper was born, smiling up at me with Steve's face, I realized my children, coming into their own as people, would have to teach me the other half of who they are. I realized that without fail they would.

Sometimes I think of it this way: my husband as some sort of math equation. One of those equations in which you know the final product but only a small part of what makes it. You need to use intuition and subtraction and you need to hypothesize in order to fill in the question mark with the correct answer. Here before me is a tall, dark, handsome poet, a man who loves words, a man with a great sense of humor, a man who is exquisite with his children. His father was Norwegian. His mother came from Cody. They met at a dance and fell in love. Many years later at a party I fell in love with their son. We had two children and now as most couples do, we're making our own life, our own story. What more do I really need to know?

AMY BLOOM

Dead, Thank God

• • •

I don't even know why in-laws matter. They are accidents. They are trim. Without dowries or kingdoms, or penniless schemers, or farms to be passed down, who cares anymore about in-laws? They are not the spouse, they're not even stepchildren, who can ruin a marriage with their Richard III routines or make someone previously childless feel as grateful and gifted as the Magi. I know people who speak of their in-laws (whether maternal or paternal) with great warmth and appreciation (often these are in-laws who bought a house for the young family, supported a daughter-in-law when the husband went MIA, doted on grandchildren, and generally made themselves useful and proved themselves kind) and even more who talk about them with the kind of vitriol usually reserved for mass murderers. (One woman said to me, "That's right, she is. She murdered our family.")

I'm with the latter group.

I hate my in-laws.

This is not going to lead to a warm, cleverly affectionate reveal: I don't really hate my in-laws; I did, but now I don't, or I thought I did, but realized I don't at all, or really, I was just nervous and now we're very close.

I hate them.

I hate their minginess, their poor-mouthing, their harsh unhappiness. I hate their grievous mix of virulent bigotry, neediness, and dependency, which created such a fireball of misery, I am amazed that Joy, my lovely spouse, their only daughter, walked out of it with only garden-variety scarring. When they found out she was gay, her mother turned all of her photographs facedown. They said terrible things about her morals, her nature, and predicted a horrible, unhappy future (they suggested she get a job as a toll collector on the turnpike, to avoid human contact). They also needed her to come home to St. Louis for holidays, to accompany them on various depressing cruises. ("This could be my last one," her mother often said. "When my eyes close, yours will open.") Her father was a mean drunk; her mother was a sad, friendless woman, who followed the CBS soaps, for thirty years. (Which is why I sometimes come home to a woman in the kitchen happy to have the TV on, a room away, unwatched but appreciated.)

I hate that they took a happy girl from black-white-Italian-Jewish Mount Vernon, New York, who had Bella Abzug's daughter Eegie as a best friend and the Abzug accent to match and dumped her in the moonscape of a concrete low-slung apartment complex in a struggling section of St. Louis, with midwestern accents, midwestern superiority, and repressive blandness. I even hate that her father worked as a dental technician, making bridges and inlays. There's no reason to hate that, it's honorable work, it's not being a repo man or a scab, but when we cleaned out his apartment, after he died in 1993, we found boxes and leatherette cases of his tools, and in their vicious points and brittle, crumbling plastic, they reminded me of nothing so much as Olivier's Nazi dentist in *Marathon Man*.

I don't hate my mother-in-law (she died in 1983, after a long illness, through which Joy nursed her) quite as much as I pity her, resent her, want to reach into the beyond and shake her till her teeth rattle, saying, You may have done your best, but how could your best have been so poor? And I do appreciate that Joy feels that, in time, the time we didn't get, her mother would have come to love and appreciate us as a couple and that we would have made her cramped, long-suffering world a happier one, and there are times when I can even see, out of the corner of a more generous imagination, us bringing her large-print books from the library, bringing her to watercolor class, and taking her out for coffee and cake. I can almost imagine that I would know the woman who named

Joy, Joy, and meant it. And maybe, like my mother, after expressing concern and a distressing hesitation over our moving in together, she would sigh, like my mother, and say, "Well, in that case, I have a microwave oven for you girls."

But, mostly, I am content to hate them. I can blame them for every quirk and bend I don't appreciate (saving of moldy leftovers; just falling short of washing and folding used tinfoil; believing that all pleasure will be followed by punishment of an Old Testament nature; low-grade but steady grumbling about the small stuff, which is, I have to say, matched by iron cheer in the face of the big stuff). Unlike so many of my friends, I don't have to hate and blame my in-laws for their awful legacy and present-day unpleasantness and then attend their birthday parties and be nice to them at Thanksgiving, for the benefit of the grandchildren. I don't have to spend hours picking out an expensive cardigan for the drunk, who won't like it; eat my mother-in-law's fish pudding; or listen to either one of them criticize their daughter, make claims about her idyllic childhood and their sacrifices, or run down the grandchildren (messy, lazy, disrespectful) as a way of running down the parents.

The first time someone asked me about Joy's parents, I said, "Dead, thank God." It was a terrible thing to say. I would have been—I would be—upset if Joy said that about her in-laws, and my parents are no day at the beach. What I really mean is that I am grateful. Grateful not to have to manage them, when my hands are full managing my own family; grateful not to have to see Joy as a wounded adolescent or unhappy child, as she sometimes has to see me (and the rapid spin from pouting girl to determinedly kind caregiver is interesting, I guess, but definitely not pretty); grateful not to have to add her parents to our family of three children (now grown, now bringing in boyfriends and girlfriends, and then maybe some babies) and my sister and her new husband and her stepsons and her daughter and my aging parents. I don't see how we could have fit in any more people, unless they were perfect.

So, Joy brought me perfect. She brought us ideal in-laws, her father's cousins and siblings, the Norwegians (which is what we all call them. I don't know what they call us. The Jews? The New Yorkers? Joy's Little Tigers?). They're so wonderful, I wish they didn't live so far away (and isn't that handy?). Her cousins are like her sisters, their daughters like our nieces, one wonderful brother-in-law, Torbjorn, of whom every woman I know, gay or straight, has said, after her first encounter with him, with sighing and eyelash fluttering of which I have to assume they are unaware: What a wonderful man. One daughter, Tone, and her husband, Glenn, have even produced a huge and beautiful baby, the little giant Oyvind (or as we say, Oiving). That's how it is with in-laws you love. You love them as you love your own beloved; you like to say their names, marvel at their accomplishments (Yes, she's an AIDS nurse! Yes, he can do anything with computers!) and their ways of being (She loves to knit! You can't get him to sit still!). And forgive, without much effort, that which needs forgiving. (I don't think it means the same thing in English. They don't do it that way in Norway.) The in-laws in Oslo are all pieces of Joy, translated into Norwegian (or back into the original Norwegian). After a couple of days with them, her speech patterns match cousin Siri's (little gasps for punctuation), and I can picture her at the family farmhouse in Vessoya, chasing the babies, making huge meals with only two burners going, and everything about her brightens, deepens, opens. I would make offerings at the Shrine of the Norwegians, if my people still did things like that, for everything they bring her, and me.

In-laws are, I think, like the gods. Like real gods: some grand, some petty, some representing our virtues, some our vices. They represent us, and our spouses, played out across the planetarium of marriage. Balder is the Norse god of innocence and light, and he shines for my whole family at the farmhouse. Hoder is the blind, dour god of darkness, and I assume he can still be found in outer St. Louis, making moldy Wonder-bread sandwiches. Valkyries, minor goddesses who decide who will die in combat (think of them as aunts by marriage, drawing lots in the kitchen), interfere, advise, and whisper. Our in-laws are our partners, inside out and writ large, and when that is a good thing, you get family get-togethers and truly merry Christmases and photographs in which people look genuinely glad to be shoulder to shoulder. They are also the demons that live within our partners, tormenting their poor child (or even worse, controlling and manipulating the poor goof, who doesn't even see it . . . no matter how many times you point it out) and forcing us to see just where the impotence, depression, photophobia, migraines, and all else comes from.

In-laws are the gifts, the dead mice, our spouses lay at our feet. Joy managed to give me love and hate as in-laws and I take them both and am glad, in my virtue and vice, for both.

JONATHAN GOLDSTEIN

Her Father Under My Skin

● ● ●

The first time my girlfriend Hettie's dad Butch ever laid eyes on me was seven years ago. I was walking down the street to meet Hettie and he was standing with her in the courtyard of her building. While I was still half a block away, he turned to her and told her two things about me. One, he said, was that he could see by my gait that I was Jewish. Two, he could already tell that I was a "good-time Charlie." That was the only time anyone has ever referred to me as a good-time anything, and to this day, despite the many negative things that man has said about me, I cherish that original misappraisal.

All I'd heard about Butch from Hettie before I'd met him was that he was the loudest and strongest man in Montreal.

"When he'd yell, things would fall off the shelves," Hettie told me. She said that when she was growing up, their apartment was so loud she had to spend most of her time outside on the fire escape with the window shut. She would do her homework out there on a wooden chessboard on her lap.

When I finally met him that morning in the courtyard, I guess I was expecting a cartoony man, a man who looked like Bluto, a man who wore skintight black turtlenecks and had continuous jets of steam coming out of his ears. Instead the man I met was just a white-haired old guy in a painter's cap.

"Good shabbos," were his first words, which he punctuated by spitting a toothpick from his mouth in my general direction. "Good shabbos" is the traditional salutation Jews use to greet each other on Friday night, after synagogue. As Butch was not Jewish, and this was in fact a Wednesday, I was left with only one conclusion.

"I don't think your father likes Jews," I told Hettie afterward.

"He doesn't like anyone," she said.

"He's old," I said.

"He could still take you."

I tried to imagine the spectacle of that: a paunchy, gout-footed man my grandfather's age dragging around a thirtyish bespectacled man in a headlock. It is an image that my mind has returned to many times over the years.

Hettie was born in Montreal, but during the early years of her life, she, her two sisters, and her parents lived all over the place—trailer parks, crummy motels, and shacks in the woods without electricity. When she was five, they moved to a commune in North Carolina. Butch was not what you'd call the hippie type. He did not do drugs, never drank, and didn't "vibe" on being mellow. He was a tightly wound spoilsport prone to emotional meltdowns when someone so much as misplaced the TV remote. But out of his love for Hettie's mom, he went to live on a commune, and since everyone who lived there was too lazy to work the land, they had to survive on the chickens Hettie says Butch stole from neighboring farms. To hear Hettie tell it, her family was a little like the Mansons, without the ambitious agenda or the leadership skills of a Charles.

When Hettie was six, her family moved to a hut on the outskirts of a trailer park in Virginia. Her father's job was to collect rent from the people in the trailer homes, and Hettie would go with him when he made the rounds. Butch's favorite part of the job was when people didn't have their rent. This was a chance for him to yell.

"What do you mean you don't have the rent?" Butch would intone in the doorway. "It's because you sit around like the king of England, watching color TV and eating TV dinners all day. Stop living so high on the hog!"

While Butch delivered his top-volume sermon on home economics, Hettie studied the interior of the trailers. Each one was like a cozy rocket ship with the whole family so close together. Hettie thought the people who lived in trailers were lucky and she wished that one day she could have a beautiful little trailer home, too—one she would never move from.

During this time her parents divorced, and for the next few years Hettie and her two sisters romanced around the south with their mother, and Butch moved back to Montreal. Her mother used to tell them that if they ever saw Butch, they were to run and hide because he was a dangerous and crazy man. She would tell them this every so often like it was a fire drill. But then one day their mother decided she wanted to be an artist, a real artist, and a real artist had to be free. Painting birds on the bathroom walls was not enough to satisfy her artistic spirit. She needed to travel, and so at the age of nine, Hettie was put on a plane to Canada. Her sisters would soon be sent too, but then it was only Hettie, all alone at the airport, meeting her father, a man she hardly even remembered. When he got down on his knees to give her a hug, she felt embarrassed about being squeezed by a stranger in public.

Eventually, when her sisters came to join her, Butch put the three together in one little bedroom, crammed in on bunk beds. They were all pretty close in age and so Butch had them share their clothes out of one big box. He called it being efficient. In the morning he woke them up with a beaten-up old bugle he found, but other times he would just wake them up with yelling. This could even be at two in the morning if he couldn't find his income tax forms and needed help looking. Some days, he would send them three miles with their little wagon to pick up cases of soda on special. He would force them to learn the entire times table in one night to make sure they weren't retarded. He gave them haircuts with a bowl and pounded their dolls with a hammer when he was upset. Growing up, they hardly had any toys. Hettie owned one *Archie Digest,* which she kept under her mattress and read each night before she went to bed. Hettie is the only person I know younger than me who had a Depression-era childhood.

Hettie escaped Butch's apartment as soon as she could. In her late teens she moved through a series of other Montreal apartments, but she still saw her father regularly. They would meet on park benches and eat Butch's homemade sandwiches.

Then a few years later, when Hettie was in her early twenties, she and her five-year-old daughter Zouzou moved into an apartment in the building where she grew up with her dad and sisters. Butch was still living in his old apartment, two floors below.

Hettie decided to move back to the old building in the late '90s, when rents in nicer parts of Montreal began to get too high; but it wasn't just that. With her father around to help watch Zouzou, Hettie could go back to college and have a bit of a life. Having to put up with the omnipresence of her father seemed like a fair trade. "Plus," Hettie says, "Jack White of The White Stripes lived in the same house all his life, too, and he's cool."

Alone with Zouzou, Hettie just felt like the old building was a safe place to be. It's a mystery to me, how Hettie could have felt that way, and how she could have willingly gone back there. Butch's pull on her is something I always quiz her about, but she just shrugs. The closest I come to understanding the whole thing is when I think about things in nature, like salmon swimming upstream to get back to their ancestral habitat or penguins marching single file in mile-long lines across the Antarctic just to return to some spot of ice they call home.

Hettie hasn't seen her mom in years. All that's left of her now are some Jean Cocteau books of essays on Hettie's bookshelf with drawings in the margins that appear to be made of either ketchup or blood. I have smelled them and I still cannot tell. Hettie's mom disappeared, but her father, for better or for worse, would always be a part of her life, and a part of her sisters' lives, too. He was the one that stuck around, and there's power in that.

Now, for the last year, I've been living with Hettie two floors above her father, too. It's the worst building on the block. Bricks are always falling off the outside walls and there are bats that nest above our window. Plus, it's had a reputation for being a bad-luck building since the time when a best man fell to his death while dancing at a rooftop wedding party in the '50s.

Sometime in the mid-1980s Butch became the building's concierge, and as it turned out, he proved to be very well suited to the job. Hettie describes the building at the time as a forlorn place where the tenants occupied themselves all day long with the elaborate writing of suicide notes. As concierge, Butch began to see himself as a kind of ringmaster to the Circus of the Damned, arbitrating disputes between tenants by threatening to evict them all. Butch treated his new job as though he himself owned the building, and when people were late with the rent, he took it as a personal slight. On the first of each month, Butch could be heard screaming in the halls and pounding the walls.

It took a while, but I started to get used to the way things worked in the building. You had to creep past Butch's door on the way upstairs, because it was as if he was perched inside with a caulking gun in his hand, ready to leap right out like a jack-in-the-box and start yelling at you about the high cost of caulking.

Butch started to slowly get used to my presence, too. He saw my working at home as a curiosity, and he'd always have questions for Hettie about what I was up to. He'd ask Zouzou, too, and no matter the time of day or what I was actually doing, she'd tell him I was still asleep. This was one of Zouzou's favorite jokes. She loved to see Butch react.

"He says he's going to come upstairs and pour a pot of matzo ball soup over your head," Zouzou reports back. "He says he is going to put firecrackers between your toes to wake you up."

"Did you defend me?" I ask.

She shakes her head no.

"He also says he can tell what sex my hamsters are by sticking firecrackers in their butts and seeing which way their eyes turn."

I look over at Hettie with disbelief, but the room is already on fire with their laughter.

Another thing I had to get used to was the fact that Butch calls for Hettie easily a dozen times a day. In this way, you always feel his imminence. Sometimes he calls to ask Hettie the time because he is too tired to get up and look for himself. Sometimes he calls to see what she is having for dinner, or he calls to have Hettie make him some insanely aggressive sign to post in the laundry room, something like "If you wash shoes in the machine, I will kill you. The Management"; but most of the time he calls and doesn't say a thing. Hettie will pick up the phone and only hear classical music playing, and she'll know it's her dad with his kitchen radio on. Sometimes I'll walk into the living room and Hettie will be watching TV with a telephone cupped to her ear, not saying a word, and I know she's on the phone with him and that two floors down, he's sitting, watching TV just as silently.

Hettie never turns down any of Butch's requests, no matter how absurd. It is just the way he programmed her as a child: to always be feeling guilty and sorry for him—sorry that he was sad, lonely, grouchy, vociferous, ill-tempered, or even in need of entertainment. It was a well-honed parenting technique. So when he wanted a television companion,

Hettie couldn't say no. From an early age, if she even started to say no, Butch would go into lasers-of-guilt mode. "When I am rotting in my grave, the worms eating my eyelashes, you will regret your great cruelty," he'd say, clutching at his heart like Redd Foxx.

When our phone line is in use and our voice mail picks up, Hettie's father will leave a dozen messages in a row. The way we know it's him is that there are no words, just the click of the phone. After about ten minutes, the fact that he can't get through starts to drive him crazy, so he walks down to the buzzers by the building's main door and buzzes our apartment. The way he sees it, why should he have to walk *up* two flights of stairs to our apartment when he can just walk down one to the lobby.

The buzzer is like an amplified dentist drill, and some-times, when you're quiet or deep in thought, the suddenness of it is like being goosed by something cold and metallic. It is the kind of sound that rats in lab experiments come to as-sociate with a terrible, perhaps fatal, error. "Even now it can buzz," you think to yourself all day long. "Or even now."

When we hear the buzzer, we get off the Internet or the telephone so that he can call.

One day, I didn't get off-line quick enough, so he went back down to the buzzer and this time he just leaned on it. I logged off and Hettie phoned him. He wasn't answering. She yelled down the stairs, but still, he would not stop. He was making a point.

I am not exaggerating when I say that he kept the buzzer going for several minutes straight, and after a while you could hear layered fluctuations and subtle pitch blends. He was like Yoko Ono on that thing.

I imagined going down there, wrapping my arms around his old withered bull's neck, and wrestling him to the ground. I imagined him biting my shoulder blade, a goatee of blood around his mouth, both of us screaming in a death embrace.

Hettie, though, in a gesture that I believe to be indicative of her philosophy for dealing with her father in general, got on a chair and hit the box above the door with a hammer. This move, although not actually confronting the source of our agony, did give us respite. The buzzing stopped.

A few minutes later, her father called. "What was so important?" Hettie asked.

Her father was quiet. Finally, he asked her if she knew what night the Oscars were on.

Hettie told him that he had gone too far.

It made Hettie's father sad that our doorbell was gone. He suggested that he and Hettie get walkie-talkies. I imagined them both, sitting in their separate kitchens, each eating a sandwich, and between long silences one of them uttering the occasional "Ten-four."

Hettie refused the offer.

"Fine," he said. "From now on I'll just go down into the basement and turn off the building's power two times, really fast. That'll be the signal for you to free up the line."

Hettie told him that that would be the signal for her to move out.

Now that we don't have a buzzer, I am constantly missing deliveries; but Butch is good enough to receive them for me. He phones up, I come down, he hands me my package and then asks me to help him move a refrigerator up a flight of stairs. We struggle it up while Butch explains to me why Jews are the worst at moving refrigerators.

It got so I began to avoid leaving the building when Butch was around for fear I'd be suckered into wasting half my afternoon moving windowpanes from one end of the basement to the other. It was in those moments, as I heard myself saying yes even though all logic and desire within me was crying no, that I felt like I was beginning to understand Hettie's definition of what family was all about. I guess it also meant that, despite everything, I was slowly coming to think of Butch as family.

Sometimes whole days would roll by and I'd stay in, peering out the window every so often to see if the court-yard was clear. In the summer Butch is a fixture out there, seated on a bridge chair in the center of the concrete. He sits in his undershirt, sometimes twirling a wrench, sometimes using the wooden end of a toilet plunger as a back scratcher, but always complaining and telling the tenants that pass by how they are doing things all wrong.

"Your shoe is untied," he yells. "That bag is going to tear." "You've missed a belt loop."

People respond to him as they would to the sudden stab-bing pain of gas.

Butch stops me as I'm going upstairs and tells me about this sink he once unclogged, and I look at him and try to see

Hettie's face in his. As I look, I slowly inch backward toward the building.

One fall day, there was a knock at the door. It was Butch and he wanted his can opener back. He was out of breath, all worked up about a fight he had just gotten into with a tenant who insisted on keeping his windows open with the radiator on. I asked him if he wanted to come in and sit down, but he declined. Instead, he sat on the stairs in the hall. He said that his chest was hurting like a son of a bitch. That afternoon, Hettie called the hospital and made him an appointment with his doctor for the next morning.

After the doctor examined him, he told Butch that he had been having a series of small heart attacks and that he was going to have him go in for a bypass the next day. He didn't even want him to leave the hospital, but Butch argued that he still had rents to collect, so, amazingly the doctor let him go. We brought him back to the hospital that night, and soon after he had the surgery.

All the following day, Hettie and I sat at the hospital, waiting for news. We feared it wouldn't be good. With his temper, poor eating habits, and stress level, it was sort of incredible that he had lasted as long as he had. Hettie and I had been calling him Heart-Attack Harrison for years. I held Hettie's hand while she cried.

Finally, a doctor emerged from the operating room. He told us that Butch's strength was phenomenal, that he was doing really well, and that Hettie would be allowed in to see him soon.

That night Hettie said that Butch kept asking for me. I thought it might be to talk about Hettie and Zouzou—things to be taken care of in the event of his death—to have some kind of conversation that would start with the words "I know we've had our differences . . ."; but it turned out he wanted to tell me that if he dies in the hospital he wants me to write an exposé about it in *The New York Times*.

After the operation, I took it as a given that Butch would be retiring from his concierge post, but he had other plans. Almost immediately after the surgery he started talking about all the stuff at the building that he had to get back to. He gave instructions to Hettie about what to say if any of the tenants started asking for him.

"Tell them Monsieur Butch will be back soon to fix everything . . . but for God's sake don't tell any of them I'm in the hospital. If they hear that they'll think they've got the upper hand on me and then I'll be finished. Just tell them I'm in the Orient. On business."

"You almost died," I said. "How can you be thinking about the building at a time like this!"

I was worried about him, but also, of course, I did not want to be saddled with picking up his slack in my role as dutiful janitor-in-law. I did not want to be a janitor. Not in that building, and I felt like that's what was going to happen next.

Hettie would start taking over his responsibilities, and out of guilt, I would pitch in, and then we'd be a janitor couple.

I could see it already. The barrage of phone calls would start early in the morning, people needing toilets wrenched open and crusted mustard picked out of electrical sockets. I am not a handy man, but I would want to make a good show of things, plus in the back of my mind I'd always know that if I didn't go, Hettie would have to.

I went home that night and lay in bed. I imagined myself in apartment 2C responding to a call to unclog the drain. It was right opposite our apartment, and I'd never been in there. I saw myself bringing along a can of Liquid-Plumr and pouring about half of it down the drain, and like magic the gurgling would start. This gurgling would become a sound I'd absolutely live for. The water would go down and there would be a thick layer of red beard hair lining the sink. I knew that Butch would have yelled like hell, saying that in his building one trimmed one's beard over a garbage can, not a sink; but I imagined the building under my governance as a new regime, a kinder regime. I would just smile and go off on my way.

I'd pretty much have to give up on doing any work at home. There would always be building stuff to do, and as it would pile on I'd start to become less peaceable about the whole thing. Eventually, when a college student would call me over to tighten a loose door hinge, I'd ask him with some annoyance if he had been slamming doors.

"Do you have any idea what slamming does to the life

expectancy of a door hinge?" I would demand, having no idea whatsoever what the answer was, but knowing I had made my point. And when the old man on the fourth floor would get drunk and start running, naked and screaming through the halls, I would go up there and sternly tell him to get back in his house because no one wanted to see his wrinkled old raisins slapping around.

It would get so that the neighbors would stop saying hi to me in the halls. They would start to associate me with Butch, their enemy. Being an enemy is something that Butch has no problem with. Being an enemy hangs from him with ease. I, on the other hand, would prefer to be seen as a good-time Charlie, a man of the people.

One Friday night, we visited Butch at the hospital. While Hettie was helping Zouzou with her homework in the cafeteria, I gave Butch all the building gossip, telling him what a pain in the ass the woman downstairs was, the way she set off the smoke alarm every ten minutes with her Brazilian incense that smelled of wet dog on fire, and how the madman in an upstairs apartment had thrown an armchair out his window and ripped down a phone line. This all made Butch happier than I had seen him since before his operation. Butch said that he needed to get back to the building. He told me that janitorial kind of work is what he's been doing almost all of his life. He told me that when he was young, he used to shabbos goy for a synagogue—on the Sabbath he turned on the lights, lit up the furnace—and the rabbi who employed him there had shown him more kindness than he had ever known.

I took this story to be Butch's version of an olive branch.

Upon his return home, Butch said he felt twenty-five years younger. "There's no more weight on my chest," he said. "Everything is clearer, like it's all gone from a twenty-five-watt bulb to a sixty-watt."

One of the things he's taken to doing since his return is wearing dress shirts. This is so that at a moment's notice he can undo the buttons and show everyone his bypass scar. When Zouzou has friends over, we send them downstairs so they can see it, and whenever they come back up they look thoroughly grossed out. I know this must satisfy Butch to no end.

MATT BAI

The Family Without Stories

• • •

Growing up in the Northeast, I imagined Orange County to be an endlessly unfurling landscape of adobe mansions in which housemaids dusted portraits of Ronald Reagan. I pictured grand swaying palm trees and tony shopping malls full of Aryan-looking kids who play volleyball. I once wondered to my wife, Ellen, what happened to the ugly kids who grew up in her part of California. "They have to become lawyers," she said.

That I might have been generalizing too liberally about life in Orange County became apparent as I made my way off Interstate 5 into Garden Grove, the sprawling, unadorned city where Ellen was born and raised. At that time, Ellen was my girlfriend, but since I was spending the week in Los Angeles for work, I had called her parents and invited myself down for dinner. It had occurred to me only as I was sitting in rush-hour traffic that this might have conveyed the wrong impression. Ellen and I had been dating for two years, and it would have been reasonable to think that I was appearing at her parents' doorstep, alone and almost unannounced, to do that thing where you ask the father for his daughter's hand in marriage. In reality, it never would have occurred to me to discuss such matters with her father. I'd met her parents only briefly, but already I had the impression that one did not broach topics such as love and devotion with George and Nancy. In Ellen's family, as in a lot of Japanese-American families of her generation, life was better left unsaid.

I found myself driving past the gates of Disneyland, down a broad boulevard where, as a little girl, Ellen had marveled at the exotic landmarks of her childhood—a motor inn with a topiary garden, a Sheraton built to resemble an Elizabethan manor. My destination was a street of wood-sided ramblers with neatly kept lawns, hard against one another, many of them now owned by Latino and Vietnamese families. A kid dressed like Eminem was riding his bike. George and Nancy came to the door before I'd finished parking.

The little house was warmly decorated with old furniture and cluttered with the kinds of random artifacts my relatives call tchotchkes. I noticed a glass case with Japanese wooden dolls of various sizes. Atop the piano was a handmade wooden clock on which Nancy had flawlessly painted an American flag and some watermelons. There were pictures of George as a young man in his Army khakis, small but sturdy, with a cocky grin. Out back, in a fenced-in square yard, George tended to trees growing oranges, persimmons, macadamia nuts, papayas, and lemons. His father and brothers had been farmers before the war. George, on the other hand, aided by the GI Bill, had become a pharmacist at the local Sav-On, a tedious job for which he showed mild enthusiasm and then retired.

He was in his eighties now, his round face leathery from the sun, his eyes blinking slowly—large, unusually wide Asian eyes like my wife's. I thought he resembled a big koala bear. He interspersed his sentences with the word "see," like Jimmy Cagney in his old movies—"I planted this tree when it was this high, see?"—and sometimes trailed off in the middle of them. You had to shout into his two hearing aids in order to be heard, but he looked twenty years younger than he was, he still golfed twice a week, and his arms suggested a deceptive kind of power and agility as he shook ripe oranges to the ground for me. I imagined that one did not lightly pick a fight with that young soldier in the photograph.

We sat in chairs in front of the wide-screen TV on which George watched UCLA or Ohio State, his alma mater, play on Saturdays. We didn't say much. I think I heard a clock tick. At my request, Nancy pulled out an album of Ellen's baby pictures, and she and George watched as I flipped through them, taking care to keep a polite, even smile on my face. What was she like as a child? I wanted to know. "Oh, she was always reading," Nancy replied. What did she read? "Anything she could get her hands on." She sure was a cute kid, I offered. "Oh, yes," Nancy said.

Ellen and I are journalists; we met aboard Bill Bradley's campaign bus a few days before the New Hampshire primary in 2000. My wife has the quiet confidence of a genuine intellectual (before stumbling into news, she acquired a master's degree in medieval literature), and she was adept at shutting frivolous men down with a blank stare and a turn of the head. Undeterred, I waited her out, until one night a week or so later, during a cross-country charter flight, when I sat down next to her and started asking her unreasonably personal questions.

At some point she revealed to me, with neither pride nor shame, that the government had interned both sides of her family during the Second World War. "Interned"—the word sounded spookily like "interred," with the same deathly connotation, and it brought back vague memories of a high school history lesson long since forgotten. On February 19, 1942, a little more than two months after the surprise attack on Pearl Harbor, President Roosevelt signed Executive Order 9066, later upheld by the U.S. Supreme Court, which decreed that no one of Japanese ancestry, whether a citizen or not, could live on the West Coast. Some Japanese-Americans fled inland to states they had never before seen, but more than 120,000 of them reported to a series of concentration camps—that is, by definition, what they were—in six western states. These families sold their homes and businesses for next to nothing, or simply left them behind for others to claim. The reasoning behind the internment was nicely summarized by Lieutenant General J. L. DeWitt, who carried out the relocation, in a letter he wrote to the Army's chief of staff in 1943: "The continued presence of a large, unassimilated, tightly knit and racial group, bound to an enemy nation by strong ties of race, culture, custom and religion along a frontier vulnerable to attack constituted a menace which had to be dealt with."

Though George and Nancy wouldn't meet until after the war, both their families were interned, passing as many as four years in the camp. The exception was George, who had already enlisted in the Army by the time Roosevelt's order was handed down. While his parents and siblings lived behind barbed wire in North Dakota and Arizona, George fought alongside other Japanese-Americans in a segregated regiment, the legendary 442nd. Somewhere in that house, probably in a dusty box, he kept a cluster of Purple Hearts.

Ellen's mother, meanwhile, went to high school in the notorious camp at Manzanar, California. "The Manzanar reception center will be a self-sufficient community, with a 150-bed hospital staffed by Japanese doctors and nurses, community kitchens, a library, motion-picture theater and houses of worship for all denominations, including Buddhism," a wire service reported cheerily as the first prisoners arrived in the spring of 1942. "From this elevation of 3,700 feet, the Japanese evacuees will enjoy, if they feel that way, some of the most magnificent scenery in the United States." In fact, these lucky internees lived in barracks without plumbing or stoves, where two families would be crammed into a twenty-by-twenty-five-foot room. They were encouraged to foster an environment of normalcy, working low-wage jobs and electing representatives of a camp government. The photographer Ansel Adams shot sparse, haunting portraits at Manzanar, where he captured the surreal quality of its small-town pretensions. One of his photos features a smiling, attractive high school student in a dress, her knee raised, twirling a baton against a foreboding, mountainous backdrop. The girl is Ellen's aunt Flo.

Far from conveying the impression that they felt angry or unjustly persecuted, Ellen's parents almost never even talked about this history with their two daughters. When her mother did make a rare, passing mention of the internment, it was lighthearted, as if such an ordeal were a fairly typical childhood experience. Ellen recalled her aunts and uncles mentioning their days "in camp," where they spent hours rolling up balls of tinfoil for recycling into metal. Ellen was a teenager before she realized that her mother hadn't been talking about the YMCA.

"It never really had any impact on us," Ellen told me. I asked what her sister was doing now. Ellen said she was an immigration lawyer. (Apparently, it wasn't just the ugly kids who went to law school.)

"And you don't think there's a connection there?" I asked.

"I guess I never really thought about it," she said.

I wanted to know where her family had been held and for how long, how her father had been hurt, why he had ended up fighting when others in the family had not. She had vague notions about all of this but admitted that she had never really felt at liberty to ask. Her father wasn't given to long explanations. Her mother guarded the most routine information as if she alone understood its hidden value; she didn't like for outsiders to know her address or telephone number, and she adamantly refused even to be photographed.

I will admit that Ellen's shadowy family history was one of the things that drew me to her. Her relatives had suffered, and this was something I could understand; Jews have elevated suffering to a kind of performance art. That Ellen's parents had risen beyond discrimination and ostracism made them, in some weird cultural way, more like my own forebears, chased by bigotry across Europe and Asia and, finally, to a new country whose muted resentments were more subtle and insidious.

What I could not understand, on a cultural level, was the secrecy. In my family, every small injustice is scrubbed and polished, like an heirloom, so it can be measured against the injustices of others. An especially harrowing trip to the grocery store becomes a tale of victimization to be repeated through the ages at family weddings and funerals. To remain silent in the face of misfortune, however petty or subjective, would be an abdication of our inheritance.

In Ellen's family, the determination not to acknowledge injustice is equally willful. When the *Los Angeles Times* published its "Photos of the Century," it included one of Ellen's grandfather, Nancy's father, that was taken the night of

Pearl Harbor. He was a charmer of a man who ran through a succession of jobs—for a while, he ran an East L.A. hotel that is still visible from the freeway—and, according to family lore, was given to gambling. On the night the picture was taken, he had just taken his three daughters to a dance recital. The FBI was waiting for him at home, though no one ever knew why. In the photo, he is sitting on a bench alongside other prominent Japanese-American men, smoking a cigarette and looking faintly bored. He wears a thin mustache, a tailored suit, and dress shoes. For eighteen months, Nancy and her family would receive only sporadic and censored letters from a series of holding facilities—from Tujunga, California, to Livingstone, Louisiana—until Nancy's father was at last "released" and reunited with his family in Manzanar.

No one in Ellen's family had seen this photograph until it was published in the newspaper almost sixty years later. Nancy did obtain a copy, but I couldn't find it hanging anywhere among the homemade crafts and family snapshots in her and George's home. I imagined it had been discreetly deposited into a drawer somewhere, alongside all the other unanswered questions.

I was thinking about that missing photo as I flipped through the pictures of Ellen as a young girl. Our conversation stalled repeatedly, but I couldn't say it was awkward. George and Nancy seemed at ease with silence. Decades of stony reticence had settled into their lives in the way that calcium deposits itself into the joints of the aging; it had hardened and filled the spaces. The drawn-out pauses, along with what little manners I'd managed to preserve in my years as a reporter, dissuaded me from asking the questions I really wanted to ask as I blithely turned the pages of the photo album. My more subtle entreaties—"How long have you lived in this house? Did you grow up in this area?"—went nowhere. George nodded. Nancy smiled.

What had become of George's boyhood farm? When he fought in the foxholes of France and Italy, did he think it was still there, waiting for his return? How narrowly and how often had he escaped death? George might have thought I had come to ask for his daughter, but what I found myself wanting—what not even Ellen had gotten—was his story.

Several weeks after the terrorist attacks of 2001, George and Nancy visited us in Washington. The occasion was a reunion of the remaining, robust veterans of Company K, which had been George's Army unit. Usually, they met every few years in Hawaii or on the West Coast, since virtually all of the veterans lived on the Pacific. But in recent years, Washington had, belatedly, honored the Japanese-American families with a memorial and a museum exhibit, and the old soldiers wanted to see those testaments while they were still able.

I asked Ellen if I could join them at the reunion. My ostensible reason was that I wanted to write an article about it, but in fact, my deeper motive was simply to penetrate some of the mystery that surrounded their lives—and, perhaps, by doing so, to peel away some of the unease that characterized my brief conversations with her parents. Ellen advised me that this would not be an easy assignment. Her father agreed readily to have me tag along with a notebook, but she cautioned me that he probably hadn't realized—either because he didn't hear well over the phone, or because the very concept was so foreign to his existence—that I intended to ask him all kinds of questions. Nancy, meanwhile, understood all too well; she was fine with my badgering George about his war service, but she wasn't about to be interviewed herself.

About thirty veterans and their wives gathered at the dreary Holiday Inn on Capitol Hill. So as not to alarm my future in-laws right away, I started by approaching other veterans and asking for their stories, which seemed to amuse Ellen's parents. "What are you writing?" Nancy would ask me, with a wry smile I'd not seen before, as our coach bus traversed the capital en route from one attraction to another. "It's all about you," I teased her, nodding meaningfully at the notebook. "I'm writing a book." Ellen winced. Her mother just laughed.

I finally confronted George in his hotel room, during an afternoon break. He sat on the edge of one of the room's two double beds, his hands planted on the flowered bedspread, while I sat facing him in the desk chair. I had to shout above the hum of the air conditioner when I asked him to tell me where he had been when the war started, and how he had come to fight while his family was kept behind barbed wire. To Ellen's surprise, her father didn't seem at all reluctant to discuss the war years. He rubbed his short-cropped hair and scoured his mind for dates and places and people. The problem was that all those years of silence, which had so deterred his daughters from probing him about his life, seemed to have corroded the mechanism of his memory, the way an old, unopened safe becomes rusty and mistimed. He remembered getting his draft notice and training at a base in Minnesota so cold that his hair froze. He could recall the names of friends who were blown up on the hills of France and Italy. Isolated facts, unmoored to place and time, resurfaced, but their connections to one another were tenuous.

Until that time, I'd never really considered the relationship between narrative and memory. Mine was a home consumed by storytelling. We all knew, for instance, about how my father had moved out of his Yale dormitory and commuted from home so that he could take care of his stricken mother; how he had been unable to work for a lot of venerable law firms because he was Jewish; how my mother's father had lost two fingers in a slicing machine in the family bakery before, eventually, suffering a fatal heart attack over the ovens—a fate, my mother never failed to mention, that the philandering dilettante deserved. These tragic little narratives, endlessly rehearsed and sharpened, preserved our collective past, even as they almost certainly distorted it.

But what happens when a family's stories aren't assiduously maintained and preserved? The avoidance in George and Nancy's home—and in the homes of so many of the other Japanese-American veterans I was meeting—had taken its toll on the past. George could still recall places and faces and moments in time, but he could no longer easily slide them into their proper order or perspective. He was in France and Italy. He was in a military hospital. He was training for war, while his family endured the camps. In his memory, he was in all of these places at once. He reminded me of Billy Pilgrim, the broken soldier in Kurt Vonnegut's *Slaughterhouse-Five;* George too had "come unstuck in time." Too long neglected, the narrative thread of his life had unraveled.

And so we began, all of us, to weave it back together. Ellen leapt in with prescient questions. Even Nancy found herself trying to restore her husband's memories to their proper shape. "Weren't you at that base in the desert first?" she would ask, prodding him along. Nancy was nine years younger than George and hadn't met him until a ski trip long after the war. It occurred to me that she might not have heard the entirety of his story, either.

George recalled that he had settled into life as a mule-driver on the family farm when he was drafted on October 19, 1941, less than two months before Pearl Harbor. (He had been born Yuichiro, but adopted the name George when he was very little as a means of blending in, just as Nancy and all of Ellen's other relatives had chosen American names in the years before the war.) The Japanese-American soldiers were like human Kevlar for the Army; it was assumed that they had yet to prove their loyalty, and thus they were deployed for some of the grisliest fighting of the war. (The 442nd would emerge as the most decorated unit of its size in the history of the country's military, testifying to both the ferocity of its fighters and the breathtaking scale of its casualties.) George helped liberate the town of Bruyères, France, then did his part to rescue the famed Lost Battalion—a Texas-based unit that had been encircled by Nazi troops in France. As German fire ravaged the Japanese-American soldiers, George heard the general in charge issue an order to the battalion colonel for the men to charge straight at the German machine-gun batteries. "That's when I thought, 'Maybe he thinks we're expendable,'" George recalled with a chuckle.

By the time the Lost Battalion was freed, Company K, which had started out with some 200 men, had been reduced to only 12, with no surviving officers. Amazingly, George's luck held out for several more months, until a mortar barrage shattered his eardrums and peppered his flesh with shrapnel.

I asked George about his family in the camps. He shrugged. He admitted that he harbored hopes that if he fought bravely enough, they would be released. When at last the Army sent him home, the home he left was a distant memory; the mules and melons now belonged to someone else, either by sale or by seizure, and his relatives had relocated to Cleveland, where they worked in factories and car dealerships, trying to start again.

By the end of our weekend in Washington, George was volunteering scraps of memory as they returned to him, filling in gaps without any prodding. The stiltedness that had permeated our first conversation in Garden Grove seemed to have dissipated as we strolled through the memorial to the Japanese-American internment, a few blocks from the Capitol, and saw the names of America's ten concentration camps chiseled into stone: Manzanar, Tule Lake, Poston, Minidoka. Even Nancy posed with me for a photograph in front of the monument's granite wall. She wasn't willing to relive her wartime experience in the way that her husband was, however. As we toured the National Museum of American History, she and I found ourselves standing in front of a life-size replica of one of the prisoner huts at Manzanar. She stared at it for a long moment. "Is that what it looked like?" I asked.

"Yeah, that's not bad," she said wryly. "Only it wasn't that nice."

The dynamic between all of us seemed different after that weekend. Months later, at the request of someone in Hawaii who was writing a history of Company K, Ellen interviewed her father for the first time and committed to paper his oral history. Nancy and I began exchanging lively e-mail. Now, when I would see George a few times a year, he would tell me stories about his days in the Army and as a student—about how he slept in the football stadium at Ohio State, because the number of incoming students had overwhelmed the housing system, or about how someone had managed to talk George into going out for J.V. football as a freshman, a decision he quickly regretted.

What remained, for me, a mystery was why George and Nancy—and, for that matter, so many Japanese-Americans—had allowed their memories to become so entombed in the first place. Not long ago, I was making this same point to my wife, by musing on the cultural differences between Jewish-Americans and Japanese-Americans. Why was there no great Japanese-American novelist to chronicle their persecution? Why were there no organizations dedicated to reminding us of the internment? All of this reticence, I argued, had made it easier for America to forget, and perhaps to repeat its crime.

"You have to remember," Ellen told me, "it's not like everyone came rushing up to apologize when they got out of the camps. Nothing changed. They still couldn't get jobs."

As I thought about that conversation in the days that followed, I decided that I might have been looking at George and Nancy in the wrong way all along. Perhaps it wasn't that their long, self-imposed silence had somehow obscured their sacrifice; perhaps their truest sacrifice was the silence itself. After all, there had been those in the camps who rose up in revolt, just as there had been Japanese-American draftees who refused to fight and litigants who challenged the internment. But George and Nancy had never condoned the airing of such grievances; if anything, they resented it. After all, they wanted the same things for their children that all Americans want—a sense of belonging. Could they really have provided that and demanded justice at the same time? Perhaps it wasn't shame that swallowed their narrative. Perhaps they bore their burdens silently so their children wouldn't have to.

I was forced, then, to reconsider the volubility of my own upbringing. We were defined by our stories, and for that reason I treasured them, even in adulthood. But the inescapable theme of our household—that we were apt to be victims, that fate would somehow conspire against us—had left an imprint, too. My older sisters and I labored, midway through the journey of our lives, to take risks in our career and in our relationships, to see ourselves as unencumbered. We were trapped, in a way that my wife is not, by the stories of our childhood.

Last Christmas Eve, my father-in-law taught me to harvest macadamia nuts and snap off the shells. I was bagging the nuts in the kitchen when, suddenly, I heard a familiar series of explosions in the sky outside. I stepped out onto the driveway, and there, overhead, were the nightly fireworks going off over Disneyland. A few minutes later, George came out and stood beside me, and we both stared quietly for a good ten minutes at the electric sky, arms folded across our chests.

"This is the finale, see," he said finally. Sure enough, blue and green stars erupted into little galaxies, and red streaks slithered toward the horizon. It was a nice moment. We stood watching comfortably in silence, the space between us filled by the light and fury of the American spectacle.

MICHAEL CHABON

My Father-in-law, Briefly

● ● ●

I didn't play golf, and he had never smoked marijuana. I was a nail-chewer, inclined to brood, and dubious of the motives of other people. He was big and placid, uniformly kind to strangers and friends alike, and never went anywhere without whistling a little song. I minored in philosophy. He fell asleep watching television. He fell asleep in movie theaters, too, and occasionally, I suspected, while driving. He had been in the navy during the Second World War, which taught him, he said, to sleep whenever he could. I, still troubled no doubt by perplexing questions of ontology and epistemology raised during my brief flirtation with logical positivism ten years earlier, was an insomniac. I was also a Jew, of a sort; he was, when required, an Episcopalian.

He was not a big man, but his voice boomed, and his hands were meaty, and in repose there was something august about his heavy Midwestern features: pale blue eyes that in the absence of hopefulness might have looked severe; prominent, straight nose and heavy jowls that in the absence of mirth might have seemed imperious and disapproving. Mirth and hopefulness, however, were never absent from his face. Some people, one imagines, may be naturally dauntless and buoyant of heart, but with him good spirits always seemed, far more admirably, to be the product of intense training in his youth, of a strict program of self-improvement—he believed, like most truly modest men, in the absolute virtue of self-improvement—which had wrought deep, essential changes in a nature inclined by birth to the darker view and gloominess that one saw crop up elsewhere in the family tree. He didn't seem to be happy out of some secret knowledge of the essential goodness of the world, or from having fought his way through grief and adversity to a hard-won sense of his place in it; they were simple qualities, his good humor and his optimism, unexamined, automatic, stubborn. I never failed to take comfort in his presence.

The meaning of divorce will elude us as long as we are blind, as I think at the start we must be, to the meaning of marriage. Marriage seems—at least it seemed to an absurdly young man in the summer of 1987, standing on the sundrenched patio of an elegant house on Lake Washington—to be an activity, like chess or tennis or a rumba contest, that we embark upon in tandem, while everyone who loves us stands around and hopes for the best. We have no inkling of the fervor of their hope, nor of the ways in which our marriage, that collective endeavor, will be constructed from and burdened with their love.

Looking back—always an unreliable procedure, I know—it seems to me to have been a case of love at first sight. I met him, his wife, and their yellow house on the beach all on the same day. It was a square-pillared bungalow, clapboard and shake, the color of yellow gingham, with a steep pitched roof and a porch that looked out over a frigid but tranquil little bay of brackish water. His wife, like him in the last years of a vigorous middle age, had been coming to this stretch of beach since early in her girlhood, and for both her and her daughter, whom I was shortly to marry, it was more heavily and richly layered with memories, associations, artifacts, and stories than any place any member of my own family had lived since we had left Europe seventy years before. Everything about this family was like that. My future mother-in-law lived in the house in Seattle in which she had been born. My father-in-law had grown up down the road in Portland. They had met at the University of Washington. Everyone they knew, they had known for longer than I'd been alive. All the restaurants they favored had been in business for years, they were charter members of their country club, and in some cases they did business with the sons of tradesmen they had dealt with in the early days of their marriage. A journey through the drawers, closets, and cabinets of their house in town yielded a virtual commercial and social history of Seattle, in the form of old matchboxes, rulers, pens, memo pads, napkins, shot glasses, candy tins, golf tees, coat hangers; years and years' worth of lagniappes, give-aways, souvenirs, and mementos bearing the names, in type-faces of four decades, of plumbing supply companies, fuel oil dealers, newlyweds, dry cleaners, men and women cele-brating birthdays and anniversaries.

God, it was a seductive thing to a deracinated, assimi-lated, uncertain, wandering young Jew whose own parents had not been married for years and no longer lived any-where near the house in Maryland in which, for want of a truer candidate, he had more or less grown up! They were in many ways classic WASPs, to be sure, golfing, khaki-wearing, gin-drinking WASPs. The appeal of such people and their kind of world to a young man such as I was has been well documented in film and literature; enough, per-haps, to seem by now a bit outdated. But it wasn't, finally, a matter of class or style, though they had both. I fell in love with their rootedness, with the visible and palpable continu-ity of their history as a family in Seattle, with their ability to take out a box of photographs taken thirty summers earlier and show me the room I was sitting in before it was painted white, the madrona trees that screened the porch before two fell over, the woman I was going to marry digging for geo-duck clams on the beach where she had just lain sunbathing.

Of course they were more than a kind of handsome package for their photographs, houses, and the historical contents of their drawers. They were ordinary, problemati-cal people, my in-laws, forty years into a complicated marriage, and over the course of my own brief marriage to their daughter I came to love and appreciate them both as individuals, on their merits and, as my marriage began so quickly to sour, for the endurance of their partnership; they had that blind, towering doggedness of the Second World War generation. I suppose it's possible that with two daughters they'd always wanted a son, my father-in-law in particular; I do know for certain that I have never been one to refuse the opportunity to add another father to my collection.

He offered himself completely, without reservation, though in his own particular, not to say limited way (it is this inherent limited quality of fathers and their love that motivates collectors like me to try to amass a complete set). He took me down to Nordstrom, the original store in downtown Seattle, and introduced me to the man who sold him his suits. I bought myself a few good, square-cut, sober-colored numbers in a style that would not have drawn a second glance on Yesler Way in 1954. He introduced me to the woman from whom he bought jewelry for his wife, to the man who took care of his car, to all of the golf buddies and cronies whose sons he had been admiring from afar for the last thirty years. He was a bit barrel-chested anyway, but whenever we went anywhere together and, as was all but inevitable, ran into someone he knew, his breast, introducing me, seemed to grow an inch broader, the hand on my shoulder would give me a little fight-trainer massage, and I would feel him, as first the wedding and later the putative grandchildren drew nearer, placing, for that moment, all his hopes in me. He took me to football games, basketball games, baseball games. He let me drive his Cadillac; naturally he never drove anything else. Most of all, however—most important to both of us—he let me hang out in his den.

As the child of divorced parents, myself divorced, and a writer trained by five hundred years of European and American literary history always to search out the worm in the bud, I have, of necessity, become a close observer of other people's marriages. I have noticed that in nearly all the longest-lived ones, if there is space enough in the house, each partner will have a room to flee to. If, however, there is only one room to spare, it will always be the husband's. My in-laws had plenty of room, but while she had her office, just off the bedroom, in which I would sometimes see her, sitting at a Chinese desk, writing a letter or searching for an article clipped from *Town & Country* about flavoring ice creams with edible flowers, my mother-in-law's appeared to serve a largely ceremonial function.

My father-in-law, on the other hand, sometimes seemed to live down in the basement. His office, like him, was mostly about golf. The carpet was Bermuda grass green, the walls were hung with maps of St. Andrews and framed *New Yorker* covers of duffers, and all around the room various hats, ashtrays, hassocks, cigarette lighters, plaques, novelty telephones, and trophies were shaped like golf balls, tees, mashies, mulligans, and I don't know what. In the midst of all this sat an enormous black Robber Baron desk with matching black Captain Nemo chair; an old, vaguely Japanese-looking coffee table on its last tour of duty in the house; a cyclopean television; and a reclining armchair and sofa, both covered in wool patterned with the tartan of some un-known but no doubt staunch, whiskey-drinking, golf-wild highland clan.

It is for just such circumstances, in which two men with little in common may find themselves thrown together with no other recourse than to make friends, that sports were in-vented. When my wife and I would visit I went downstairs, flopped on the sofa, and watched a game with my father-in-law. He made himself a C.C. and soda and sometimes to complete the picture I let him mix one for me. Like many men of my generation, I found solace when unhappy in placing quotation marks around myself in everything I did. There was I, an "unhappy husband," drinking a "cocktail," and "watching the game." This was the only room in the house in which I was permitted to smoke—I have long since quit—and I made the most of it (a man's den often serves the same desublimating function, in the household, as Mardi Gras or Las Vegas, in the world; a different law obtains there). We spent hours together, cheering on Art Monk and Carlton Fisk and other men whose names, when by chance they arise now, can summon up that entire era of whisky and football and the smell of new Coupe de Ville, when the biggest mistake I ever made came home to roost, and I had, for a moment, one of the best fathers I've ever found.

My ex-wife and I—I won't go into the details—had good times and bad times, fought and were silent, tried and gave up and tried some more before finally throwing in the towel, focused, with the special self-absorption of the mis-erable, on our tiny drama and its reverberations in our own chests. All the while, however, the people who loved us were not sitting there whispering behind their hands like spectators at a chess match. They were putting our photographs in frames on their walls. They were uniting our names over and over on the outsides of envelopes that bore anniversary wishes and recipes clipped from newspapers. They were putting our birthdays in their address books, knitting us socks, studying the fluctuating fortunes of our own favorite hitters every morning in the box scores. They were working us into the fabric of their lives. When at last we broke all those promises that we thought we had made only to each other, in an act of faithlessness whose mutuality appeared somehow to make it all right, we tore that fabric; not irrecoverably, but deeply. We had no idea how quickly two families can work to weave themselves together. When I saw him some time later at his mother's funeral in Portland, my father-in-law told me that the day my divorce from his daughter came through was the saddest one in his life; maybe that was when I started to understand what had happened.

I haven't seen or spoken to him in years, for a lot of not very good reasons. He's grown much older now, I suppose. His mother lived well into her nineties, and he favors her, so I can imagine the way in which he must be aging. Sometimes I wonder if he'll live long enough for me to see him again. Would we know each other? What am I, now, to him? How can it have felt to have been divorced by someone he treated like a son? These are not considerations that comfort me or make me especially proud. I try to remind myself that in the long course of his life, I occupied only a tiny span of years, toward the end, when everything gleams with an unconvincing luster, moving too quickly to be real. And I try to forget that for a little while I formed a layer, however thin, in the deep stratigraphy of his family; so that some later explorer, rummaging through the drawers of his big old desk, might brush aside a scorecard from the 1967 PGA Northwest Open signed by Arnold Palmer, or an old pencil-style typewriter eraser, with a stiff brush on one end, stamped QUEEN CITY RIBBON CO., and turn up a faded photograph of me, in my sober blue suit, flower in my lapel, looking as if I knew what I was doing.

COLIN HARRISON

The Deal with Nana

● ● ●

"We can't live here and have Nana *there*," I told my wife,
Kathy, meaning her eighty-nine-year-old grandmother who lived in Los Angeles. "It's a disaster waiting to
happen."

We were walking through our leafy brownstone neighborhood in Brooklyn after dinner, trying to figure out what
to do with Nana, who was making our lives increasingly difficult. Voice cracking with fear, some of it ginned up for dra-
matic effect, Nana now called my wife whenever she had a
problem, which was every day: she couldn't get beef heart at
the butcher's shop to grind up for "the girls," her Persian

cats, or the garden tools were disappearing from her garage, or, most ominously, she had scraped the pump in the gas station with her Lincoln Mercury Grand Marquis, the biggest one they ever made, a car so large that it appeared to be driverless as Nana boated through the neighborhood. Clearly she was having difficulty living on her own.

"We can't move to L.A.," I said, just in case anyone might think such a thing were possible.

"That'd kill me," Kathy agreed.

Nonetheless, the situation was becoming urgent. Earlier that day Kathy had received a frantic phone call in her office in Manhattan when Nana had stumbled to the floor in her kitchen. Kathy had sat in her office listening to her grandmother crawl back and forth across the floor alternately wailing for help as if she were going down in the *Titanic* and muttering to herself about needing to feed "the girls." Eventually Nana had pulled her diminutive self up on a chair and returned to the phone, but by then my wife was a wreck, tearful with worry and frustration in equal measure.

We had moved to Brooklyn in our mid-twenties, and the problem of Nana, what to do about her, or *for* her, or, most worrisome, *with* her, was a dilemma we'd conveniently subordinated to the excitement of getting married, starting new jobs, and forging an existence in New York City. Kathy's mother, an only child long divorced, was dead, as was my wife's grandfather, and thus Kathy was Nana's only living relative, but for a couple of cousins twice removed, one living in Paris. They could not be the "responsible party," nor could any of Nana's friends, who ranged from the aging gay hairdresser who gave her a rinse each week to the kindly and yet increasingly ineffectual Mexican housekeeper, herself no spring chicken, to the various doctors Nana saw, including the "toe man," a wizard with the arthritic knobs and bunions of Nana's feet. To put it plainly, the people Nana communed with on a regular basis usually expected a check for their services.

Moreover, Nana was by any measure difficult, by virtue of her age, her temperament, and her upbringing. She had lived long enough that the circumstances of her birth were of another era; she had been born in Shanghai in 1899, the second daughter of a wealthy Jewish family who lived in the British concession. Their mansion was so large as to require the assistance of forty Chinese servants. And this was just the beginning: she'd ridden the Orient Express across Russia before the Russian Revolution; she'd seen death, suffering, and pestilence as a girl in pre-Communist China; she had hobnobbed with and rebuffed some of the richest young men in Asia, infuriating her father ("I could not possibly marry a man who calculated sums on the cuff of his shirt! Can you *imagine*?"); she had lived in Nice in the '20s and '30s, driving huge motorcars and conducting love affairs and then, aware that the Nazis were coming, moved to London. For reasons that had always remained mysterious, she had then moved from London to southern California of all places, and found herself a strapping widower who had no money but was a gentleman in every respect, and then had her first and only child at the age of forty-two.

Nana had been wealthy and intrepid on three continents,

and no small measure of her sense of entitlement remained, even a generation after the money was mostly gone (poorly invested, wasted, frittered away), the Oriental carpets sold off, and the once grand antiques spattered by the snot of the Persians, which, overbred for show competition, suffered from a strange feline sinus malady and sneezed constantly. Nana herself, every wit still in place, was razor-tongued, never hesitating to tell anyone of her mistreatment at the hands of fate. She felt sorry for herself, having outlived her husband and only child. I'd met her only a few times, on each occasion somehow amazed that I was now related to this old woman. She fascinated me, but I didn't exactly like her.

"There's no sort of assisted-living situation . . . ?" I began again, euphemistically.

"Nana won't go into a nursing home." My wife shook her head at the horror of the idea. "And I don't want to put her into one. We both saw what happened to my grandfather."

We headed home to our one-bedroom apartment that we quite liked. It was large enough that it had not only tiny office spaces for each of us but also a garden out back that was ours to use. The previous summer I had turned over the whole plot by hand and built four raised beds in which I planted twenty-odd kinds of vegetables, including corn. Not many cheap apartments in New York City have gardens large enough to grow corn. And on top of this, my wife and I both had great jobs and New York City was exhilarating, having reached one of its periodic heights of frenzied prosperity. We were not going anywhere, no matter what.

"Suppose we moved Nana here?" I said, scarcely believing what I was saying.

"You must be insane," my wife sputtered.

"It will only get worse out there," I told her. "You'll be flying to L.A. constantly. She's going to blow up the gas station one of these days, plow that car into the pump."

"Don't," Kathy pleaded, laughing. "It's not funny."

"I know it's not funny."

"Oh, *fuck*," she said. "I spent years getting *free* of her!"

Yes, this was certainly true. My wife's mother had become accidentally pregnant at age eighteen, submitted to a quickie marriage and divorce, and then more or less deposited her newborn baby into Nana's hands as the price for her release. Kathy's mother had moved away from Nana, never living at home, always residing at some temporary and sometimes unknown address. My wife's father, still a boy really, had been banished forever and drifted to Texas, where he later remarried. As my wife had grown up in Nana's house, the three of them—grandmother, mother, and daughter—had engaged in an ornate yet ferocious battle for autonomy, control, and identity. In this struggle, which did *not* end when my wife's mother died of breast cancer at age forty-three, money was a weapon, love always provisional, and screaming a constant. So far as my wife was concerned, her real life began when she had escaped her grandmother's house. Any extended time spent with Nana meant revisiting a long, painful childhood.

We walked farther, passing one grand, four-story Victorian home after the next. Brooklyn's brownstone neighborhoods had appreciated nicely during the boom, and it would be many years, if ever, before we might afford to buy one. Around us we saw people coming home late from work, couples with babies, folks going out to dinner.

"Where could she live?" Kathy asked.

I stared at her.

"No," she said. "Not with us. We're *newlyweds*. This is our first year. I don't want to take care of my eighty-nine-year-old grandmother."

"Just an idea," I said.

An idea I'd been quietly studying. As the Brooklyn real estate market steadily floated upward, the L.A. market had become an insane speculators' bazaar. The upward rise was bound to crash sooner or later, but until then Nana's ranch house, even with its earthquake damage, cracked swimming pool, and walls stained by cat mucus, had appreciated dramatically in the madness.

"Did you know," I ventured, "that the value of your grandmother's house would probably cover a good chunk of a house here?"

My wife looked at me, aware that my motivations were decidedly mixed. She smiled. "You would think of that."

"Hey, maybe we could do a good thing, but maybe that could be good for us, too," I said. We were going to have to take action, one way or another. We either initiated change or had it forced upon us. My wife, I also knew, really didn't want to deal with Nana's aging. But she was also selfless to the point that she would never think of a way to help her grandmother and herself simultaneously.

"I can't live with her," Kathy said. "She'll drive me crazy."

I didn't especially want to live with an eighty-nine-year-old woman myself. I'd seen what had happened to my own grandmothers, the family angst that their descent had caused; my mother's mother had gone blind, her heart slowly shutting down because of congestive heart failure, her knuckles swollen into misshapen paws by arthritis. She'd died alone. On the other side of the family, my father's mother had drifted through the decades into an inchoate, medicated senility in which she was only able to make sorrowful gobbling noises from her bed in the nursing home. Although unable to talk, she was quite capable of feeling, and when her roommate of many years passed away my own grandmother decided to stop eating. Which she did, successfully.

No, I certainly didn't want to live with an old woman and have to take care of her. I was twenty-eight years old, for Christ's sake, and running out to dinner parties with my beautiful young wife and working hard, playing in a basketball league at night, and generally having the time of my life. The idea of living with Nana *was* insane. What had gotten into me?

But now my wife was thinking about it. "Nana has no one else," Kathy said. "She's frightened. That's a big house to go to sleep in by yourself each night."

"She'd be happy if you moved there."

"But she knows I won't."

"So why is she calling so often? I mean the reason under the reason?"

We stopped walking. No matter how difficult her up-bringing, my wife had said many times that the bottom line was that her grandmother had always taken care of her, shel-tered her, paid for school, college, everything.

"Nana is asking me to fix it," she said slowly. "She doesn't know what to do. She's afraid she'll just *die* there in the mid-dle of the night and no one will know. Which could happen, I guess."

Within a week, my wife had proposed to Nana that she move to Brooklyn. She would sell the ranch house and help us buy a brownstone, where we all would live, Nana in her own ground-floor apartment, the two of us above her. The plan now excited Kathy, and I could see why: it offered a way for the two of them to be together in a set-ting other than the one where so much familial destruction had occurred. Maybe a little redemption might be possible. The plan possessed a certain theoretical elegance, but its enormity scared me. Executing the two transactions would be entirely my responsibility; not only were the sums in-volved considerable, but I would have to sell real estate in Los Angeles while buying it in New York almost simultane-ously. It would involve lawyers, wire transfers, bank inspec-tions of the properties, and so on. If one part of the plan failed, the whole thing failed. I had never done such a thing, and yet I had assured my wife that I could pull it off.

"We'll take care of you," my wife told her grandmother.

"I'm not moving," Nana said.

"What will you do?"

"I'm fine. Someone will take care of me."

"Who?"

That was when the crying began. "Nana, I am absolutely not moving to Los Angeles," Kathy would say. "I'm *young*. I have my life here."

Nana wouldn't budge.

"Tell her that's the best we can think of," I said.

"Nana, this is the best we can think of. The best we can think of for *you*."

"Tell her nursing homes are six thousand dollars a month."

Kathy put her hand over the phone. "I'm *not* going to tell her that."

"Tell her—hell, I don't know what to tell her."

A month later my wife and I flew to Los Angeles, having made no headway with Nana, even though there had been more incidents. Something about the car and a large bush. Another time Nana had become lost while driving on the freeways, finally needing a police escort home. She had dropped one of her $800 hearing aids in the kitchen disposal. And so on. Meanwhile the L.A. real estate market was teetering at wild heights, ripe for a crash, while at the same time the Brooklyn market was still rising. If our plan was to work, it needed to work *soon,* before the markets went in opposite directions.

"This is it," my wife said when we arrived, pointing to an

uninspiring two-story house with stucco siding built into a sliver of hillside. I could see that someone had once doted on the bougainvillea and the lemon trees, that someone being her grandfather, but that otherwise the place had fallen into a kind of sunbaked suburban shabbiness. Nana's enormous car sat half parked in the garage, and a quick glance upward showed that the roof was losing its thick cedar shingles at a precarious rate.

Nana met us at the door, looking even smaller than when I'd last seen her at our wedding.

"Oh, at last! At last!" she cried. Stooped and so thin her vertebrae lifted her sweater, she was no more than five feet tall in her heels. Her relief was immediate, and she clung tearfully to Kathy.

Inside my wife showed me the earthquake damage, the wall-to-wall carpeting streaked with dried beef heart drippings. Every conceivable nook and cranny in the kitchen was jammed with bills, canceled checks, newspaper coupons, supermarket receipts, and hearing aid advertisements.

"If I go, we must take my darlings!" Nana announced, and I assumed she meant her three Persians, who now inhabited what had been my wife's old bedroom, their enormous exercise furniture draped with sub-sanitary clouds of cat hair. But I was wrong, or rather, my awareness was incomplete. Nana led us out to the kidney-shaped swimming pool, and once past the cracked sidewalk around it pointed at some handmade elfin headstones arrayed in the weedy bed.

"My darlings!" she repeated, and my wife explained that

this was the graveyard of innumerable cremated Persians, each tiny tin of ashes carefully labeled and dated before burial. Each rusty tin would have to be disinterred and brought to Brooklyn, I was to understand.

Left alone by the pool, I realized somewhat distractedly that if Nana tripped on the cracked sidewalk and fell into the water she lacked the strength to get herself out. And no one would hear her cries. In my distraction, I noticed a piece of paper flutter. It was a blank check from Nana's checkbook. A quick inspection showed that an entire box of loose checks had been left on the table by the pool and that any number of them had blown down the hillside, lodging in the ivy beneath the lemon trees, conveniently available to anyone who might want to make use of them.

I came inside a few minutes later, a fat wad of blank checks in one hand. Nana and my wife, meanwhile, had continued their inspection. "Nana," Kathy said, "where are all the tools in the garage? All those shovels and saws and things?"

"A few are still there, I think?"

But they weren't. In fact, every last thing that one could carry away from the garage had been carried away, but for the washer and dryer, and the monstrous, scraped Lincoln itself. I stood in the cool shadowed space thinking how odd it was that I could someday soon live with Nana, that we had proposed such a thing. Life, I was just old enough to know, was mysterious. Things happened that no one might predict. My wife had already said that I didn't have to go through with it, that I could change my mind. But that was no longer possible, I knew. Kathy was Nana's blood. I was married to Kathy. The thing was knotted up; it was what it was.

That night, we discussed the plan with Nana.

"I might do it," she said.

Kathy had brought pictures of the Brooklyn brownstones we were looking at.

Nana held them in her bony hand. "Like London," she noted.

I called a real estate agency and asked that they send over a representative the next morning to talk to us about selling the property. In a hot market I didn't suspect that it much mattered who the agent was. At precisely the appointed hour a white Mercedes convertible pulled in, and out jumped a statuesque and totally stacked blonde in a white miniskirt and white pumps. She was a perfect L.A. goddess. She offered me her hand, itself a small piece of artwork, draped as it was with diamonds and featuring creamy long nails. Every man has his weaknesses, and I certainly have mine; I could feel stupidity flood my circulatory system.

"My partner will be here in a minute and then we'll get started," she breathed.

"Partner?" I said.

A moment later an identical white Mercedes convertible pulled in behind the first and an identical woman jumped out.

"No, we're not twins!" they announced brightly. "We just like the way we both look!"

They said many beautiful things about the property that I instantly forgot and allowed as how they really wanted to represent it, and suddenly I understood that in a pretty hot real estate market, there was competition among agents for houses and that it didn't hurt to be pretty hot yourself, no matter how many of you there were.

You might be handed the grave responsibility to sell Nana's house, I reminded myself as the two women tottered in their heels over the cracked sidewalk around the pool, you have never done this before, and these cantilevered buxotics are messing with your head.

After they left, I called the real estate office back. "I want someone I can deal with," I said. "Send over a potbellied middle-aged man."

Which they did. He arrived that same afternoon. His car was nice, his watch expensive. But I looked into his face and saw a tired guy who had been beaten around a bit, probably survived a few down markets. "Listen," I said after he'd met Nana and politely inspected the cat cemetery. "We're not going to fix this house up. If we sell, it's as is. My wife and I live in New York."

"Got it," he said.

"I don't want super top-dollar. I want super fast-dollar."

He nodded. "I can get you super top-dollar, though."

"You can? Why? Look at this place."

He smiled. "It's perfect."

"Why?"

"Tear-down. Everyone wants one."

I nodded slowly. Nana had not quite made her mind up.

The idea that her house would be demolished by bulldozers the day after she left might spook her, underline the impermanence of things. And really, who could blame her? She'd lived in the house for twenty-five years, many of them good ones. Her husband had spent thousands of days grooming the flowers and trees. She'd buried a dozen-odd cats there.

"We would, of course, not need to mention this to Mrs. Jacobs," said the real estate agent.

I nodded again. That would be prudent.

"Are you selling?" he said.

"I don't know," I told him.

That night, perched on the edge of her antique chair, Nana said she had been thinking about the idea of moving to Brooklyn and leaving her "lovely California."

"I'll do it on one condition," she told us. "Only one."

Kathy and I looked at each other. We thought we had covered all of the angles. "What?" Kathy asked.

"That you have a baby."

"What?"

Nana's expression was defiant. "If you promise to have a baby as soon as possible, then I will move. That's my offer."

We were taken aback. But we could see that Nana was serious, and I grudgingly admired her willingness to deal in the most ultimate of terms. This was not a demand of a weak old woman but rather the forceful wisdom of one who had *lived*. Born in another time, she knew things that we did not. For one, she knew how young we were, and how old she was. She knew the wheel of generations, the magic of a newborn. A baby would send her own family's flesh forward in time, and in the face of her advancing years, it was a consolation.

All this was in Nana's old face as she sat waiting for an answer. My wife looked at me. We'd barely discussed having children. But it was a question that would come soon enough. On the other hand, Nana's request was enormously self-indulgent; it presumed that her happiness was more important than her granddaughter's, a selfishness typical of Nana. And yet, to argue it another way, Nana had seen her only daughter's marriage blow up quickly, and here we were, married less than a year ourselves. Maybe in Nana's eyes having a baby would help cement the marriage, make it stick. Moreover, I felt that there was a deep female logic to all this. My home for yours, your baby for me. Warm new life before cold, certain death. The equilibrium was complicated, but it made sense. My wife wanted deeply to care for her grandmother, and later, when it would be too late to change anything, she also would need to have tried to make things as good as possible. She would need to know that she had done her best. And if a baby could help to tear apart a family, might not a baby also help put one back together?

"Yes," my wife said.

"What about him?" Nana asked. "He might not like living with a baby and an old hag at the same time."

"I can handle it," I said. Brave words, to be sure, but cheap, too. I didn't know enough about babies to be properly scared by what it meant to agree to have one. I'd never changed a diaper in my life. Plus, it all seemed a little abstract and off in the distance. What did scare me, though, was

what I'd already seen in my brief visit. Nana was barely func-
tioning as an independent adult. If she slipped five or ten
percent further, there might be a fire, a car accident, a bad
fall. We'd arrived just in time, and I knew that I would say
just about anything to get this problem fixed now.

I called the real estate man and told him to sell Nana's
house. The L.A. market was hanging in the firmament
like a rocket about to fall to earth. But . . . not yet. The bro-
ker held an open house for Nana's property and it sold, for
full price, in eighteen minutes.

We moved into our Brooklyn house, a big creaking
brownstone, in May 1989. Four floors. Seven bedrooms, three baths. Seven mantels. Walnut detail throughout, never painted. Sure it needed a little work, they all do.
We were deliriously excited. This was our house now? In the
hours just after the closing my wife and I lay on the dusty
parquet floor of the empty living room gazing up at the impossibly high ceilings. How would we fill this big house?
How would we populate it? What life would we live that otherwise would never occur? These questions were impossible
to answer.

Meanwhile Nana had to be moved east three thousand
miles. As promised, I did in fact dig up the cat cemetery
around the pool and bring the encrusted little urns back to

Brooklyn. I toted boxes filled with decades-old canceled checks, shopping fliers, and Christmas cards from the 1970s. These boxes often contained cat hair of unknown vintage, important documents such as birth certificates, and a fine yet unidentifiable granular matter, perhaps Nixon-era kitty litter. Nana followed a few weeks later. Her cats were flown by *personal courier,* at a cost that made me want to bang my head against the wall. Ah, well.

We settled in. My wife catered to Nana's every need, which delighted Nana. Once a week she was bustled off to a local hair salon, which she quite liked, sitting under a giant hair dryer among the ancient widows of Italian longshore-men who'd worked the docks of Brooklyn in days gone by. Despite their disparate backgrounds, they shared the same osteoporotic stoop and shameless application of rouge. "The hags!" Nana exclaimed when she returned, her hair a blue cloud. "You have no idea!"

After living alone for the better part of a decade, now Nana's anxieties eased considerably. We had dinner parties and she conversed brightly with people almost sixty years younger. She pretended to clutch her stomach and complain in French about her liver. While sitting in a lawn chair next to the front stoop she engaged the mailman in small talk and charmed whoever happened to go by, which in Brooklyn can be anyone, including murderers and thieves. She called everyone she knew in California and bragged about the mar-velous house she lived in with her "most beautiful and smart granddaughter." It was, for her, a genuine adventure, as if she had departed on a very long cruise on an ocean liner as big as Brooklyn, with a stateroom the size and configuration of a brownstone.

Meanwhile, the Los Angeles real estate market cratered, dropping thirty percent. (I congratulated myself, *oh yes I did.*) California itself went into an enormous recession, followed by the rest of the country. A neighbor sent a photo of what remained of Nana's house: a slab of concrete where the garage used to be, and a few two-by-fours sticking up from a pile of rubble. Nana never knew or cared. She was happy and secure. She would hear me hammering or sawing or drilling something elsewhere in the house. Her cats ran amok in her apartment. She complained about my wife's cooking but begged for more of it. Little did we know that she would insist that we inspect the inside of her nose by flashlight each night before she went to sleep. Somehow I did not mind doing this. She insisted on a variety of goopy cat food so obscure and expensive that it was not sold anywhere in the borough of Brooklyn. Some of this molten beef sauce ended up on her glasses each day. She consumed box after box of English cookies. She tended to fall asleep on the sofa after dinner, her swollen ankles set together. She dropped food constantly in her apartment kitchen and I was sure she was going to set something on fire. She complained that I was "a lout," and when my wife got angry at that, she cried for forgiveness and kissed her hand and said her life had been saved. But this was minor. We settled into a routine. My wife and I worked each day and came home to Nana, who spent innumerable hours during the day examining her mail, tidying up the kitchen, making tea for herself, and writing small checks to the large number of animal charities that had already discovered her new address. I spent the weekends working on the house, fixing up the top floor, spending long hours in the hardware store. Nana would come upstairs once a day for dinner. She didn't mind a little drink beforehand, and she would sit at one corner of the couch and prattle on about her cats while Kathy cooked. The whole thing felt easy and domestic as the weeks slipped by. Nana had made the move—just as she had once moved from Shanghai to France, France to London, London to California. My wife and I wondered if something a little bit fantastic had happened. Nana was happy. And my wife was happy.

Maybe that's why she got pregnant so quickly.

On February 5, 1990, almost exactly nine months after we had moved in, my wife had a baby, a daughter we named Sarah. Nana beheld this newborn creature in her lap a few days later, too nervous to lift her. "My hands are no good," she cried happily. Not only was the baby precious but the meaning of the baby was precious, too. Two generations removed, this flesh was her flesh, as well as that of her father and mother, her husband, and of course that of her daughter, dead too soon.

From there Kathy and I fell into the difficult time of being new parents. Working, taking care of a newborn *and* a ninety-year-old, the days slipped past in a blur of sleep deprivation. My wife worked herself to a deep exhaustion, losing weight, running the baby to the doctor's office, shopping, cooking, cleaning. Sarah was fat and cackling and we loved her more than life itself. The deal we had made with Nana seemed completely logical in retrospect, preordained even. Each piece had fallen into place.

Except the last one, the most obvious piece. Our baby girl was not ten months old when it became clear that Nana had started to fail. She was tired, she was weak, she was irritable. Getting her to and from the hairdresser became more difficult. She didn't want to go out to shop anymore. To get her out of a chair, I would take both her hands and gently pull her up. She wobbled alarmingly upon standing. Her skin was now so thin that it tore easily if she lurched against a piece of furniture. Her mood deteriorated as well. Now Nana complained about her food and even sometimes spit it out on her plate as if my wife had tried to poison her. Now she said that we spent most of our time and energy on the baby. There was a measure of truth to this, but, then again, she had insisted that we have the baby in the first place.

My parents, visiting, expressed their alarm at the stress my wife and I were under. "I can see it in your faces!" my mother said. "Your wife is nursing a baby, and she has to put up with *this*?"

Yet what were we supposed to do? There were no other family members to rely on. We had chosen this predicament. We hired a woman to help look after Nana during the day, a woman as patient as was humanly possible, who cleaned and straightened and made tea, but the situation worsened. Now I carried Nana up the stairs for dinner and then down again. Sometimes she urinated in my arms. I didn't much mind. She had given me my house and in a way she had given me my daughter. But we were never free from her. If we wanted to take the baby for a walk, she cried piteously on the sofa and wouldn't look at us. "Nana, we're just walking around the block," my wife would say soothingly.

"Just go and leave me!"

As the weeks tumbled by, my wife and I sliding along, dumbed by exhaustion, Nana required ever more care. My wife bathed her every day or so, changed the sheets. I would check her nose with the flashlight, adjust the blinds, the heat, the blanket. But none of these things could address her looming terror. She began to scream at night, a kind of frightened wailing that rose and fell. Two floors above, my wife would lift her head.

"Oh, *fuck*," she'd say. "I can't take this anymore."

I, the fool who had suggested the whole arrangement in the first place, would stumble down the stairs and stroke Nana's forehead and promise her that if anything happened I was there. In the darkness, Nana would cry a little and then passionately thank me, and then maybe she would fall asleep and maybe I would, too, or not.

I would slowly climb the stairs again, taking a quick look at the clock, to see how many hours remained until morning, not unaware that I had become a shelled-out version of myself. I had once been an athlete able to run eighteen miles in the hot sun; I had dug ditches with a pick-ax, had worked two and three jobs while attending graduate school. I was only thirty years old. But taking care of Nana was the most difficult physical thing I'd ever done.

At the top of the stairs, I'd listen, then find my way into the bed. Sometimes that was it, and we'd sleep through. Other times, not. This went on for months—how many I can no longer remember.

Then came the next-hardest part, when we had to stop kidding ourselves. We had promised Nana we would take care of her to the end, but now she was losing blood from her rectum and losing consciousness. My wife took her to one doctor after another, but soon the doctor's visits became hospital stays. She was dying, her doctor told us. Her heart was failing, and she might live another six months. This meant that she would either die at home, or she would not. Either option was bad, but one of them was worse, given the circumstances. I began to look into what a nursing home might cost.

And finally, we did it. Nana went to the hospital one more time, and once stabilized, never came home. She was a little confused but mostly fearfully complacent. She had lost the ability to walk. We placed her in the nearest nursing home we could find, a hulking institution about a mile from our house in a bad neighborhood. It was the only place even remotely close that had an open bed, and we tried to look on the bright side: we could visit with Nana, we could take her out in a wheelchair onto the roof garden when the weather turned warm. . . .

My wife was able to visit Nana nearly every day, but wept as soon as she entered the door. I visited at night on my way home from work. Panting weakly most of the time, Nana had lapsed into an uneven delirium, in which she complained about the food and then said that she'd seen red roses growing out of the wall. If she wasn't in bed, then I would find her in the floor's dayroom, slumped over in her wheelchair, tied up in order that she not fall out, with a dozen other women, many with urine bags under their seats, all asleep or staring at the wall-mounted television. Her eyes would be half open and she would slowly lift her head at my touch, the corner of her mouth caked with gummy white stuff, able to say something or not.

Had we done this to Nana? Were we—was I—to blame for this suffering? I was not sure. Had Nana never moved from Los Angeles, Nana would still have suffered heart failure. But somehow this was no consolation to me. She was here, now, in human torment. I looked around. They all were in torment, strapped into their wheelchairs, being spoon-fed soft food by the attendants. Meanwhile, one of the few ambulatory patients, a gray-skinned and haggard woman, shuffled along the halls ceaselessly, looking for her lost children, crying, "I'm so tired, I'm so tired."

I visited Nana alone in the nursing home every night after work, night after night until I thought I would go mad, stepping from the elevator into the long waxed hallway so often the desk attendant didn't even make me sign in anymore, just waved perfunctorily. Many times Nana didn't even know I was there. Sometimes I stayed awhile, sitting next to her bed, yet many times I did not. There was absolutely nothing noble or redeeming or virtuous about my visiting Nana. It changed nothing, except that I could tell myself and my wife that I had visited. I did not go with a glad heart, I often resented it, I sometimes resented Nana, I resented myself, and most of all I wanted it all to end. I wanted *my* suffering to end. Perhaps in later years I would have undertaken this duty with more charity and perspective and patience. But that wasn't the case now. I was tired, working all the time, fed up, sick of trudging from the subway each night. I wanted Nana to die, yes, I did. I admit it now, even if I could not have done so then.

Then came the last hospital stay, when the nursing home called an ambulance. My wife and I arrived at the hospital and I noted the lack of urgency in the manner of the nurses and staff. They had seen this moment many, many times. It was the place the nursing home sent such patients. My wife and I made the decisions, we signed the forms. Do not resuscitate, do not tube-feed.

Always we would remember the way Nana looked in the bed at the end, chin high, mouth open, eyes half shut. Life leaving her. Her emaciated chest barely rising. Born in Shanghai in the nineteenth century, dying in Brooklyn ninety-one years later on a hot August afternoon, a mercy.

Fifteen years gone, Sarah wears lipstick and has probably already kissed a boy or two. She has a younger brother and sister. There are two cats and a dog. My wife thinks she needs glasses. We see couples in their late twenties walk the neighborhood, some with babies in a stroller.

We are in the same house.

SUSAN STRAIGHT

A Family You Can't Divorce

● ● ●

We will gather in the driveway on Memorial Day forever, though we are not even married anymore to
the men whose father owns that driveway, though we are not
even always cordial to them, though we will roll our eyes
later tonight when they break out the Hennessy and domi-
noes and start hollering and leave us to clean up. The four
sons will have done the big-time barbecuing for hours, in the
oil drum, and we women will have brought our signature
side dishes, the greens and salads and rices. There will be
more than a hundred of us from four generations, in varying
shifts all day and into the night when the concrete finally

cools and the metal folding chairs get rearranged into our usual circles. It will already be hot in May out here in Riverside, California, sixty miles east of Los Angeles, on the border of the desert, where our parents all settled from places faraway, but where most of us were born. We will gather in my father-in-law's driveway because even when you get divorced in a family like this, you can't really break away. We are not legally entwined now to these men, all of us women sitting around, but we will gather here forever.

I have been sitting in this driveway for twenty-seven years. I was sixteen on the first Memorial Day my boyfriend brought me here in 1976. It was my first opportunity to see that on this strip of concrete everything is filtered through the male. I was partly terrified and partly amused, in my halter dress navigating the male relatives who raised their eyebrows and said, "Is that *you,* cuz?" That's how they called it, when you were with someone—not dating, or courting. "Aah, cuz, is that *you*?" Does she represent you, your choice, your taste, your dreams or fears?

There were one hundred people in this driveway and house back then, too. My boyfriend's father was the third of four sons, and my boyfriend was the third of four sons. All the uncles and aunts and cousins, the distant relatives and the neighbors who were called relatives, the godmothers and godfathers of this extended clan whose roots were Oklahoma and Mississippi and whose branches and leaves were Los Angeles and Riverside. I remember how afraid I was; I was introduced to so many curious faces and dubious nods and even a few baleful frowns: I held out my hand but was refused by two women—Tina, my boyfriend's older sister, and Margaret, his older cousin, who said, "I don't believe this."

I was the only white person there. Most of the time, I still am. But now, after twenty-seven years, my married family has forgotten that I am white. (Last year, while publicly excoriating a white woman my brother-in-law dated, my former sister-in-law started in on her hair. I said gently, "Now, give her a break. I'm blond, too, remember?" The three women with us looked at me blankly, then sucked their teeth and said, "No you're not," before going on about the conversation.)

But I remember that first holiday, how in the driveway, the men were fairly gleeful at the prospect of a small blonde with Farrah Fawcett hair holding hands with a six-four basketball player with an Afro the size of a giant tumbleweed. I remember how inside the house, in the living room, the aunts and other women were fairly mistrustful of my ability to cook properly or be polite, as white people were not known for their home training. I chafed to get to the kitchen, where I would meet my future mother-in-law. With all the food I'd seen piled on the table, I knew there were dirty pots, and I knew what to do.

I knew how to clean, not just wash the pots but wipe down the stove and even the burners, erase spatters from the plastic-encased clock above the stovetop.

My future mother-in-law, Alberta, had beautiful white teeth like tiny refrigerators, and she smiled at my braces. She said what she said to me for the next twenty years: "Did you get you a plate?"

After I ate, I washed the pots that had been emptied and cleaned the counter, including the area behind the faucet, which I scrubbed until the hardwater clouds left the metal. Alberta put her arm around me and led me back out to the living room, where she confirmed my suitability by saying, "She's so sweet, you should look at the kitchen. He found a good one."

I was Dwayne's girlfriend from the time I was sixteen until we married, when I was twenty-two, and we stayed married for fourteen years, the longest anyone in the clan stayed married besides his parents.

My father-in-law, General Roscoe Conklin Sims, Jr., was born in Tulsa, Oklahoma, and his father died when he was seven. His mother had to split up her five children; the older ones ended up in Los Angeles with her sister, and the younger ones stayed in Oklahoma with an uncle. After he made his way to Los Angeles, General entered the military and was stationed at Camp Pendleton. Visiting his brother in Riverside, he met Alberta Morris, who was a senior in high school. They married directly after her graduation in 1953.

Alberta Morris was the third of four daughters, and no one ever really knew where she was born: perhaps Mississippi, where her mother was from; perhaps Arkansas, where her mother arrived in the 1940s after her own mother was run down accidentally on a dirt road by white teenagers; or perhaps Calexico, the California town on the Mexican border where a relative's car broke down and so much of the family stayed. But Alberta was raised in Riverside, and she fell in love with the great dancer and charismatic man who was part Indian, Irish, and African, whose face was reddish and tinted with so many freckles that his nickname is Specks.

Mr. Sims, as we all still call him, is retired now, but he has always been the social force on his street, given his love of alcohol and music, his conversational finesse, his encyclopedic knowledge of black history and culture. He was a gardener who worked for many rich white families, judges and doctors and lawyers and contractors, and so he knew everything about the city, and loved to impart his knowledge to any and all in his driveway while he fixed lawn mowers and engines. He had forty-seven mowers in the back and side yards when I met him, and worktables covered with tools, machine parts, jars of screws and nuts and nails and found treasures.

But while people talk, they get hungry. My mother-in-law could cook. Between her skill and generosity, she fed countless people every day. Not just her own six children, and the nieces and nephews and cousins who came to live with her when they had problems with their own parents, but any of her children's friends, neighbors, even a little white girlfriend who drifted into her kitchen that Memorial Day.

My mother-in-law made entire hams, not small canned portions. Her pots, for neckbones and rice or for collards and ham hocks, were huge compared to the pots in my house.

But I knew how to cook, too, and my mother had also taught me the virtues of ham hocks: the knuckly portion that boiled for hours to lend green things flavor, the pink slivers extracted and tender. When I took apart a hock in Alberta's kitchen, she grinned in approval.

My own house was different, though not that far away, in a neighborhood bordering the orange groves. My mother was Swiss, my stepfather Canadian, and in addition to raising three kids of their own, for twelve years they fit pairs of foster children into our family like puzzle pieces. Five kids from ages one to five—I was the oldest and learned to cook and clean the kitchen early in life. We ate *raui roesti* (Swiss fried potatoes) and *salzhardapfeli* (Swiss boiled potatoes) and lots of liver. My dad had his own junkyard, behind his laundry equipment shop, and he owned several laundromats, which we made lint-free and sanitary every Saturday.

Dwayne and I were instant comrades when we met on the bus coming back from a field trip during our freshman year of high school. We started meeting at the playground to shoot hoops and the breeze. We talked about his work on his father's gardening truck, where he and his brothers sat atop the mountain of trimmed branches and grass all the way to the dump, because his father didn't figure he needed a cover to hold down the debris. Then we talked about my work in the laundromats (always looking for spare change) and how my little brother got bit by our junkyard dog and it was his thumb but he held the finger to his jeans fly as he ran to my dad and all that blood on the denim made everyone assume he'd lost the family jewels.

Dwayne and I were both schooled the same way: hard physical work for men, hard domestic work for women, only a few clothes to rotate all week—and stories. Dwayne took the story of the bloody zipper to the driveway, and I stood beside him while it conferred respect on me and my family.

I fit into the driveway just fine, even though I looked wrong. I talked sports with my future brothers-in-law (I knew about Cornelius Greene, the black quarterback for Ohio State University, and what he meant). I helped the dubious holdouts, Tina, my future sister-in-law, and Margaret, my future cousin, in the kitchen, and my mother-in-law always had my back, teaching me how to make smothered steak, admiring my prowess with Ajax.

Dwayne and I married at the end of my first year of graduate school. It was the same summer his oldest brother, General Roscoe Conklin Sims III, married Lisa. We were in each other's wedding. General III was our best man, and on August 20, 1983, we circled the city lake in their cousin Newcat's Cadillac. The horn didn't work, so my new brother-in-law shouted, "Honk, honk, damnit, these people just got married." His reception toast was "Be fruitful and multiply."

But he went first. He and Lisa had four kids (the oldest is General IV), and then she got a job as a correctional officer in Sacramento. General III lasted only six weeks up north before he came back home to Riverside. We in the Sims family do not leave Riverside, but unfortunately, that doesn't prevent us from leaving each other. General was divorced from Lisa, and later had relationships with four other women and had four other children. Lisa eventually transferred to a local prison and moved back to Riverside with her four kids when they were teens.

But back then, every holiday in the driveway, people would tease Dwayne and me because we didn't have babies yet. I got an MFA, began teaching, Dwayne got a job as a correctional officer, and the week after we got health insurance, I got pregnant. We had a daughter in 1989, and another in 1991, and somehow I was confined to the living room and kitchen with Alberta and the women, and Dwayne spent more and more time in the driveway.

All those conventions of our immigrant families (and yes, at one family reunion Alberta's cousin stood up and said, "We moved here from Mississippi, y'all, that was a third-world country")—the divide between the sexes, between domestic and physical labor, between freedom for men in the driveway and the tight confines of the steamy kitchen for women—helped wedge us apart.

How did people like Alberta and General stay married for forty years? I always wondered. The physical geography of their marriages gave them room to breathe. Alberta had her leather club chair near the TV and she had the kitchen, from which she produced plates for General in the driveway—a place she otherwise rarely ventured. All up and down their street, and mine, back then in the 1970s and '80s, men had their garages and cars and driveways, and women their patios and sewing rooms and kitchens. That's why they stayed married, even Dwayne and I can admit now.

In the beginning, Dwayne had his own driveway, at our

house, and when his friends and brothers gathered there while they pounded U-joints into submission or rebuilt engines, I did what I was meant to: I brought tin pie plates full of food for everyone. But after we had two daughters, and when I became a published writer, I couldn't do it. I wanted Dwayne to sit inside, with us; I wanted him to fix our dryer, rather than spend all day in the driveway fixing his brother's car. He wanted me to never miss a holiday in the driveway, and I began to travel for my books.

And Dwayne tried hard. Once, his father happened to visit while Dwayne was actually ironing my black skirt for work. (He worked graveyard at an institution; I taught days at the university.) His father never let him live that down.

But Alberta did her best to keep us together. She watched my babies when I went to work, and I came to her house at lunchtime to nurse and watch one soap opera. When Dwayne chafed under the endless responsibilities and tried to escape to his brothers' single company, she told him, "You have the best woman you'll ever have. You ain't spending even one night on my couch, so take your sorry butt home right now. Go."

He told me that, later.

Dwayne and I were not set up to have separate lives, like our parents. We were very frayed by 1994, and I had been wanting another baby for some time. But Dwayne was adamant: if I got pregnant, he'd get a Harley. I took this for a veiled threat of imminent escape by injury, and when repeatedly pressed by Alberta for another baby to watch (she passed them on to Dwayne's godmother when they could walk too far and take her away from the soaps), I told her about her son's reluctance.

"Why you even asking him?" she said, incredulous, her voice rising high. "He ain't gotta know. When the baby gets here, he'll be fine."

Around that time Alberta started to have searing headaches. She knew her blood pressure was dangerously high but wouldn't tell anyone or visit the doctor. One morning she had a stroke. Over the next five days, she had a series of strokes, which got progressively worse, and while she lay in a coma, we all gathered in shifts in the ICU room, the women cooking in rotation in Alberta's kitchen. One night, in a care facility a few blocks from our house, Dwayne sat by her side and whispered to her that I was pregnant. We hadn't told anyone, as I was just a few months along. He read a children's book to her and then, when he left, she slipped away, just as I was arriving to sit by her bedside with five of the women from the driveway—sisters-in-law and cousins.

We fretted about Alberta's manicure, ragged now, and her hair, the gray fringe she hated beginning to show. Some women did her hair and nails and makeup for her funeral. I did not. I took care of her kitchen, with the women who were good with kitchens, like me. After the service, and the formal reception at the church, we had the family in the driveway. Just the close family—a hundred people.

All the food. All the foil-covered dishes, our specialties,

and a ham that made me cry. Afterward, I wiped the counters, the Formica that Alberta had been so proud of for the one day it was new and unmarked—that first evening her husband left a lit cigarette on it, the brown halo of her anger at the mark, the way she touched it for years. The spoons. Never enough serving spoons for all the people. The linoleum. I scrubbed at the linoleum floor furiously with Lisa, my sister-in-law for life.

Things fell apart in the driveway for a time after Alberta died. Her own sisters-in-law had moved from Compton and Crenshaw and Inglewood to the high desert, leaving their houses to escape crime, and leaving to others their traditional three holidays (Labor Day, Fourth of July, and Super Bowl Sunday, a Sims national holiday). The drive was too long and somber without Alberta's face there in the driveway or the kitchen to greet them. Mr. Sims cleaned up the driveway, too, after Alberta was gone. No lawn mowers or engines hanging from a chain in the trees, no barbecue. He didn't want company for a time. So we gathered at a brother-in-law's, at a park, at a cousin's. The second year, on Memorial Day, there were several arguments and near-fights, between women and men, between General's exes, between relatives who had drunk too much in their sorrow over Alberta's absence.

And my husband, without the tether of his mother's home as an alternate anchor to our own, left for several trial periods—to a motel, to his sister's, and finally, to a one-room apartment. He needed, he said, to be independent for a time, to try out solitude.

When our youngest daughter was two, we divorced. He didn't have his mother to reassure him that these hard days of young children and work were the way life was laid out for us; he didn't have his father in the driveway for stories and companionship, because his father, in his grief, had left his house for a one-bedroom place he built himself on a rental property.

But Mr. Sims moved back into his own house two years later, ready to try to make it his own again. And that May, he spread the word that Memorial Day would be held as before, in the driveway.

This past Memorial Day, Lisa came by, as she always does, without her companion. Not to see her ex-husband, though she checks out him and his new wife. She comes to pay respects to Mr. Sims, and to see us, all the sisters-in-law.

Lisa hugs me long and hard. We are the originals. As General III's other women tend to glare and shift and gather in their own factions, we sit together and talk about old times.

We have to laugh, watching our father-in-law hold court' at the head of the driveway by the rubber tree plant. I think his rubber tree, in its pot, has been next to the front door all twenty-seven years I've sat in that driveway.

My father-in-law and his contemporaries let the kids begin the music. My nephews' generation: Jay-Z, Usher, Alicia Keys.

Then my ex-husband and our kind take over, later in the afternoon: Marvin Gaye, Parliament, Chaka Khan.

But eventually, my father-in-law gets out his old records. His favorite is Earl Grant, a jazz organist whose name I only hear in this driveway. Charles Brown. And then Bobby Blue Bland, when they break out the homebrew. (My father-in-law has been experimenting with his own orange wine for some thirty years now.) I look at the stretch of cement, bordered on one side by wrought iron and a strip of grass with roses in their water wells, and on the other by the patch of lawn and the ancient perfectly pruned olive bonsai and a cement-block wall against which the most looped men rest their chairs by the end of the night.

My own family is scattered now. My brother, who used to love to drink and visit in the driveway, died in 2002. My half brother lives in Washington state, and my foster siblings are all gone. My parents eventually left our old house and bought a brand-new home in a tract on the edge of the city. Holidays there mean ten or twelve of us at a long formal dinner table (including my ex-husband).

My daughters are fifteen and thirteen and nine now. The youngest one, who was born after Alberta died, looks so much like my mother-in-law that everyone remarks on her winged brows, her generous square smile, and her obsession with shoes. My girls hear our stories while we all sit in the folding chairs. They hold their plates on their laps and study our offerings.

They asked me one night why every dish but the fruit

salad contained meat. Shirley's barbecued beans had bacon and hot links, Doris's greens had fatback and bacon, Terri's potatoes and green beans had ham hocks, Mrs. Walker's blackeyed peas had chicken necks, and my rice had hot sausage. (These side dishes accompanied the ribs, chicken, hot links, hot dogs, and hamburgers. For a kind of dessert we'd make asada, grilled beef.)

I told them that our family had not always had meat. They had heard the stories in the driveway, about grandparents and ancestors who had gone days and weeks without meat, with only grits or cornbread and greens. They knew that the elderly man sitting near their grandfather had killed a pig at seven, with a hammer, because his mother was so hungry.

Of all my "sisters in law," Shirley is the one I see most. She was with General III after he and Lisa divorced. They never married, but she had a daughter, Erika, with him, and rented the house next door to her father-in-law early in their relationship, nine years ago. She has never left, though General hasn't lived there for years. Shirley's and my father-in-law's driveways are separated only by a black wrought-iron fence three feet tall. She cooks and drives and argues with General's kids, whom she treats as her own, given all the time they spend in the driveway. She leans on that wrought-iron fence to chat with Mr. Sims and she takes him to the doctor. She makes him eat when he doesn't want to.

Now we women stand behind the long tables in our

aprons and uncover the pots and bowls containing our dishes. They are our specialties—we don't bring anything else by now, because the dishes are part of who we are.

When I came to Memorial Day as a rookie, I used to bake, and I made great brownies, but they were not signature enough—not Aint Sister's peach cobbler or Terri's Seven-Up Cake. So I simmered saffron-yellow Mahatma rice with red-hot sausage and black beans and blackeyed peas, with curry and garlic and Creole seasoning and black pepper and sugar.

I spoon out my rice to the hundred or so people who have gathered here today to honor tradition and forgiveness and eye-rolling and stories. My rice, the one Alberta loved because I'd finally made up my own dish. You bringing your rice? My rice. My family.

My daughters eat their meat. They visit with their uncles and older cousins who have sweated for hours at the drum barbecues along the wrought-iron fence. Huge slabs of ribs, like so many xylophones, lie on the long table and are chopped separate with a small axe.

"She look just like Alberta," someone says about my youngest daughter, who holds a single rib like a harmonica between her teeth.

Though on paper, legally, we are not family now, we will be forever family. Not in law. In food and blood and the driveway.

ANTHONY GIARDINA

My So-Called Jewish Life

● ● ●

Jewishness—not the religion, but the state of being—first appeared to me as the most desirable thing in the world during the summer of 1964. I was hanging out in the home of my best friend, Stanley Slotnick. His mother, Janice, was reading the paper in one room; his father, Ruby—a pharmacist, rarely present—must have been in another, because Janice's voice suddenly rang out, with characteristic Slotnickian hauteur—"Ruby, let's go see this movie *Nothing but the Best* tonight. The paper says it's a witty and wicked satire!"

Understand that I was a fourteen-year-old Italian boy, the child of immigrant parents, and I was obsessed, in ways that were probably not healthy for a fourteen-year-old, with what might then have been referred to as "middlebrow" culture. Foreign imports like *Nothing but the Best* that played at the Exeter Street Theater in downtown Boston were to me the essence of a world I wanted to get to but which seemed far beyond my reach. All it would have taken was an easy bus and subway ride into Boston from my suburban Waltham home, and the two or three dollars the Exeter charged. But the psychological gulf was huge. Going to the Exeter would have meant taking a brazen leap above my station into a world I didn't yet know how to annex.

So to hear Janice Slotnick declare, with evident blitheness, her easy access to this world was a revelation. It, along with other habits of hers—her avid reading of fat middle-class bestsellers, for one—seemed to be mysteriously connected to her Judaism. I knew nothing at all about the religion except that Friday nights were off-limits to Stanley. But being a Jew seemed to confer something that my Italian parents couldn't come close to: some in-synchness with the larger world of "culture."

In high school, I dated all three of the Jewish girls available to me—Barbara Dinoff, Gayle Polimer, Ellen Weinstein. Whenever I picked up Barbara Dinoff for a date, I had to endure her mother's unmasked trepidation at the sight of me: me the unwashed, the unacceptable. Looking up from the vantage point of the driveway, where I had just gotten her daughter settled in the car, I was always treated to the sight of Mrs. Dinoff clutching the drapes at the bay window of her house, not making the slightest attempt to hide from me her baleful witness, lest I hop her daughter then and there, and not only adulterate the Jewish race but ruin her daughter's chances of marrying the nice doctor Mrs. Dinoff had picked out for her.

What made all this endurable—even worth it—was something these girls had had planted in them by their mothers, something that I, even in my non-Jewish state of being, shared: a sense of aspiration, of heading toward a life beyond the confines of Waltham. I had by then stormed the gates of the Exeter Street Theater; I knew now that merely sitting among urban sophisticates didn't make you one of them. In the company of these girls I had the sense of being one of the chosen. Together, we could debunk our little town and have fun doing it, knowing that we were soon to graze in richer pastures.

I decided early that my own grazing had to be done in New York, but Columbia rejected me. So I ended up at Fordham, in the Bronx, a school not exactly noted for producing urban sophisticates. A few semesters in, however, something began to dawn on me. It would never be enough just to be close to culture. I wanted to create the thing itself. My ambitions, in other words, had turned literary. I read critics, I read novelists, and I soon came to feel that the essence of the life I'd always vaguely aspired toward was an essence I came closest to when I read Lionel Trilling, or Saul Bellow, or Philip Roth, writers who pointed me toward a serious life, a thought-filled life, an undeniably *Jewish* life.

I got a job while I was at Fordham driving a cab. My favorite neighborhood to troll for fares was the Upper West Side of Manhattan: Riverside Drive, West End Avenue. I loved the look of those streets, the severity and intellectual depth embodied in the heavy stone buildings. The life of the mind was enshrined in that neighborhood. It was thrilling to think that at any moment an arm might reach out from one of these apartment buildings, flagging me down, and the arm might turn out to belong to Hannah Arendt, or to Trilling himself! I developed a fantasy on those long, slow swoops down West End Avenue of someday finding a Jewish girl—it had to be a Jewish girl—and moving into one of these brownstones, and in her company finally committing to paper my own *Dangling Man,* my own *Goodbye, Columbus.* The fantasy went further: on Sundays her parents would visit, her good intellectual Jewish parents would come and offer their approval. They would introduce me to the right people, and confer on me their blessing. Life, my perceived Jewish life, was a thing of order and intellect, to which I wanted to hitch my star.

My aspirations, as I said, were literary, but what I actually did in college was act. At the end of my junior year, I was introduced to the producers of a small summer stock company nestled deep in Pennsylvania farm country. I was hired for the summer, and when I asked about transportation, the producers suggested I contact a young actress in the company, who might be willing to share a ride.

It would be wrong to say that the Jewishness of Eileen Bonder was what initially drew me to her, though, let's face it, it didn't hurt. Instead, I like to think it was her belt. That summer, while we rehearsed musicals like *Gypsy* and *Carnival,* and stale sex farces like *Plaza Suite* and *Your Daughter, My Son,* she seemed to always be wearing the same red belt, one in which a parade of dogs chased each other around her waist. More likely, though, it was the way she wore it, or moved in it, an implied attitude of cool rebelliousness. She was seventeen that summer, far, far too young. But I was very quickly smitten.

She was herself smitten with the company's gay set designer and would be for the next two years. But by summer's end, we had at least become friends—enough so that she accepted a ride back to New York with me and my college roommate. We drove through the night, arriving on the outskirts of the city just as dawn was breaking.

A kind of invisible cowl came over Eileen as we got nearer to Co-op City, the industrial-looking high-rise development in the Bronx where she lived. The summer had been exquisite freedom for her, the first time she'd ever lived away from home, and now she was returning to a neighborhood she loathed. I hoisted her bags into the elevators and accompanied her up to the fifth floor.

My memory of the moment the door opened is of a woman—round-faced, beaming, dressed in her morning *schmatte* and probably inching it closer around her to cover the weight she was always concerned about. Instead of a Dinoffian mother scowling at me disdainfully as she attempted to fold her daughter back under her wing, Eileen's mother—a dead ringer for the later, increasingly zaftig Shelley Winters—offered me an enormous smile of greeting and ushered me to a seat at the breakfast table. This woman—her emotions bubbling over like a pot kept permanently under a high flame—emptied the cupboards and kept asking *What else? What else can I get you?*

The Bonder home did not much resemble the Jewishness I'd come to revere. For one thing, there were very few books in this apartment: an early Chaim Potok or two, *The Joys of Yiddish,* and a book called *The Art of Serving Food Attractively,* which, given the culinary habits of this family as I got to know them, must have been there for decorative purposes only. Where Barbara Dinoff and Ellen Weinstein had always seemed to exist, within their houses, as shrouded and protected as sultan's daughters, Eileen seemed to live in a far less ordered world.

The Bonder apartment was in fact a monument to disorder, to clashing styles. I knew that Eileen's father owned a dry-cleaning store on Belmont Avenue, very near my Fordham neighborhood. I knew that they were far from rich. But lack of money did not quite explain the gestalt of the Bonder apartment. I felt like I had walked into the home of the anti-Trillings. Clearly something else dominated here, something that was the antithesis of what I'd come to expect from Jews.

As I got to know them over the course of that year—I kept showing up in the role of Eileen's "friend" while she conducted her hopeless long-distance relationship with the set designer—I came to see that emotions were what was stockpiled here in place of books. To sit at the table and listen to Eileen's mother Ann tell a story was a kind of Mozartean experience: I hadn't been aware that so many emotional notes could be hit in so short a space of time. She would travel from the death of a departed loved one (instant tears) to a recounting of the most hilarious thing that had ever happened to her, back to (the tug was always there) death and loss, then surging again, in a cascading line, toward hilarity. It was exhausting, but it was the lingua franca here, in this household of four daughters. Ann rarely finished her sentences, but gave the impression that this was not because of a failure of language but because of *the* failure of language. "I only wish . . ." and "I only hope . . ." were two of her favorites, yet what exactly was wished, what exactly hoped? Something so ineffable, partaking so much of emotional depth, that words, in their inadequacy, could never quite capture it. Her initial acceptance of me only thickened over time, so much so that I came to believe that, should things between Eileen and me begin to develop romantically, I would face no resistance at all from this family.

Then, when spring came around, Eileen invited me to her family's Passover Seder. I had no idea what a Seder was, and Eileen's description of it was disconcerting. A pious, solemn occasion involving something called a "shank bone." But I was always up for a free meal in those days—I was twenty-three, and living on my own in the city—and I thought it could do no harm to show this family what a respecter of Judaism I was.

My first memory of that Seder scene is of glassware shaking on the Seder table as a child ran by (two of Eileen's sisters were married by then), of soup nuts in profusion, of too many people working at cross purposes, while Eileen's mother, in the kitchen, conducted a kind of performance art: How much uncertainty could the act of cooking encompass? How much self-doubt could be brought to bear on the creation of a kugel? By the time she placed food on the table, she seemed to be trying to disown it, as if nothing made by her could possibly be worth anything. But at the center of all this, I remember a newly daunting presence: Mr. Bonder at the head of the table, patiently waiting, in close proximity to the fabled shank bone.

It was during that Seder that I became aware of a change in Eileen's father. He'd always been friendly enough to me. But now, here, was I imagining it or was he not, out of the corner of his eye, watching me—or, more accurately maybe, was he making sure *I* watched *him*? It was as though this scene had been set up to point out something to me: Don't be fooled by the openhandedness here, the bear hug of welcome. Here at the Seder table was the essence of the thing itself, the hard kernel and nut. Jewishness was not, finally, the Exeter Street Theater or the heavily draped Dinoff living room. It was not the Upper West Side or *Dangling Man* or even *Portnoy's Complaint.* You could penetrate all these things, make them more or less your own; what you could not penetrate was Judaism itself. In this family, it seemed, Judaism did not exist as an intellectual construct at all; it seemed to me instead a simple *force,* unquestioned, immovable, one that did not have to justify itself intellectually.

Sure enough, when, a year or so later, Eileen and I finally became lovers, her father took her one afternoon out onto the apartment's "terrace," a tiny porch just big enough for two, facing the other Co-op City towers. On that terrace, he laid down the law: if you get serious with this guy, if you marry him, that's it, I'll disown you. I can imagine that scene: the seriousness, the gravity, the old-worldness of it, a father calling his erring lovestruck daughter back into the fold. I can imagine the setting, too: those high towers Eileen found so repulsive. For her, Judaism was inseparable from milieu: it was this drab outpost of the Bronx, it was the small-mindedness of her relatives, it was the men who would not let her sit downstairs in the synagogue when she'd come, a nine-year-old Yeshiva *bucher,* to meet her father. She'd turned away from the faith early, and I can imagine precisely how she turned away from her father that day after receiving his ultimatum. "Fine" is what she said. There it was, the rebelliousness I'd seen in the way she'd worn that dog belt at the Millbrook Playhouse. "Fine." She turned, and left the terrace, and went inside.

Nothing more ever came of it. He'd delivered the same ultimatum to Eileen's two older sisters when they'd started dating non-Jewish boys, and they'd obeyed him. But here, with his third daughter, he was clearly up against something else, and he backed down without a fight.

When Eileen told me about what her father had said, I couldn't believe it. "What does he mean, I'm not a Jew?" was practically my reaction. Did he not know I'd been worshiping at the altar of cultural Judaism since the age of fourteen? Was he not aware that I lived on West 107th Street, in one of those fabled brownstones, that I kept a volume called *The History of the Jews* in my bathroom, near the tub?

And did it not matter that, were she to marry me, Eileen was, by the crudest, Jane Austenesque social accounting, moving a notch upward on the social scale? My parents had by that point gone from being hardworking immigrants to becoming solidly successful middle-class suburbanites. When the two sets of parents met each other, they were astonished by their similarities, down to sharing the same names ("Ann and Phil"), until, on their first visit to my parents' abode, the Bonders realized that this other "Ann and Phil" lived in a world of cabin cruisers and in a home that, in Ann Bonder's house-hungry terms, counted as a "palace."

And if this did not matter, how about the fact that, in marrying me, Eileen was marrying Aspiration itself, that she was indeed headed toward another class, one governed less by the money we would make than by the circles we would soon begin to move in?

It was soon clear that I'd become more of what I considered the classic Jew—the writer, the reader, the *aspirer*—than the Bonders had ever had any interest in becoming. Not all Jews, it would appear, got off the boat clutching a prayer shawl in one hand and *The Adventures of Augie March* in the other. Some got off clutching *The Art of Serving Food Attractively* in one hand, while with the other they clutched at something always out of reach—a handhold, maybe, a sense of security. The Bonders were the Diaspora—transported, not always by choice, from one place to another, and as uncertain of the new place as they'd been of the old. Further, they carried the Diaspora as a way of thinking about the world: always fearful of the new, always deeply uncertain. Over the course of forty years, they had gone from Academy Gardens in the South Bronx (until the "neighborhood changed"), to Black Rock Avenue in the mid-Bronx (until Co-op City had opened) to this farthest outpost, these towers built, as it turned out, shoddily, another state governmental promise run afoul. It would be easy to lay this sad journey to their sense of timidity, but they remained true believers. The promise New York State had made to lower middle-class Jews in building Co-op City was that you didn't have to be enterprising, a pioneer, didn't have to move out to Long Island or New Jersey and risk the entire nest egg in order to protect your family. The city—the Bronx—wanted to keep this class of Jews within its borders. Weren't these towers the physical evidence of that? Within a few years the towers were covered with scaffolding, the sidewalks were coming apart (the buildings had been erected, apparently, on an inadequate foundation), and the halls smelled of urine. Yet they stayed.

They stayed because their identities were fixed in time. For Ann, Eileen's mother, I knew that Judaism didn't amount to very much beyond that unquestioned identity. Brought up in a family of legendary poverty, under a father who followed religious dictates to the letter—to the point of inviting strangers in to eat even when there was not enough to feed his own brood—she had gravitated toward a less rigorous philosophy, one that allowed for at least the possibility of plenty ("Live Laugh Love" read the necklace she wore until her death). Death itself—the loss of her parents— seemed to unmoor her from whatever religious beliefs she may once have had. When, five years after Eileen and I were married, death took beautiful Sam, the thirty-four-year-old husband of her beloved second daughter Lorraine, that was the end. I never heard her utter a religious sentiment afterward. Indelible to me is the memory of her clutching the rabbi's arm at Sam's funeral, asking, as if it were some state secret confided only to rabbis, *why* God had chosen to do this.

There were times, in the Bonders' presence, when I felt pulled back to something even more primitive than the immigrant life I'd grown up in. It was impossible not to be close to these people—the emotional ties were too strong, too insistent—yet it sometimes worried me that our attempts, Eileen's and mine, to move into the new world were going to be retarded by their pull on us.

Once, when Eileen and I were headed to a production of a play of mine in Washington, D.C., a production that signified a major leap forward in my own career, Eileen's mother insisted that we take a pot of her matzo ball soup with us on the plane ride. We had a new baby going with us: what were we going to eat when we got to Washington? Inconceivable to Ann that when we were picked up by the theater's producers at the airport, we might feel a little embarrassed holding this pot of soup. Nonetheless, we took it—how could we refuse this woman?—and yes, we were embarrassed, and some of it spilled on the plane, so that the smell of the soup pervaded the compartment, as it by then had begun to pervade our lives.

Nonetheless, we connected, even in ways that were surprising. Ann Bonder worshiped the theater. To watch the Tony Awards with her was to see her revel in every cheesy, gloppy musical number. It was all ecstasy for her, though she frequently got the mile markers wrong ("I thought they were Chinese children," she said once, while we were watching a scene from *The Sound of Music*). And like the fourteen-year-old boy I had once been, she considered Broadway itself—a mere subway ride away—as remote as Bali. Making her way through Times Square alone terrified her, and her husband didn't like to go with her. So she watched the Tony Awards, and pined.

At a certain point I became a member of a playwrights organization called New Dramatists, one of the side benefits of which was free tickets to every new Broadway play while it was in previews. There is a way that even someone who had been as hungry for such things as I had once been can become glutted by them, and I usually turned these tickets down. Then it occurred to me that Ann might like them. So we developed a little ritual. Late in the week I would call her and ask her if she was interested in seeing what was up that week: Joanne Woodward in *Candida,* maybe, or Suzanne Pleshette in something called *Special Occasions?* "Are you kidding?" was always the reply. Then, on Saturday afternoon, she would take the special Co-op City–to–Manhattan bus that dropped her off near the theater district, where I would meet her and take her to Chock Full o' Nuts. Afterward, I would walk her to the theater lobby, and watch her go in. She always looked a little uncertain doing that, as if this world, so desired by her, had some kind of rules—arcane, unspoken— she had to obey. But of course the whole world was like that for her. I imagine it must have been a relief when she got to her seat, and the lights dimmed, and no one could anymore deny her this pleasure by saying her ticket was invalid, or that it was in fact not meant for *her* but for the young man who had escorted her here.

I never went in with her. I was too sophisticated by that point to waste a Saturday watching Joanne Woodward in *Candida,* or any play with a title like *Special Occasions.* I wonder now how I passed those afternoons, what more important thing I had to do than sit with her and take in her pleasure.

How much would it have hurt me to do that, to make her feel that little bit safer in this alien world? I thought it was enough that I could act the Big Man, the dispenser of blessings, a kind of Janice Slotnick to her.

I see how it would be tempting to end here, to close on this scene where I had achieved at least some of my goals, gotten to the center of the cultural life I had so craved, and was able to give this gift to the least entitled woman I had ever met, a Jewish woman, no less. To end here would seem to close the circle nicely, except that it would imply the relationship was all one-sided, me the giver, Ann Bonder the taker. And this wasn't true. Because I was drawn to that uncertain woman in the theater lobby in complicated ways; I *identified* with her in ways that had something to do with love but a great deal more to do with a surprising and not always acknowledged need.

In fact, our relationship had grown a bit thornier over the years. After my initial affection and fascination with her, she had become a sometimes maddening force in my life. I hated the lack of self-worth she felt and had imparted to her children. As I came to know Eileen more deeply, I came to see how that feeling her mother had about her cooking— that nothing she could make could possibly be worth much—had been more or less helplessly passed on to her daughters. I knew Eileen was loved, but the snob in me couldn't help but want her to have had more of a classic Jewish upbringing, one where she'd been pushed toward the sorts of high-end goals so many of the women of her generation had embraced. Having been deemed bright enough to take the entrance exams for prestigious Hunter High School, rebellious Eileen had blown off the exams, whiling the afternoon away at a Marx Brothers movie. Did her parents ever check up on her, or even ask the authorities how she'd done on the tests? Of course not. For them it was good enough that she finish out high school at her dangerous local Bronx school, then move on to the far less prestigious Hunter College, the tuition for which was a whopping $68 a semester. Her mother had always given lip service to achievement, without having the faintest idea how you got your children to actually perform: to do so would have required her to ask them to suffer, an impossible request for her to have made. Yet as maddening as all of this had become over time, I had also come to see what it came out of: the primitive, purely intuitive helplessness of someone who *only* knows how to love. That love, in its depths, had come to embrace me, too. I was, in her view, someone who *got* her. What she couldn't know—what I myself wasn't able to figure out for years—was that I needed the chaos she brought with her.

I described, earlier, the life of a fourteen-year-old boy whose Italian immigrant parents would have regarded their son's excursion to the Exeter Street Theater as the most pretentious act possible, the gesture of a young fop. But there are all kinds of pretensions. My father's climb to prosperity had begun when, in his forties, he began to buy small businesses—a rooming house, a laundromat—that, added to his insurance salesman's salary, eventually allowed him to fulfill his dream of building a big, showy new house for my mother in a big, showy new development. As a couple, they began consorting with the lawyers and wealthy developers who lived in their new neighborhood. Their secret was that they never had quite enough money for the lifestyle they adopted. My father was always, as he phrased it, "borrowing from Peter to pay Paul." He was also always working. So from the wild and chaotic but mostly happy emotionalism of my childhood (an emotionalism I associated exclusively with Italians), we moved to a life where it seemed my mother was always shouting at my father, as he escaped, usually with me at his side, to attend to one business or another. They could have gone on shouting at one another for the rest of their married lives, but that phase of their marriage ended with my mother's stroke. She was fifty-four at the time, and she survived it. But she was never the same afterward. She was Valiumed out; things became placid in the house, too placid. The woman who used to chase me out to my car, when I went out on dates, making an Anna Magnani–ish scene of her attempt to hold me back, now sat in the light-filled den, attending to her plants. Meanwhile, their lives as middle-class "successes" went on. The cars got bigger, the "affairs" they attended more lavish. In a way, I am exaggerating; they were always warm and loving people; they did not exactly exchange their identities for a piece of the American pie. But in another sense I am not: I know exactly how much they paid for the life they attained.

Growing into my own adolescence and young adulthood, I witnessed this as if it didn't matter. But it mattered; of course it mattered. Carrying ambition into our adult lives, we sometimes carry two ambitions, often at cross purposes. We want to make good, and we want the world we are leaving, if it was a good world, to remain the same, to keep its best and sweetest elements intact. Philip Roth famously wrote that a (male) writer spends the first eighteen years of his life trying desperately to get out of his parents' house, and the rest of his working life trying desperately to get back in. Why? Because the things that happen to us in our first eighteen years are always the truest: the tenor of family meals, the curling linoleum in the corner of the kitchen, these are the things that you can afford to ignore when you are in the midst of them, but which, after they are gone and irretrievable, you would give your right arm to get back again. In my case, the loss was weirdly slanted: I could still go home, but the tenor of those meals had changed, the linoleum replaced by its more high-end cousin Congoleum. My parents had achieved a nullification of the past.

But that past (albeit the Jewish version) had been re-created at the Bonders'. In their kitchen, in their Bronx outpost, with the scaffolding below and the cracked sidewalks and the continuing threat that Co-op City would become unlivable, forcing another retreat, they nonetheless managed to remain, to the end, exactly what they had always been. They insisted you could take matzo ball soup with you wherever you went; they kept a past world alive. And though it was not exactly my parents' past, or my parents' world, there were elements that brought me right back to my own childhood. I was the beneficiary of what had *not* happened for the Bonders. Because they had not achieved worldly success, their striving was caught, frozen in a kind of Bronx amber. Those words of Ann's—"I wish"—still haunt me. I know, on the most basic level, what she wished for. She wished that one of her daughters had married a doctor, had married, at least, wealth. Though she loved all her sons-in-law, and though each of her daughters achieved a level of prosperity beyond hers, none of us was ever able to provide the setting of physical splendor—the Gatsbyesque Long Island mansion—that would have made her believe the daughter in question was truly safe in the world. She wished that her husband had had more "luck." She wished above all that they could have afforded, in the last years of her life, to be "snow birds"—to keep, in other words, two residences, one in the north, one in the south, so that she could be near her daughters and grandchildren more of the time. Instead, they uprooted and moved south after Mr. Bonder sold the dry-cleaning store, first to a small town house on Hilton Head (the only HUD housing on the island, right across from the Bi-Lo), then to a development called "Sunrise" in Fort Lauderdale. There were visits—we came south, they came north—but they were never long enough. She died, at the age of eighty, still wishing.

But the larger thing she wished for—the thing there were no words for—was, I think, what gave rise to her emotional outpourings: she wished for some way she might order the world, make it yield. The discipline, the coldness necessary for such a thing were entirely foreign to her; she didn't respect those things enough—not at her core, anyway—to try to incorporate them. She wanted love to have a power it rarely does, at least not by itself: to protect people, to make their lives good.

She was frustrated by those unfulfilled wishes, but I can't think of her life as tragic. She lived it too authentically, too richly for tragedy, and she gave me something I didn't fully realize I still needed. The tenor of the house I'd grown up in—the yearning, the outbursts—was a thing I believed sophisticated people no longer wanted: the whole thrust of life was to get away from it, into the cooler, more ordered world. I thought the Jews—those cultured, ordered people— were going to help me do that. Instead, it was the gift of these particular Jews, my in-laws, to bring me right back in.

DANI SHAPIRO

My Mother's Four Rules of Family Life

● ● ●

When I was thirteen, on the night before my bat mitzvah, I heard my mother shouting at someone on the phone. I couldn't make out what she was saying, but I could hear the nonstop flow of words. I was upstairs in my bedroom; I cracked open my door and quietly made my way down to the landing of the staircase. I peered through the wrought-iron banister, straining to listen.

"Goddamnit, Shirley," I heard my mother say. "The flu? Can't you come up with a more original excuse than that?"

I rested my forehead against the cool iron of the banister. We knew a few Shirleys.

"And you call yourself religious," my mother spat.

Well, that narrowed it down. There was only one religious Shirley. That would be my mother's sister-in-law, my father's younger sister. I snuck farther down the stairs until my bare feet hit the cold terrazzo floor of the foyer. Where was my father? In the distance, I heard the muffled sound of a television. Was it possible he couldn't hear what was going on?

"Do you know what I think?" my mother went on. "I think you've always known you weren't going to come to Dani's bat mitzvah. Your grown children didn't even have the common courtesy to respond to the invitations I sent them. Do you realize that I sent each one of them—Mordechai, Henry, Joanne, Esty—a separate invitation? Now, that's class. But did your classy, religious children even—"

She stopped. "Hello?" She paused. "Hello?" Then she slammed the phone down in its receiver.

"Paul!" Her heels clicked down the hall. I raced back upstairs to my room, my heart pounding. A door creaked open, the sounds of television abruptly stopped, the door closed, and my parents began what was, for them, a regularly occurring pas de deux of angry whispers.

My mother's rage against my father's family had been a part of my life for as long as I could remember. Oh, she was angry at other people, too. Strangers, friends, institutions. The butcher who kept her waiting too long, the friend who forgot a tennis date, the phone company for its general ineptitude. But it was the particular alchemy of the relationships with her in-laws—that strange, strained forced intimacy—that really set her off. Her rage was the sputtering, irrational fury of a toddler. I remember, as a child, tracking her face for the warning signs, the way a weatherman might be on the lookout for a gathering storm: first, a slight crease between her brows, a frozen expression of disbelief. Then her pupils would start to jiggle, as if the disturbance was occurring from deep within. And finally, the torrent of words. Terrible, unstoppable. It was as if she didn't understand that words have meaning and heft, that they would live on in the consciousness of the person at whom she hurled them. Or perhaps she knew it—but the force of her own anger was so extreme that she just didn't care.

And so I was raised in a house divided. There was *us* (the tiny unit of our nuclear family) and there was *them* (the family that my father came from). My grandparents were out of the picture early: Grandfather, dead. Grandmother, bedridden after a series of strokes. That left my aunt and uncle— my father's two younger siblings. By the time my bat mitzvah rolled around, they were just about out of the picture, too. Pushed out by the sheer force of my mother's animosity. She called my uncle a crook, my aunt stupid, and the whole lot of them a bunch of religious hypocrites. I grew up not knowing my cousins. In the hermetically sealed bubble of my childhood home, it was just me, my father—who, increasingly, turned to a series of prescription drugs—and my mother's philosophy of family life, her four rules, which went as follows:

1. You can trust no one except your family.
2. Your family is defined by those related to you by blood.
3. In-laws are interlopers, therefore
4. They cannot be trusted and must be kept at a distance.

I grew up having no idea how to be part of a group. *Part of.* It simply wasn't in my vocabulary. Groups larger than two made me nervous. I didn't know where to look, whom to talk to. High school cliques, camp, college dorm life all went by in a blur. I did my best to belong—and on the surface I seemed to fit in—but, in truth, I was a solitary planet, orbiting in the dark, lonely universe of my own mind. I even, at one point, joined a twelve-step program I didn't belong in, just so that I could sit on a folding chair in a church basement, a person among people.

My father died in a car accident when I was twenty-three, and with his death, I had a new and unwelcome identity: I was the only child of a widowed mother. I spent most of my twenties and early thirties speaking to her several times a day. I lived only a few blocks away from her. I had relationships with men, and friendships with women, but my mother was always first and foremost in my mind. But then, at the age of thirty-four, I met the man with whom I knew I would spend the rest of my life. Until that moment, I hadn't fully realized that my mother and I had an unspoken agreement. I could love other people, but not too much. Not more than I loved her. Other people could be important to me, as long as she remained the most important. *I am your mother!* she would sometimes scream at me. What she really meant was *I am everything to you!*

When my mother met my future husband, I think she sensed, with the instincts of an animal in danger, that she was being threatened. The insults began as no more than a whisper. It was the way she spoke to my husband, with a vague but unmistakable whiff of condescension. The way her eyes glazed over when he spoke. The way she interrupted him. But it wasn't until his parents—my in-laws—entered the picture that the full force of her primal rage truly began to assert itself.

It began much in the same way, I imagine, as her relationship with my father's family had begun many years earlier. At first, she tried to charm them. In the early years of our marriage, the times she spent with Bill and Bunny (my mother-in-law, the youngest of five sisters, is the kind of warm, easy person who never shook her childhood nickname), my mother put on the full-court press. She dressed magnificently, in stylized cashmere and tweed, like a 1950s movie star. She broke out the good jewelry. She wore her large, emerald-cut diamond solitaire, her engagement ring which she had rarely worn since my father's death. Her hair was artfully, professionally done. Everything about her self-presentation was a seduction and a challenge: *Look at me, admire me, and don't fuck with me,* it all was saying. She would talk about her travels and her art collection—both things in which my in-laws, also Jews of a certain liberal, intellectual, privileged ilk, shared an interest.

"We've also been on safari," my mother-in-law, Bunny, would interject at some point, leaning forward, eager to connect, her sweet, round face crinkled into a smile.

And my mother's eyes would glaze over. I would see a flicker of annoyance just beneath the surface, signaling to me that the conversation wasn't going exactly her way.

And then my mother would change the subject. "My husband wanted to buy me a mink coat, but I insisted that we buy a Mary Bauermeister sculpture box instead. That's how we began our art collection."

"Really," said my father-in-law, Bill. "We started with prints—"

Now, I should mention here that my father-in-law is an imposing man. He has a thatch of snow-white hair and a big white beard, and looks a lot like Santa Claus in a bad mood. He has a booming, gruff voice. Usually, he intimidates people.

"And then we bought a Joan Mitchell oil," my mother soldiered on, as if my father-in-law hadn't spoken. "You must come over to my apartment to see it." Conversation was a chessboard, and she was the queen. She moved strategically, with only checkmate in mind.

At the same time that my mother was doing her damndest to keep my in-laws at a distance, I was trying to break free of my solitary confinement. I liked my in-laws—

particularly my mother-in-law, who had been incredibly welcoming to me, the new wife of her firstborn son. She recognized, in her unassuming but razor-sharp way, that my husband and I were well-suited. She saw that I made him happy, and that was all she wanted. It was that simple. I liked my husband's whole large, noisy extended family. His brother, sister-in-law, their three kids. His sister, brother-in-law, their two kids. Compared to what I was used to, it was a huge tribe. If my childhood had been spent alone in a room, joining this new family was like being plopped, without ceremony—or rather, with the ceremony of marriage—into the middle of Grand Central Station, during rush hour. People came and went. They laughed and argued and insulted each other, jostling, stepping on toes without the fear that anyone would actually get hurt.

Hey, Mikey! Put on some weight? my brother-in-law might say. *Yah, fuck you.* Or Bunny would ask, *Should I put together a little dinner?* And someone would say, *No, thanks, Mom. Frankly, your cooking sucks.*

Once, when my in-laws were visiting us in New York City, I started to cross the street before the light turned green. *Hey, watch it!* My father-in-law pulled me back to the curb. *We don't want to have to break in another one.*

But no matter how easily and warmly my husband's family accepted me into their midst, whenever we visited my in-laws in their comfortable, suburban ranch house north of Boston, I often found myself hiding. I didn't quite know how to be among them, how to be absorbed by them. And so I'd go to the bathroom. Ten, fifteen, twenty times a day,

I'd lock myself in my mother-in-law's powder room, surrounded by old bottles of perfume and air freshener, and a year's worth of copies of *Hadassah* magazine, and try to take some deep breaths.

"Are you all right in there?" my husband would say, knocking on the door.

"I'm fine," I'd call out to him. Which was basically true. I was fine—just overwhelmed and confused, as if I had lost my way on a familiar road. I wanted to belong to this new family, but I didn't exactly know how to go about it. Every time I felt that thing that separated me from them—that constant, droning, angry whisper—I struggled against it. But the harder I struggled, the louder it got.

I hid our trips to the suburbs of Boston from my mother. She hated it when we went up there, and made me pay for it for weeks afterward.

"But you never bother to visit me," she'd complain.

There was little point in reminding her that she lived six blocks from us in Manhattan, that we saw her all the time.

"Isn't Bunny a little . . ." She'd trail off, ingeniously leaving it to me to fill in the adjective.

"Don't insult my in-laws, Mom."

And then there would be a brief nanosecond of silence, like the pause at the top of a roller coaster before the plunge.

"What did I say? I didn't say anything! Oh, *right*," she would snap. "Protect your in-laws. Leap to their defense. But when it comes to your own mother, you have ice in your veins."

Ice in your veins. Cold-hearted. Frozen. Cruel. Ungrateful. My mother's language became increasingly harsh and melo-dramatic as I tried to pull away from her. Our battle was a daily fact. Every night, at dinner, my husband and I would go through a debriefing, sifting through that day's diatribe. It went on this way until, a couple of years into our marriage, something came along that tipped the balance: we had a baby.

Here's a moment from those early, blurry days spent in the hospital, after my son was born: the windowsill of my room is overflowing with flowers, baskets of food, "It's a Boy" balloons. A steady trickle of friends stop by, their cheeks pink from the cool, glorious spring day. I'm in bed, propped up on pillows and nursing my tiny baby, deliriously happy, groggy from painkillers after my cesarean. My mother is there, of course. She has been there, pretty much, since a few hours after my husband called her with the news. If she is happiest when she has me completely alone, to her-self, with no outsiders around, these days in the hospital are sheer torture for her. My husband is there constantly (the baby's father!)—an endless source of irritation, except when he goes downstairs to get her a cappuccino. Friends are not paying her the proper respect; they're more inter-ested in the new baby. But peace is maintained until my in-laws arrive.

"Where's the little *ketskelah*?" Bunny coos as they walk

through the door. Their arms are laden with FAO Schwarz shopping bags, a furry teddy bear poking its head out of one of them. "Where's our boy?"

Our. Had I been looking, I would have seen the parade of warning signs march across my mother's face. The jiggling pupils, the glazed expression. Of course, I should have seen it coming. But with a kind of willful naiveté, I had chosen to believe all those people who had told me that babies bring families together.

"He has Michael's chin!" Bunny says. The baby does, in fact, have my husband's chin—pointy and delicate. I have handed Bunny the baby, and she is holding him easily, comfortably—she has been holding babies all her life.

"He has the Shapiro forehead," pronounces my mother. "In fact, he looks exactly like Dani." She pauses. *"Exactly."*

Bunny blinks at my mother.

"You know, there's a reason why people always say babies look like their fathers," my husband says. "In traditional cultures—"

My mother shoots him a look, and he goes quiet.

I, in the meantime, take my baby back to bed with me. I look down at his peaceful, sleeping face and am overcome by an image of him being pulled apart, yanked violently limb from limb.

"How long will you be staying?" My mother turns to Bunny and Bill.

"Why? Trying to get rid of us already?" Bill jokes. Except we all know perfectly well that it isn't a joke.

Over the next couple of years, my in-laws continued to try to befriend my mother. When they came to the city, they made a point of calling and inviting her to dinner. They included her in holiday celebrations, family weddings—it would never have occurred to them to do otherwise. They saw her as part of their family. But it was never enough for my mother. She was not interested in being *part of* any family—something which was hard for Bunny to grasp.

"Why can't she take pleasure in you?" Bunny asked me. "If you were my daughter, I would be so proud of you. I *am* so proud of you. And what about the little *ketskelah*? She and I share that beautiful little boy—but when I call her up and try to talk about him, she just cuts me off."

I understood perfectly. My mother didn't want to share the title of grandmother. She wanted the little *ketskelah* all to herself. And she wasn't—couldn't possibly be—proud of me. Any accomplishment of mine, any happiness, was perceived as one step further away from her.

"Just stop trying," I said to Bunny. "You don't need to include her—no matter how hard you try, it's never going to make any difference." I felt cruel for saying it, but I knew it was true. My mother and my in-laws were never going to be friends, and all I could hope for was that they wouldn't become enemies.

Finally, on one winter visit to New York, Bunny and Bill had planned to have lunch with my mother. Bill was feeling unwell—he had been up sick all night, and Bunny was worried, but still, she met my mother for a quick lunch. She explained that Bill was sick, back at the hotel. After lunch, my mother suggested that they go to an exhibit at the Metropolitan Museum.

"I'm sorry," Bunny said. "I've got to get back to Bill."

On her way back to the hotel, Bunny slipped and fell on an icy patch of sidewalk, badly injuring her knee. When I called my mother to tell her that Bunny had fallen, she sniffed. She didn't actually say it, but still I could hear what she was thinking: *serves her right.* And she never bothered to call Bunny, after that, to see how she was doing.

My mother died a sad and lonely death when my son was four years old. Those four years between his birth and her death were among the most painful in our long and rocky career as mother and daughter. Instead of bringing us closer, my son's existence in the world tore us apart. Instead of forging a bond between the two families, the shared grandchild created a rift. Jews even have a special word for the two sets of in-laws that a marriage creates: *machetunim.* Bunny and Bill, who had begun their relationship with my mother so optimistically—who even, initially, had been taken with her—finally stopped calling. *Bunny's just plain dumb,* my mother spat into the phone during those years. *She's completely suburban. And Bill's—let's face it—a nasty man. He has insulted me more times than I can count.* Although they never knew the extent of her anger toward them (and would have been unable to imagine it), my in-laws gave up. The lines of communication dribbled to a halt, punctuated only by Bunny's annual Happy New Year card.

As soon as Bill and Bunny heard the news that my mother had died—which, though she had cancer, still had the shocking quality of any death—they left their home north of Boston and headed down to our house in Connecticut, three hours away. They wanted to be with us—with *me*—to step in as parents, now that both of my parents were gone.

And while I was comforted that they were coming, I asked my husband where they were going to stay. Usually, when they had visited us in our new home in Connecticut, they stayed at a nearby inn.

"The inn has no rooms available," my husband said.

"You're kidding. Are you sure?"

"I tried everything."

Panicked, I called a friend across the hill who had a guest house. I felt an intense need for solitude, for control over my environment. I knew my in-laws meant well, but they were loud and boisterous, they had their own way of doing things, and I had nothing inside me to give them. Nothing.

"Can my in-laws stay with you?" I practically begged my friend.

"Of course."

But then they arrived. Bunny enveloped me in a hug, and I breathed in her by now familiar powdery scent. Bill's voice was gruff, choked-up when he kissed me hello, his white beard scratchy against my face. As they walked into our kitchen, bags in hand, I realized that of course they would stay in our house. Of course. Anything else felt perverse. And so we stuck together—my husband and I, his parents—as the hours and days passed before we buried my mother. Bill and Bunny played with our son, their grandson, keeping things as normal as possible while I made phone calls and funeral arrangements. They protected me, by creating another, larger, more porous circle than the kind I had been used to with my mother.

We sat shiva for my mother at her apartment on the Upper West Side, surrounded by the fine art collection that had mattered to her so much. Her apartment was full of people—but almost none of them had ever met her. Oh, her attorney, her accountant, and her stockbroker paid shiva calls. But mostly, when I looked around I saw my friends and colleagues. I felt guilty and sad at the abundance of my life, and the paucity of hers. In the weeks before my mother's death, whenever I answered the phone in her apartment, it was almost always a sales call, or a wrong number.

In the middle of the first day of shiva, the doorbell rang. I opened it, and there stood my mother's sister-in-law, my aunt Shirley. She was an older woman now—the same age as my mother—and she held the arm of her eldest son, my cousin Mordechai.

"I'm so sorry, Dani." Shirley hugged me. Mordechai—whom I barely knew—shook my hand. He was now a prominent rabbi, and looked it in his black suit and hat.

"You came," I murmured. "I can't believe you came."

They stepped into my mother's apartment for the first time in their lives. Shirley and my mother hadn't spoken in decades—certainly not since my father's death. I brought my aunt and my cousin over to meet my in-laws. And as I walked across the rug of my childhood, past furniture I had grown up with, walls covered with photographs of my mother, father, and me—I wondered what my mother would think. Would she have appreciated the gesture? More likely, she would have found it empty, hypocritical, or worse. I could hear her voice in my head: *Look at them. They're just here to gloat. They don't have a genuine bone in their bodies.* I shook off my mother's voice—it will be the work of the rest of my life to shake off my mother's voice, when it chimes in, unbidden—and searched instead for what I thought.

My aunt and cousin—just like my in-laws—had come for a very simple reason: It was the right thing to do. They had come to heal, to smooth over, to connect. They had come for my mother, for themselves, for me. They came hoping that my mother had not passed down to me her reflexive need to destroy—to turn love and decency into something parched, tense, and fearful. Shirley, Mordechai, Bill, Bunny, my husband, and me—we were all connected, however tangentially, by the witnesses and ceremonies that echoed through our shared history. These fragile, hopeful moments had made us each other's family. My mother had tried her whole life to erase that. But she had failed.

DARCEY STEINKE

Hot Head

● ● ●

Early in our relationship my husband told me that his parents were midwestern squares and hard-core Republicans. They disapproved of his bohemian lifestyle and had refused to pay his college tuition. Even in his black jeans, motorcycle jacket, velvet porkpie hat, I saw how Michael's elegant frame grew brittle as he talked about his parents. He'd worked his own way through school and was currently bartending and making house music records. Michael lived in a loft with a couple of goth teenagers and a drag queen. He made Super 8 movies, lived hard, and could play any song off the radio on his black electric guitar.

While I was already attracted to Michael, his parents' dis-approval was like an aphrodisiac. Stories from his midwestern childhood were endearing, but my mind seized most on his estrangement from his parents. I was empathetic: my mother disapproved of my writing and I knew what it was like to struggle without parental support. I began to fantasize about how I'd safeguard Michael's avant-garde existence, his thrift-store aesthetic. I'd buoy him up. I'd keep him from any pain. I'd defend him to his conservative cookie-cutter parents.

The day I arrived at my in-laws' home for my first visit we sat around the walnut kitchen table eating cold-cut sand-wiches and drinking root beer. In New York, I lived across from the projects in a broken-porch brownstone. Michael's parents, on the other hand, lived in suburban splender: a big open living room with cathedral ceilings and a railing with an open corridor that led to the bedrooms. Over the stone fire-place hung a macramé owl. The house in every detail was trapped in the '70s. There was a room with a wooden hot tub surrounded with hanging ferns, and in the basement the crate furniture had orange cushions; one wall displayed my father-in-law's beer can collection.

My mother-in-law had on a kitty-cat sweatshirt and pink Keds tennis shoes, her hair was short and frosted. My father-in-law wore khakis and a duotone velour sweater. Weeks be-fore this first Thanksgiving visit, Michael joked about his fa-ther's terrible temper. The smallest thing could set him off, someone interrupting him or that there were no more filters for the coffeemaker. That day in the kitchen, his parents lis-tened while Michael talked about the record he was making, how he had bought a new synthesizer and was starting to DJ in clubs around New York City. Little lines began to form on his mother's upper lip and his father's ruddy Germanic face took on a look of startled displeasure. Michael, sensing their disapproval, started talking about me, how I worked at a Montessori school and lived in my father's rectory in the Williamsburg section of Brooklyn. Though we hadn't talked about it, I knew that in bringing me home, Michael was offering an olive branch. Though I had my funky side, I wore motorcycle boots and thrift-store dresses; basically I was a Lutheran minister's daughter, somebody both he and his parents could agree on. While his mother listened with some interest, his father was just as suspicious of the details of my life as he was of his son's. While Michael kept talking, I could tell he was discouraged; his long face had taken on a desperate patina that brought out the physical resemblance to his family. As I went to bed I realized that my mission as protector would be hard to pull off; to defend Michael would embarrass him and seem aggressive to his parents.

The next morning my father-in-law, discovering a Tupperware container in the refrigerator that had been left open, cried out and swung his body sideways. I thought he had been hurt, stung by a bee or cut himself. His round face got red, and his body became like a flame as he jerked around the house ranting about wasting food.

My mother-in-law stood very still. She was a soft-spoken religious person. She prayed every morning, attended church on Sundays, and brought casseroles to neighborhood families in crisis. She collected dolls and made quilts by hand. She was enamored with Billy Graham's book *Angels,* and she suffered from diabetes. She would occasionally go into insulin shock, and during one recent episode, she'd crashed her car into the gas pump at the service station. Here in the room, her eyes filled with tears and she continued to stand perfectly still as if any movement on her part would provoke a direct attack. She suffered through his accusations for twenty minutes, until he burned himself out and retreated to the TV room adjacent to the kitchen. Michael took the broom from his mother, who had begun to sweep the kitchen. Michael's father walked back into the room and began to criticize how he held the handle, the lack of strength in his broom stroke.

"Why not just let him sweep?" I said, vehemently.

"You think I should let him alone?" he said. I could see by his blotchy neck and bulging eyes that he was sliding back into the tantrum.

I nodded.

"You think you know this guy," his father said, "but you don't. I raised him, I'm the only one who really knows him." He turned on his heels and clambered down the basement stairs to his meticulously organized workbench. Hammers and screwdrivers hung on the walls around him gleaming in fluorescent light. I knew Michael's father felt his son was irresponsible, that he was just wasting time playing music, but from this exchange I saw how complete his father's disapproval was, he felt Michael was poisoned, that there was nothing he could do right.

"Thanks for *finally* sticking up for me," Michael said once his dad was gone.

It surprised me that the word "finally" had the most emphasis. Michael didn't seem particularly grateful that I'd come to his defense; he seemed angry, as if it was my fault I hadn't been there the other times his father ridiculed him. Though he knew it was impossible, it was as if he wished I'd been able to defend him when he was a little kid. I could tell he was glad I'd seen the painful conflict played out between him and his dad, but he was also sheepish and embarrassed by it.

Michael's parents were pleased when we announced our plans to marry; finally their wayward son was settling down. My mother-in-law planned a wedding shower and they paid for our honeymoon to St. Martin. When our daughter, Abbie, was born, my in-laws flew over from Chicago, stayed in a bed-and-breakfast, and came over daily to hold the baby. My relationship with them began to ballast. The baby solidified our familiar connection and gave us something to talk about. We visited them once or twice a year. At first I always arrived with my spurs on, ready to defend Michael from his father's belittling. According to his father, Michael couldn't scramble eggs, didn't know how to drive, and wore the sort of clothes usually reserved for clowns in the circus. I'd refute his accusations. He'd look at me, his eyes bulging, his mouth twisted into a knot, as I listed Michael's accomplishments, what a caring father he was, how he could play any song by ear. My father-in-law said I didn't know what I was talking about as he retreated to his basement workbench, where he worked obsessively making birdhouses, wooden candlestick holders, and spice racks.

Becoming a member of Michael's family gave me some sympathy for his dad. During family gatherings, I'd see how Michael's grandmother and aunts teased his father relentlessly. In hysterics, they told a story about how one day, when he was a boy, he got so mad that they held his head under the bathroom faucet to cool him off. He was the only member of his family to attend college, and he commuted an hour and a half each way every day to his job as a neon-sign salesman.

My mother-in-law clearly enjoyed our visits. She bought the root beer and German onion rolls she knew Michael liked. She'd show us the newest addition to her doll collection: a rare Cabbage Patch doll, or a Crying Cindy. She'd tell us inspirational stories from the Christian magazines she subscribed to. Sometimes as she spoke in her cheerful girlish way, I wondered if she was for real. Her marriage was arduous, even emotionally abusive, she had a severe case of diabetes, but she remained naive and positive. I was still angry she hadn't protected Michael, but I also felt a growing affection for her. She sent me clippings from her town newspaper about local artists and reviews of theater productions, as well as packages filled with Florida oranges and homemade chocolate chip cookies. She sewed Abbie sun hats and jumpers.

As my relationship with Michael's mother stabilized, my relationship with my husband was reaching a pressure point. The stress of parenthood highlighted our fundamental differences. We'd initially been united in our common belief that life was sad. Michael dealt with this melancholy legacy by playing his records, drinking beers, wisecracking; nobody was more fun at a party. At first I'd been enthralled by this strategy. In the early months of our relationship, Michael and I sometimes spent whole weekends in bed; other nights we'd stay up dancing till dawn. But since having the baby I was developing a fledgling interest in religion. I still felt life was sad, but rather than fighting off sorrow I was trying to see it as a conduit to God. Michael felt, predictably, that religion was for squares. He went out a lot and left me alone with the baby, and we began to fight nearly every week. One of the worst arguments occurred one morning after he'd stayed out late. I hadn't slept all night when I finally heard his key in the lock at seven o'clock in the morning. He went right into Abbie's room, picked her up out of her crib, and put her into her high chair in the kitchen. Wearing my flannel nightgown, I walked into the kitchen and asked where he'd been. At first he insisted he'd been home for a while, but I told him I'd just heard him come in.

"I was out with friends," he said. "I didn't call because I didn't want to wake the baby."

I started to cry, and I saw how Michael's body straightened and his face got red like his father's. "Why are you always making such a big deal about things? I didn't do anything."

This was his usual line; as long as he wasn't actually sleeping with anybody, he didn't see why I should be upset. As he saw it, staying out all night was just his attempt to have a little fun. My emotions always made Michael angry; I think he saw them solely as restricting his behavior, as censorious. I found myself, that morning, as I had so many times before, trying to convince him that he'd hurt me. He just got stiffer and more accusatory; his anger was more contained than his father's but equally terrifying. He accused me again of making a big deal of everything. I continued to cry. I saw his pupils dilate and he retreated, getting spacey like his mother. He sat there on the kitchen stool, his eyes filled with tears. He wouldn't answer any of my questions, just stared at Abbie, who was picking up Cheerios one by one and putting them into her mouth.

I was beginning to see that in mythologizing Michael and his relationship to his parents, I hadn't seen Michael clearly. I still admired his passion for underground art and music, his aesthetic sensibility that could transform a thrift-store coffee table into an object of wonder with a little gold paint, his relentless collecting of first editions and soul music on vinyl, but I'd underestimated the effect of his father's constant disapproval. When Michael was a kid, any show of vulnerability was attacked rather than comforted. Emotions, he told me many times, were dangerous things best kept to oneself. Once when I asked him how he withstood a particularly exacting boss that he had at work, he told me he just thought of himself suspended in space looking down on the planet earth. From this position his boss's negative comments seemed meaningless. As a child, in order to withstand his father's ridicule, he'd had to cultivate remove. Often this remove made him seem hermetically sealed. His defenses had not melted as I'd hoped under what I thought were the warm rays of my love, not at all really. Michael was just as impermeable as ever.

While things were going particularly badly, Michael's sister's husband died. At the reception after the funeral at a bar in rural Minnesota, his parents stood awkwardly talking to the minister, who wore a ski jacket over his clerical collar and black shirt. Michael wore a thrift-store suit made from shiny blue polyester; it was slightly too small for him, and with his black Chelsea boots and tall slender frame he looked like an aloof British rock star. Ever since my in-laws arrived, whenever Michael's sister was out of earshot, my father-in-law reiterated how he'd lent his son-in-law money when he couldn't make the mortgage. I'm not sure which was more disconcerting, my father-in-law's badmouthing or my mother-in-law with her big wet eyes as she nodded in agreement.

The minister left. "What a nice man," my mother-in-law said. Michael watched his sister; the circles under her eyes were dark as eggplants, and she was shaking and disoriented even as she tried to make small talk. She was speaking loudly and swinging her arms around like a rag doll in the dim light at the end of the bar.

"I'm concerned about your sister," Michael's father said.

Michael looked at him warily. He and his sister, while not close in the conventional sense, shared an intimate understanding of their difficult childhood.

"I raised her," his father continued. "I know her dark side."

I realized it wasn't only Michael—my father-in-law thought his daughter was damaged, too.

Michael was too angry to talk at first, but then, apropos of nothing, he said, "Jesus was gay, you know."

"That's ridiculous," his father said, his head sunk down in the space between his shoulders and his eyes bulged out.

"No, it's true," Michael said, "scholars have all confirmed Jesus was definitely gay."

"I don't know about gay," I said, trying to make peace between them, "but he was definitely androgynous."

Michael glared at me. "Shut up, you don't know what you're talking about."

I turned toward my mother-in-law, who was staring at her husband. A Garth Brooks song was playing on the jukebox, and the TV over the bar showed a mute hockey game. Men padded up like monsters hit each other with wooden sticks. I don't know why I was surprised. If you walk out into cross fire, eventually you're going to get hurt.

Now that I was experiencing Michael's temper firsthand, I realized how hard it must have been for my mother-in-law all these years. At the time, we were in touch by phone and mail; she wanted to hear every detail of the development of her new granddaughter. When my babysitter went on vacation, my mother-in-law flew in to watch Abbie. She was helpful, doing the dishes in our deep old-fashioned porcelain sink and straightening up the living room of our cramped apartment. Away from her husband, she laughed more and seemed less sad.

I began to look forward to her visits; she'd get the baby in the mornings so I could sleep, and it was fun being with somebody as crazy about my daughter as I was. She came for Abbie's second birthday. A few days into her visit I got a sinus infection. I walked to the doctor's office in a snowstorm and then to our drugstore. The pharmacist informed me they no longer took our prescription card. I was exhausted and feverish, and rather than search for another pharmacy, and though I knew we couldn't afford it, I paid $160 for the antibiotics. When I got home I told my husband what the drugs had cost. His face grew crimson. "Do you think we're millionaires? This is ridiculous. You bring these back and find a place that takes our insurance." I protested. My mother-in-law was in the room, eyes wet and glittering, her body in the familiar stance of fearful stillness. She watched me grow weary of fighting, put on my down coat, and head back into the snowy street.

I thought I could feel her empathy. Her husband and son, she was trying to tell me through her eyes, had brutalizing tempers. But she wasn't willing to say something, to stand up for me, and any emotional connection between us was compromised by her passivity. After that, the only time I felt close to her was when she went into insulin shock, which would happen periodically when her blood sugar got too low. Her eyelids drooped, her head bobbed loosely on her neck, and her speech slurred. She'd say she liked my leather jacket, and call my father-in-law "that guy." At these times she was freed from the timidness and fear that usually bound her. These episodes terrified my father-in-law. His face blanched as he rushed to the refrigerator and poured the small glass of orange juice that in minutes restored her to her more conventional self.

The last time I saw Michael's father have a tantrum was when we were all vacationing in Orlando. During the day we roamed the Magic Kingdom, and at night we hung around the condo talking and watching television. Everyone took turns cooking. When it was my turn, I shopped for fresh seafood and imported tomatoes. My father-in-law came in late from playing golf. He glanced at the plates piled with ziti and shrimp and said that he only ate angel hair pasta. All the symptoms of a fit began to manifest: his face got pale and then pink, and his body volcanic. He stomped into the kitchen and poured himself a glass of wine and sat on the salmon-colored couch under the pastel abstract painting in the living room.

He asked how much money Michael made. By then, Michael was the production manager for a small publisher. His father snorted when he heard the amount. "How are you going to raise a family on that?" Michael looked at me pleadingly, but I felt too exhausted and angry from all of our fighting to stick up for him. Before, our island of intimacy sustained Michael against his father's assaults, but that safety zone no longer existed. I carried my daughter down the hall-

way to our bedroom. When Michael came in later, I pretended to be asleep and we both lay there listening to the
cars on the highway running past strip malls filled with
make-believe: crocodile wrestling, water slides, medieval
restaurants, fake French bistros.

A few years later, Abbie and I moved out to an apartment in the Fort Greene section of Brooklyn. It had
become clear that staying together was futile; Michael and I
were like two different species, a fish and a rabbit, trying to
communicate. The hardest thing about leaving my husband
was that I worried his father would use our breakup as evidence that his son really was damaged goods. Some protector I turned out to be. Not only did I feel that I'd failed at
marriage, but I also felt I was delivering Michael into the hands
of his tormentor. I was also worried that his father's temper
would at some point turn on Abbie, and that like his mother,
Michael would be powerless to intercede on her behalf. I
mentioned this to Michael, who just shrugged his shoulders
and called me a worrywart. I know he's a good father: Abbie
lights up when she sees him and she's always telling me how
her daddy takes her to the movies, helps her with her math
homework, and lets her win at chess. Still, it's hard for me to
come to terms with the fact that now that I share custody of
Abbie I can no longer protect her all of the time—though
every parent comes to this realization eventually.

When Michael told his parents that we were splitting up,
that I wasn't happy, his father replied, "Who's happy?" I

haven't seen my father-in-law since the break, but one day I brought flowers over to the apartment, where my mother-in-law was visiting with Abbie and Michael, and I could tell that while awkward and shy, she was happy to see me. When I heard she had breast cancer, I wrote her a letter and she wrote me back a warm reply. Other than the occasional note, we don't have much contact. Sometimes, through Michael, I hear news of his family: how his uncle died, how my former niece was accepted into an elite drama school. Though mostly information filters through my daughter. Grammie taught her to sew last summer, and she sent her stickers in the mail. Grampie built her a stool and helped her fly a kite. When I asked if her Grampie ever lost his temper, she nodded. It's scary, she told me, he goes coo-coo. She jerks her small body around in miniature of her grandfather's tantrums. What does Daddy do? I ask her. She giggles and tells me that later, after Grampie has gone into the basement, Daddy pops his eyes out and stamps his feet, mimicking his father. It's really funny, my daughter tells me, everybody laughs!

KATHRYN HARRISON

Keeping Vigil

● ● ●

September 18. We've barely settled into the routine of a new school year, our children still chafing under the attempt to get them to bed whole hours earlier than we did during the summer. When the phone rings, at ten-thirty on this wet Thursday night, my husband answers with a sharp tone, quick to assume it's one of our older daughter's friends, calling too late on a weeknight. "Yes," he says after a silence. "All right." At the change in his voice I look up from the laundry I'm folding. I watch his face as I listen to his side of the conversation.

"Give him my love, okay? And tell Mom I'll talk to her in the morning." He replaces the handset in its cradle on the bureau. "Go back to bed," he says when he turns around. All three children are standing on the stairs outside our bedroom door.

"What is it?" they ask, almost in unison. "What's wrong?"

After a mostly sleepless night, the two of us get up early. I stand behind my husband, watching his reflection as he shaves around his beard. I can't find anything in his eyes beyond their attention to the razor. But when I hug him good-bye, his body feels different. It feels vigilant. As if his flesh had acquired consciousness.

During the afternoon, while he travels by train from New York to Washington, D.C., I find myself preoccupied by the picture I have of my husband in his seat. I see him among the Friday commuters, his work lying untouched in his lap. He stares out the window at the familiar scenery blurring past, the little houses with their fenced-in yards and laundry lines hung with clothes, the occasional bicycle lying on its side in the grass.

He calls me from the hospital. He's eating in the cafeteria with his mother and brother. Behind his voice I hear silverware ring against china, other people's conversations, their laughter. His father will remain in the ICU for a few days, he tells me. Morphine seems to be working a little better than OxyContin, and as soon as he's stabilized he'll be scheduled for exploratory surgery. Nothing in my husband's voice tells me how to feel; it's my mother-in-law's determined good cheer that fills me with apprehension.

For months, doctors have interpreted my father-in-law's relentlessly increasing abdominal pain, as well as changes in his bowel and bladder function, as the unfortunate fallout of radiation he received years before, in the aftermath of prostate cancer. Now, suddenly, his kidneys have failed.

A storm has left much of Washington, D.C., without electricity. My husband and his mother use candles to find their way around in his parents' dark house. I picture them together, their faces lit by that inescapably devotional light. Can either of them have put a match to a candlewick without helplessly consecrating the little flame to my father-in-law, to his recovery, or to his release, to whatever is possible?

My husband calls the next morning. He's been up since five, he says. When his mother came to breakfast she found him in the backyard, raking up what the storm had blown down. Doing as his father would do. Their shared awareness of this, of my husband's slipping into his father's role, must offer both of them comfort, and a measure of grief. In the past year, as his health continued to fail, my father-in-law asked my husband for some of his business cards to keep with him, in his wallet—like prayer cards, almost, talismans that demonstrate his son's currency in the world.

That my father-in-law's physical deterioration began with prostate cancer; that surgery not only failed to remove it completely but also compromised his potency; that hormone therapy diminished the heft of his muscles and the hair on his body and face: for my husband, these assaults on his father's masculinity have felt personal, even unnecessarily mean. They've hurt him, as gender-neutral ailments would not, and this aspect of his grief has shown me something of the primal, unarticulated psychic transactions between a father and a son—knowledge that arrived as an epiphany, making me feel foolish. Why hadn't I assumed my husband would have an experience parallel to mine with my mother, to the indelible impress her breast cancer left on me? But then, I'm the only daughter of an only daughter, raised in the absence of a father. Most of what I know of men I've learned from my husband.

An explosive, stupid fight when my husband returns to New York, a rerun of one of the stock two or three of our marriage, but louder and more profane than usual. Whatever sets off the conflict isn't the real catalyst—we know that. It's that even in the absence of a diagnosis, this hospitalization is different from my father-in-law's previous ones, his symptoms more ominous. I go on crying long after we reach our exhausted truce.

The following day, as if by plan, my husband and I take the afternoon off from each other, and from our anxious speculations. He heads up to the park with our son, a football under his arm. I go shopping with the girls, continuing our thirteen-year-old daughter's quest for the perfect pair of jeans. I'm not looking, but in Bloomingdale's I find a pair I like enough to buy. "Hey," my daughter says when she sees them, and she shows me what she's found: same style, same designer. Worried that my wearing jeans of a design identical to my daughter's might spoil her pleasure in them—that proximity to my mother-body might neutralize whatever hip qualities they possess—I consider returning them to the rack. But she encourages the purchase. I sign the receipt, aware that as much as it's a record of sale, it also documents a wish: To be as my daughter is on this afternoon. To be as young, and as far from thoughts of death.

Here's what I don't know, not yet. The death of my father-in-law will leave me prey to concerns about my own father, from whom I've been estranged for most of my life. Having never, in the past twenty years, attempted to contact him, a few months after my father-in-law dies, I'll track down my own father's address. I'll pay an Internet company called Peoplefinders.com $39.00 for the results of a "Comprehensive Background Check," which will provide me not only the names of my father's relatives, associates, and neighbors, but banks, schools, and storage facilities in his community. Neither my mother nor I will be listed among his relatives, and I'll wonder how a person might go about erasing the records of such connections.

I won't call whoever lives in the house next door to his. I won't ask what he looks like, or if his hair is now gray. Does he seem to be in good health? Is he friendly, or does he keep to himself? What kind of a person do you think he might be? There's no limit, really, to the questions I won't ask. Instead, after many drafts, many misgivings, I'll send my father a letter, wanting reassurance that no matter who he is, he does, in fact, exist. It won't be a long letter, just a request that someone please notify me in the event of his falling seriously ill. The subtext will be obvious—*Give me a chance to say good-bye*—the hostility of his response useful in that it will underscore the wisdom of our estrangement, the relative comfort distance affords me from our attempt, and failure, at being father and daughter. But for now my father-in-law is still alive, for now—a little longer—I am spared such preoccupations.

I don't know how much my father-in-law has given me in the years since I married his son. He'll be dead before I understand that all the fires he built, meals he praised, trees he planted, branches of buds he arranged on the table, and hugs he gave—especially those, tighter and longer than required for hello or good-bye—added up to something more than his affection for me.

Here's what I do know. I love him, unreservedly. Blood kinship could not make my feelings stronger. My father-in-law's thirty years as a Quaker headmaster, the last twenty at Sidwell Friends, in Washington, D.C., has won him the respect of a great many people, as well as the love of generations of students who, as news of his illness travels, write to thank him for his presence in their lives. I'll read these letters, some out loud to my father-in-law, one recollection after another of his intuitively knowing and giving students what they needed, words and gestures that, somehow, made all the difference. One letter in particular will remain with me: a description of my father-in-law walking home at the end of a workday and glancing up to see the letter's author sitting alone in the open window of his dormitory room. My father-in-law stopped walking to contemplate the boy. After a silence, he spoke. "You will be all right," he told him. These words, and their sincerity—spoken by someone else, they might well have sounded facile—changed everything for that student. Changed his life profoundly enough that, years later, he felt compelled to write and tell my father-in-law that somehow he'd heard the simple reassurance, and believed it. My father-in-law had been the catalyst for his transcending what had felt like hopeless confusion.

This quality of my father-in-law, his talent for silence, for feeling and understanding the state of another person's soul: others must share it, but I don't know them.

So, yes, I love him. I love his generosity of spirit; I love that he isn't judgmental—not that he struggles and overcomes the failing, but that he doesn't judge. And I have a crush on him, one that began the day I met him, not long after my husband had learned my family history: an absent father, a teenage mother who left me in the care of her parents and who died when I was twenty-four. "Well," my husband said, and he took me in his arms. "I guess I'll just have to give you my parents. They'll be your mother and father, too." I didn't answer what I heard as a hope rather than a promise: generous, chivalrous, and not really possible.

But I was wrong. When we married, I wore my husband's mother's wedding dress, remade to fit me, and at the end of the ceremony my father-in-law stood to read the Quaker marriage certificate, the first, after my husband and me, to announce that I was now a member of his family. Neither my mother-in-law nor my husband begrudges me the kind of crush I have on my father-in-law—benign, daughterly, reverent. Probably they know what I don't, that he is the only person who could put back together what my own father broke.

September 22, a Monday, nine a.m. I come in the front door after taking our younger daughter to school. My husband is sitting at the dining table, sitting very still, the cordless phone in his hand.

"Come here," he says, and I know from his voice, absolutely flat, that whatever it is, it's bad. "They operated late last night, because he was in too much pain to wait for them to schedule an exploratory surgery. It's cancer, and it's—it's everywhere."

We look at each other.

"Two," he says, answering my question, the one I can't ask. "Two months."

Silently, we stand from the table. It's as if we've decided to begin crying only in each other's arms. Sobs, very nearly inaudible, shake my husband's broad back. I've seen him cry, of course, but rarely and never like this. The awful, intimate, and unfamiliar feel of his grief, his strong back heaving within the circle of my embrace—this is a thing I won't forget.

We go to the couch and sit together, repeating over and over what is impossible to conceive, that my husband's father is dying, dying very quickly. Two months: a simple prediction. But we repeat and repeat the words as if they represent an impossibly complex formula we are trying to understand. After a while we fall silent. Then, when we begin to talk again, it's of practical issues. We list every commitment we can postpone or cancel in order to free time to be with his parents.

What can I do? I ask my husband. I am his wife, and I love him—he knows that—but how can I possibly help him at a time like this? His answer is one I should know by now, one that always seems too simple to be true.

"Have sex with me every night. That will help. That will help with everything."

"It will?" I ask, having assumed that only something rare and difficult to provide could assuage grief as keen as this.

"Every night." He pulls me into his arms.

"Okay," I say, nodding my head against his chest. "Every night. I promise."

My husband's crying: what might relieve me of the physical feel of it—so much more wrenching to me than my own? I know my grieving; by comparison, his is exotic. It's like seeing a man embark on a walk across embers: how will he bear this, I find myself wondering, how will he stand the pain?

I keep losing track of the date, the month, even the season, and have to deliberately think my way back to where I am in time. And every observation, even the most pedestrian, is affected by my anticipation of bereavement. I can't clean out a closet or plant a flower bulb without thinking: The next time I do this, my father-in-law will have died.

Already I'm helplessly archiving memories of him, polishing and placing them carefully in my head, ready for retrieval. My favorites are of his intensely charming, look-at-handsome-funny-me capers, as when he danced the funny, high-stepping, arm-swinging dance to make his grandchildren laugh. Or delivered a tragicomic monologue while holding up my husband's empty Christmas stocking, the year all the grown-ups focused so intently on the children that we overlooked one another. "Wait!" my husband said, and he got the video camera. As always, the little red light that showed that the camera was recording excited my father-in-law to an even more delightedly ham performance.

As for fantasies of the future, all the Christmases and Thanksgivings and summer vacations we were to spend together; the graduations; the weddings; the trips—to Oaxaca, to the Galápagos; the party I was going to throw for my mother- and father-in-law's fiftieth wedding anniversary: all these pictures and narratives have to be edited. As with writing a novel, the removal of a main character changes everything. All the stories I've told myself, told over and over, like bedtime stories, each one has to be reworked, reimagined. It's both automatic and exhausting; I get tired but can't turn it off.

I drop the lid to my grandmother's sugar bowl. It breaks into seven pieces, and I begin trying to glue them together. I should be packing my younger daughter's lunch, dressing her and myself for the walk to school, but I can't wait to fix it, can't allow it to stay broken for even an hour. Over and over, the glued pieces come apart in my hands, and I grow increasingly tense, losing my temper at each setback, even starting to cry with frustration.

"That has a doomed look to it," my husband says over my shoulder just as I'm considering throwing the lid away. But the word *doomed* makes defeat unacceptable. I waste more time regluing the pieces and wrapping the sticky, ugly mess in rubber bands. Four times it comes apart under the bands' tension; four times I start over. We leave for school a half hour late, the unevenly reassembled lid balanced on a paper towel on the kitchen counter, forced to recover even though it can barely be held together.

I remember this involuntary shift toward magical thinking from the death of my mother, the mind taking every opportunity to fashion what amounts to a spell in order to reshape an unbearable outcome. How can I allow the lid to remain broken if there's a chance of repairing it? How can my husband permit even one of the many trees his father has given us to fail, when new branches and buds predict the spring, life emerging from what looks like death? If we align one small propitiation after another—and isn't this what's implicit in making love every night: our thwarting death with the act that conjures life?—if we make everything around us into a prayer, doesn't this represent some power, if nothing more than our refusal to accept what we don't know how to endure?

I wake early, at four, and get up. I try not to sleep away these quiet hours, before I have to rouse the children for school. My study is next door to our son's room, and before I go to my desk I look in at him, sleeping with his face wedged into the corner formed by the mattress and the wall. Although I straightened his room just the previous morning, the floor is strewn with baseball cards and bits of unassembled models, things I'll pick up later, before I vacuum. The house tends to be significantly tidier during a crisis; the solace inherent in setting things straight overcomes my usual disinterest in housework.

At my desk, I sit, staring out the window at the street, still dark. It's hard to work when I'm preoccupied by thoughts of my father-in-law in his chrome-railed bed, caught in a snare of tubes and wires, outside his room a corridor that never sleeps, never darkens. Perhaps he's awake, too, and it's just the two of us, alone and thinking.

Angioscarcoma, from the Greek, *angeion,* blood vessel, and *sarkoma,* fleshy excrescence. A rare and insidious malignancy that arises from vascular tissue, growing slowly, for as long as twenty years in the case of my father-in-law, and typically diagnosed too late to cut out or radiate or blast with chemicals. Twenty years. Twenty years would mean that when I met my father-in-law, his future, *this* future, was foretold. This future embraced me and it.

Of course we knew it couldn't have been the return of his prostate cancer—my father-in-law's PSA levels were consistently low, as they would not have been had that cancer recurred and metastasized. In fact, it was those exemplary PSA results that encouraged physicians to dismiss his pain, weight loss, and the problems with his bowels and bladder— all of them classic signs of cancer—as "post-radiation syndrome," common among cancer patients, like my father-in-law, who received broad-spectrum pelvic radiation.

September 30, my first visit to my father-in-law. From now until his death, my husband and I will see little of each other, and we can't make love every night. Typically, my husband will be with his parents from Friday night through Sunday afternoon and I'll spend two or three weeknights in Washington, relying on a babysitter to care for the children after school, while my husband is at work.

To make a seven a.m. train to Washington I have to be on the subway before six, where I sit with people on their way to work. A number of them wear nurses' uniforms, making me feel as if we're all traveling to the same destination, a vast hospice waiting at the end of a dark tunnel.

As a gift, I bring my father-in-law a delicate and unwieldy bonsai, a nine-inch Fukien tea tree I spent a whole day acquiring: researching various species and their availability and traveling ninety minutes in either direction to get a perfect specimen, its trunk beautifully gnarled, each tiny bough thick with dark, glossy foliage. The tree's safe arrival seems both essential and unlikely; on the train, I hold it in my lap.

When I arrive at Union Station in D.C., sleep-deprived and overwrought, I find myself walking toward the first of many absences to come. My husband's father isn't standing at the end of the platform, as he has for years, his arms open before I reach them.

At the hospital, I see that the window in my father-in-law's private room has a view of woods, above them a bright sky. Next to his bed is a big convertible chair that can unfold flat to accommodate whoever stays the night with him, so he is never in the dark, alone, without one of his family. I drop my backpack on the floor—in it a book I won't read, work I won't do, pajamas I won't bother to change into. I set the little tree on the sill while I wait for a nurse to maneuver him into a position that is tolerable, something so elusive that it leaves enough time for my mother-in-law and me to hug and keep on hugging. When we pull away, it's without having spoken; neither of us has any words for this occasion. I dry my face, kiss my father-in-law hello, and rest my cheek against his. "There," I say, "that's good, I'm tired of loving you from afar." He smiles. It's a real smile, radiant and flirtatious.

"You're good at it, though. I can feel what you send me." I'd cry if I weren't smiling, and how can I not answer his smile when I see how happy he is that I've come? My mother-in-law leaves in search of coffee, and I take her place in the chair by the bed. When I look into his eyes I see that they're dilated from morphine, but it isn't enough. Enough would render him unconscious, unable to communicate. So he uses less, and there are groans he can't suppress; he pants to brace himself against the pain. Already it has changed his face. How alike we all look in suffering: we bare our teeth in the same grimace, whimper the same whimpers, helplessly pick at the bedclothes.

Nightfall on the day I leave the hospital. In the taxi's rearview mirror I see the driver wincing in response to my uninterrupted crying; finally, he turns on the radio. At Union Station I catch sight of myself in a shop window and see that I look as I feel, exhausted and strung-out, like a child who's lost the hand she was holding.

It's nearly midnight when I get home. I leave my shoes by the door so I can run up the stairs quietly. I climb in bed on top of my husband, awake in the dark. Still in my street clothes, I shove my face into his neck, his beard prickling my eyelids. It's an hour before I let go of him long enough to undress.

I hang a string of lights over the double doors that separate our living and dining areas. They're unusual, each bulb painted so that it looks like an illuminated glass paperweight, the kind made in Italy and crowded with tiny flowers of many colors. I bought them last spring to celebrate a visit from my husband's parents, and hung them around the mirror over the guest room's mantel. My father-in-law, who loves candles and lanterns and holiday lights, was already frail enough to elicit tenderness, a desire to provide every possible pleasure. The visit was timed to the Little League calendar; our son, nearly eleven, was to pitch in two baseball games that weekend, and my husband wanted his father to see him play. As it happened, the games were rained out, but it didn't really matter; they brought my father-in-law to our home, for what would be the last time.

The lights are pretty in the new location, a festive counterbalance to the shortening days, and because I bought them for my father-in-law they have a private votive quality. I can plug them in, and no one need know that this, too, is a little prayer.

A Sunday night, October 5. My husband has just returned from a weekend in Washington. We haven't been able to agree on the right moment to tell the children what will be the outcome of this illness that has required so many visits to their grandparents' home. I want to do it as soon as possible—I wish we had told them from the beginning—because I'm not good at disguising emotion, and already they suspect I'm hiding something. But my husband wants to wait until they've had a chance to see his father, one that isn't made awkward by defining it as a goodbye. And, though he doesn't say this, he wants to preserve a part of us, our family, that doesn't know what we know.

The children, however, settle the question for us by being so obnoxious at the dinner table that it seems as if they are trying to dismantle whatever poise we've maintained against the strain of the past weeks. Finally, after asking ten or more times for a little peace in which to eat, my husband strikes his open hand against the table and says that he's had a terrible weekend and that all of them must shut up immediately.

"What was so bad about it?" our son asks him.

"Granddaddy is very sick."

"Well, yeah, but he's getting better, right?"

"No. No, he's not. He is not."

"But, but he's not going to die or anything."

"He is. He is dying."

Abruptly, the clamor and fidgeting collapses into stunned silence. Our son puts down his fork and covers his face. Tears drip down from under his hands, which I notice have not been washed, fingers still grimy from playing basketball. Our older daughter turns to me, also crying soundlessly, a complicated look of betrayal on her face, not one directed at me for having kept the news from her, so much as at life, at fate, at whatever *It* is that takes away what *It* has given us. This adult anguish is the property of her eyes. From the nose down she's the little girl she was at five or six; her chin wobbles as she tries to hide the fact that she's crying, a thing she tries not to do and is never willing to admit. Generally speaking, the keener her unhappiness, the more fiercely she guards it. Her little sister—ten years younger, she grants our older daughter the status of a parent, albeit an unusually fun one—gets up and goes to our son, talking softly to him from outside the hands still pressed over his face. "Don't worry," she says, "it will be all right," and she repeats this over and over, she strokes his head and kisses his dirty fingers.

The incision gets infected. The surgeon who performed the operation, his scalpel cutting from just under my father-in-law's ribs, detouring around his navel, and continuing on down to make an opening some twelve inches long, removes the staples holding the two sides together, and, after cleaning the wound, leaves it open to heal. On my next visit, when I arrive I find a nurse bent over the bed, changing the dressing. I pause at the open door and knock.

"Come in," my father-in-law says. "I want you to see this." At this, the nurse looks up. She raises a gloved hand in protest.

"I don't know if that's—I don't think—"

"It's all right. She's interested in medicine," my father-in-law tells her. And I am. But the nurse was right. I only just manage not to step back in shock. My eyes fill with tears; I can't stop myself from covering my mouth with my hands. It's not—it can't be—that my father-in-law wants me to see what I'd find interesting. No, he needs witness to this, this hole, so long and deep that I think the word *seppuku,* Japanese for ritual disembowelment. A word that will never again seem literary and mannered, the property of an effete foreign novel.

"Oh," I say. "Oh, God." I come to the head of the bed, take his hand and kiss it, hold it to my face. "A Purple Heart," I say. "Two." And then I say, "Never mind. A hundred aren't enough." Not enough to acknowledge what has to be the horror of looking down into his own split-open body, a gash that's red and glistening wet and so, so big.

Back home, I ask my husband not to look. "Not unless he asks you." And I tell him the truth: that it is worse than any wound I've ever seen, even in photographs. That my husband's looking at it can only hurt him, and to what end?

"Listen," I say to him the next night, before he leaves again for Washington. "Every day since I saw it," I tell him, "some of that day—some of me—disappears into that hole."

October 10. My father-in-law turns seventy-one. A tissue sample from one of his tumors is sent to the Mayo Clinic for analysis. I tell someone this and hear that "Mayo" tone in my voice, betraying both respect and desperation.

It's as if I'm referring to Lourdes—a mythic destination of last resort, the best that our secular gods can offer, the hope for a new, different interpretation: a miracle.

My husband has put two big tomatoes from his father's garden on the windowsill over the kitchen sink. They are ready to eat, almost overripe, but neither of us has cut into one. "Save the seeds," my husband says now. "Save the seeds from my father's tomatoes."

"Do I dry them out on a paper towel?" I ask, but he doesn't answer my question.

"You'll have to be prepared for some major relic collecting," he says, looking out the window. "Seeds, sweaters, shirts, pens . . ." He trails off.

But I don't need to prepare. I didn't part with my mother's old nightgowns until eighteen years after she died.

It's that many years and more since I've waited by the deathbed of someone I love. Still, how familiar it feels— as if a version of me has continued to exist, uninterrupted by the death of my mother. I take my place in the chair by the bed, slip off my shoes, and tuck my feet into the warm seam between mattress and pad, careful, without even thinking about it, to do it so gently that the bed doesn't even quiver. "Egg crate," that pad was called when my mother was dying, because the foam that helped protect a patient's skin from bedsores was molded in that shape. My father-in-law's is state of the art, filled with moving air, humming industriously, with a set of buttons to control its temperature and the degree of its firmness. How differently everything might have turned out had I been a grown-up when my mother died. Had I not needed her too much to comfort her. Can this be why this incarnation of me persists—the girl keeping vigil—so I can get it right this time?

I fall into place beside my mother-in-law, each of us massaging a foot, providing whatever sensation we can to distract my father-in-law from pain, talking and talking about nothing, a quiet back-and-forth that he hears without listening, his eyes closed. "Don't stop," he says whenever we pause. "I like to hear your voices."

Without conscious intent, we allow ourselves to weep in the hall and then, immediately, without having to try, we stop as we walk through the door to my father-in-law's room; we resume our quiet conversation, our foot-rubbing, ice-chip-proffering, forehead-stroking, blanket-fetching, hand-holding presence. Sometimes, in the company of this man whom so many people love, their gifts and flowers and letters multiplying over every surface of his room, I find myself wondering what happens to people who don't have hands to hold as they die. Do they do it more quickly, so as to get it over with? Or do they linger? Do they wait to be touched?

Worlds within worlds," my father-in-law says. He's trying to tell me something about the nature of time. Either that, or the nature of love. Both, really. That love can't be measured by the clock of the body. The clock of his—and, one day, my own—dying body. All of us who love one another have always and will always love one another. His words are cryptic but deliberate—his eyes are locked on mine, his hold on my fingers adamant, fevered—and I'll return to them in the days and months to come. I'll revisit conversations we've had about Meister Eckhardt or Saint John of the Cross, searching for their antecedent in mysticism. Some of the happiest evenings of my life have been with my father-in-law, sitting in front of a fire he built (often just to please me, as it wasn't cold enough to need its warmth), drinking wine, and talking about things that none of the rest of the family has much interest in. As soon as one of us mentioned a theologian, or began to puzzle over the writings of a favorite mystic, my husband drifted out of the room, his brother picked up the paper, my sister-in-law went to the kitchen to help with dinner.

October 16. A few roses still bloom, and nearly a month remains to my father-in-law. He comes home to die in the room that looks out on his trees and his flower beds. It's a sunroom, with big picture windows, and the gold leaves that drop from the maples float down onto the deck just beyond the glass door, every day a new carpet of them to sweep away. With fall's drop in humidity, the light acquires the season's characteristic intensity, and as the branches bare they allow more and more sun to come through them. Sitting with my father-in-law, neither of us speaks. Sometimes, I lay my head next to his. It seems to me that the shorter days are becoming ever brighter, as if they were burning themselves out more quickly.

One evening when I arrive in Washington, my mother-in-law tells me that earlier that day my father-in-law said he was sick of long faces and directed her, her sister, and the nurse to stand around his bed and sing, which they did. He told them which songs he wanted—Quaker hymns, mostly, and a few favorite folk songs: "'Tis a Gift to Be Simple." "Michael, Row Your Boat Ashore."

With my mother-in-law's sister running the house, and friends bringing in meals, I make no effort to do any chores when I'm there. Instead, I stay beside my father-in-law every minute I can, leaving only to give him privacy with his wife or his brother or one of his sons. More often than not, I'm at the foot of his bed, massaging his feet. The comfort this gives both of us is such that I do it for hours, grateful to be able to provide what feels good to him and communicates my love as words cannot. Sometimes I read him a letter from an old student or friend. My mother-in-law's sister logs them as they arrive, about seven hundred so far.

November 8. On the last weekend of his father's life, both my husband and I are with his parents. Knowing what's coming, we've left the younger children at home with a sitter, and brought only our older daughter with us. On Sunday, my husband comes down to breakfast just as the sky is beginning to lighten. He finds me at the foot of his father's bed, eyes closed, rubbing his feet with oil. My husband puts a hand on my shoulder and I open my eyes. "Have you been here all night?" he asks.

"He likes it."

"But you're tired, sweetheart. Take a break. Come have something to eat with me."

"I will. In a minute, I will." I go on rubbing. My father-in-law opens his eyes and smiles at my husband, who comes to take his hand.

"I'm tough competition," he whispers, and my husband bends down to kiss his father's forehead.

We are trying to fill each remaining minute with love. Enough to split time open, to make love run backwards and forwards. Enough that my father-in-law can feel what he knows: that we've always loved him, and we always will.

January, February, March. In the months after his death, I dream of my father-in-law every night. In the dreams there are two of him, one dead, one living. The dead man is in his casket; the other sits among the mourners. I find this unusual, but not impossible, as it would be were I awake. The dreams are crowded with people—family and friends who have come to attend his funeral and who fill a church or an auditorium. Once it's a movie theater with rows of plush red seats; he sits on one side of his wife, and I am on the other.

Usually, the funerals are bungled. There are not enough pews, or we seat the wrong people together, or forget to order food for the reception. We don't give out song sheets, and no one knows the words to the hymns we pick. Each time something goes wrong, all of us are distraught, particularly my mother-in-law, who weeps with frustration. My father-in-law shrugs. Never mind, he tells her. What does it matter?

In one dream, the service takes place at a hunting lodge, and my husband lies down in a fireplace, among the burning logs. He curls himself up in a fetal position, and his legs catch on fire. "Stop him!" I say to my father-in-law, and I grab him by the arm. "Please don't let him do that!"

Another time, we lose my father-in-law's body; it's been stolen and shipped overseas, where a chemical extracted from his tumors will be used to treat other sick people. Before we can have a funeral, we must get it back. My father-in-law paces in this dream, and I worry that he's growing impatient. I know he can't linger forever in hopes of a funeral that doesn't go awry.

And he doesn't. There's a huge picnic, a family reunion, in a place I've never been, grassy and pleasant. I walk among the people drinking and eating and talking together, but I can't find him. Just as I begin to cry, a phone booth appears, and the phone begins to ring. "Please don't," he says when I answer. "I don't want you to cry."

TA-NEHISI COATES

The Fraternal Order
of Unmarried Dads

● ● ●

Early one August morning, I stand and pledge a shamed
fraternity—The Order of Unmarried Dads. I am the
prototype: a college dropout with bad credit, a man who
can't hold a steady job. I'm also twenty-four, arrogant, naive,
and convinced that "good father" and "husband" are not
synonymous. It's around six a.m. and I am sitting in a maternity ward in Wilmington, Delaware, beside Kenyatta, my
pregnant partner, waiting for a nurse to finish a battery of
tests. Every day some nervous father-to-be wheels a groan-

ing woman into the ward, only to find out it's a false alarm. Our nurse assures us that we probably fall into that category. But ten minutes later, she walks through the door smiling and I catch the sign—in the bowels of St. Francis Hospital, I am up.

All year I've studied for this moment, leafing through *What to Expect When You're Expecting, What to Eat When You're Expecting,* and *The Expectant Father.* I've humored the old women and their blind predictions of boy or girl. I've worshiped protein and iron, spurned sushi and smoky clubs, mastered rhythmic breathing, all to prove myself a responsible father, and the iconic Dad for these modern times. Never let it be said that I am simply the lunk who swills Guinness and cheers on Emmitt Smith. Let it be said that I swill Guinness only after ensuring that Kenyatta receives the correct allotment of folic acid.

Now I sit at Kenyatta's bedside, feeding her ice chips from a plastic cup, watching the meter for contractions, holding her close when it spikes. When she grunts and whispers, I untangle the web of IV tubes, toss her arm over my shoulder, and help her to the bathroom. Across the way, a woman is screaming like the goblins have gone to work on her. But from blood to bone, I am steel. Occasionally our nurse checks in—*We should have you on payroll. You're a really good birthing partner.* Not good. The best. And this is me drumming solo, beating the buzzer, embracing my moment, claiming my manhood.

Still a mountain looms—excluding the soon-to-be grandparents from the actual birth. In birthing class, Kenyatta and

I watched a woman go into double labor on film—first, with the baby, and then with her family. Eyes loomed everywhere, a scrum of relatives milled about, and in the midst of all the pointing and smiling, the expectant mother groaned and glared. It looked miserable. And so Kenyatta and I formulated a policy—grandparents are welcome at the hospital for support, but nonessential personnel won't be allowed in the birthing room.

I easily explain this to my parents. With seven kids between them, and grandchildren popping off biannually, they are fine with sitting this one out. But for Kenyatta's mother, Camille—the in-law who isn't—this is a loaded proposition. When Kenyatta was two, her father walked out on his family. He never returned, but his ghost walks with Kenyatta and Camille, dredging up ancient issues of trust between black men and women. And so for their mutual protection, Camille has forged a secret pact with her daughter—it's the two of them against the world. Nobody, especially not a man, can save them.

I want to believe that I've given both Camille and Kenyatta reason to think differently about me. I don't close down the clubs, or run the streets. I have a passion for cooking and reading, which makes me a natural homebody. Most important, I love Kenyatta. And I also feel bound by her pain. Her father's sin of abandonment, so common among black men, feels like some sort of burdensome family debt. On my honor, I'll have that debt paid. But I want to do it as I see fit—without fanfare and pomp, without grandiose titles and pronouncements, without marriage.

That's where I run afoul of Camille. Her own father was emotionally abusive and a serial adulterer. She was nineteen when she got pregnant with Kenyatta, and her parents told her that marriage was the only next step. But things fell apart before Kenyatta was even born. Kenyatta's father joined the Air Force, and shacked up with another woman. After Kenyatta's birth, he'd make the occasional half-ass effort to check in, but even that never amounted to much because of the considerable anger Camille held toward him. She only kept two pictures of him—one in which she's sitting on his lap looking very unhappy and another from his days as a collegiate basketball player.

Kenyatta is the only good that came of that relationship. In a life filled with disappointments, Kenyatta will always be Camille's rock. Smart, ambitious, and compassionate, Kenyatta is Camille's greatest and surest investment, a monument to Camille's determination and strength. Camille has long dreamt of the day when she could properly release her daughter into the world, but she hoped that release would come with some sort of guarantee. For Camille, marriage is at its core an insurance policy. That this guarantee did nothing for her own situation doesn't seem to matter.

Kenyatta and I rejected that notion of marriage early on in our own relationship, feeling that looking at matrimony from that perspective made the wedding ceremony resemble little more than an elaborate pre-nup. Besides, I doubt all promises made in the grand fashion of a wedding. A relationship is about the day-to-day work. Save the ring money, I reason, and make a down payment on a house.

But in a community rife with daddies on the lam, my theorizing sounds like the prequel to a great escape. I've only been with Kenyatta two years, not nearly enough time to make Camille into a convert. And now here I am about to phone her and explain why, at Kenyatta's most vulnerable moment, Camille will have to leave everything she's ever loved in my hands.

At first when I call Camille, there is joy, mostly because I've just told her that today her daughter will deliver. There is a quick conversation about logistics, about how to get her from Chicago to the hospital in Wilmington. But it goes sour as soon as I tell her that she will have to stay out of the birthing room. Camille is a hard woman with a soft exterior. Her style is curt and polite. So she does not explode on the phone—she simply tells me that she'll speak to Kenyatta when she gets here. I hang up, unsure and ill at ease.

When I turn to Kenyatta, she is only half-lucid and approaching an ugly contraction. *I don't know what to do with your mother. I tried to tell her, but she said she wanted to talk to you.* Kenyatta looks past me, hyperventilating, and squinting her brow. When the contraction subsides, she looks over at me, and now the steel is all in her. Her voice is low and impolite. *Ta-Nehisi, I can't deal with this right now. You have to handle it.*

After setting me straight, she leans her head to the side, half-burying it in a pillow, searching for some relief. Every so often a nurse walks into the room, asks Kenyatta if she needs more painkillers, and then checks her dilation. The thick drapes in the room are drawn tight, and between the darkness and the air-conditioning, I start to lose track of time. Kenyatta is fully aware only at the moment when a contraction peaks and punches its way through her trunk.

I met Kenyatta while we were students at Howard University. I was a romantic back then, with a preternatural ability to fall for girls I hadn't exchanged two words with. Lucky for me, when I finally did exchange words with Kenyatta we had a lot in common. We both fashioned ourselves intellectuals, and loved nothing more then to get drunk, get high, and then argue over some obscure point about debt-peonage, or feudalism. This is how I knew I'd found my match.

We also both believed in iconoclasm. So when Kenyatta got pregnant in early 2000, even though almost no one our age was having kids, we decided to go full steam ahead. I had no idea where that decision was headed. But I did know two things: 1. If I started having kids at twenty-four, I could have my life back by fifty. 2. A man who doesn't raise his kids is only half a man.

I grew up in West Baltimore. I had two working parents, and I never wanted for anything. My father was a very active— if eccentric—parent. And in my extended family, I was surrounded by strong men. It was different for most of my friends, who either didn't know their fathers, or only had trivial contact with them. This was not just a matter of class. At Howard, many of my friends also had troubled or nonexistent relationships with their fathers. Whenever my friends talked, I could hear a bitterness toward their absent half that chilled me. I felt a communal sense of disgrace, and desperately wanted to be some part of a solution. Had there been an army for black fathers, I'd have rushed to the front lines.

In the birthing room, sitting next to Kenyatta, I think about how I've turned having a baby into a political statement. For my son, I picked a name invested with meaning—Samori Maceo-Paul Coates—Samori for a Mende prince who fought off the French, Maceo for the black Cuban revolutionary Antonio Maceo, Paul for my father, and Coates for his clan. I fancy myself part of some grand plan to rebuild the bonds within the black community. In my relationship with Kenyatta, I've seen my own small but essential step toward that end. In making a child from that union, I've seen something larger, a chance to live for all those black fathers too broke-down to live up to the title. The revolution will be televised—if only on sonogram.

When Kenyatta first told her mother she was pregnant, Camille was mostly happy. Whatever happened with me, at twenty-three, Kenyatta had proven to be capable of handling herself. She had a steady job as a copy editor and paid her own rent.

A few years after Kenyatta was born, Camille took a job at Federal Express. She's worked there steadily for over twenty years, slowly climbing the ladder, and securing Kenyatta's needs. Her work ethic meshes well with black America's image of its women, not as domestic caretakers, but as the economic engine that keeps us moving. We believe our men to be generally flaky, but our women are always there in the crunch.

And yet in placing herself in that mold, Camille gave her youth away to her daughter. After getting pregnant, Camille never graduated from college, and though Camille never talked about it, Kenyatta would often get a vague sense that Camille had ambitions that went far beyond FedEx.

But that never affected Camille and Kenyatta's relationship. In college, Kenyatta's friends would tease her because she talked with her mother for hours, like she was talking to an old girlfriend. When Camille came to visit us, she would hover around Kenyatta, plying her with tales of Chicago, aunts who were expecting, and cousins who'd had their cars towed.

I came from a different world then Camille and Kenyatta. Though Camille and Kenyatta are very close, Camille's family is large, but scattered and only slightly interested in each other's affairs. Camille seemed hardened by the distance in her family, as well as the general distance that having a baby creates between the mother and non-mothers her own age. I come from an equally large and disjointed family—seven kids by four women. But my father was a strong thread, making sure all the kids were tight, and refusing to allow us to use the term "half brother" or "half sister." I came to my relationship with Kenyatta believing in family. But Camille and Kenyatta's experiences with their respective fathers left them suspicious.

Camille flew from Chicago to our home in Delaware twice while Kenyatta was pregnant. Her visits were pleasant and awkward, mostly because she spent half her time praying her daughter was not revisiting the sins of her mother. Always I could feel a dull discomfort emanating from Camille, and I often felt like an intruding guest. Our conversations were generally brief. We'd talk about food or Chicago. Whenever Kenyatta left the room, Camille would leave with her. I should be fair and say that I wasn't that social myself. Part of it is my nature, but a larger part was that I felt that much of the difficulty in my relationship with Kenyatta stemmed from my in-laws, both the one that was accounted for and the one that had skipped out all those years before.

One night about a month after Kenyatta and I started seeing each other, we were heading out to see a movie. She asked me a question about how her hair looked. I made some offhand remark about liking it better the way she had worn it the day before. I spent the rest of that evening attempting to douse Kenyatta's anger, and convince her that I thought her hair looked fine. At the time, I wrote that episode off as typical male-female miscommunication of the "Do I look fat?" variety. But as we moved into our relationship, it became clear that a part of Kenyatta saw me as the mastermind of a mad plot to pull her into my clutches— and then trample over her feelings. In everything I did she saw clues of this conspiracy. She routinely set out to test me.

She would walk into a room and pick a fight, or accuse a female friend of ours of trying to steal me away. To her, this was simply self-defense—she never wanted to experience anything like the pain that resulted from having a father who walked out. So she'd assume the worst and keep her hopes at bay, thus lessening the approaching and imminent heartbreak. Camille's rage toward her ex-husband had also rubbed off on Kenyatta, and I was catching the worst of it.

My parents and my younger brother drive up from Baltimore. They pick up Camille at the airport in Philadelphia, and then make the trek to St. Francis. Kenyatta hasn't dilated much since they first brought her in. She shifts in and out of consciousness. Camille calls to tell us that they are just moments away. I'm scared, because the last thing I want is a fight with Camille in the maternity ward. I think back to some advice my dad gave me after the baby shower. The time there with Camille had been uncomfortable. Once again, I felt judged and I told my dad as much, hoping for a bit of affirmation. He was unsympathetic. *Kenyatta's her whole world, man, and you've gotta understand that. I could see it in how she looked at her daughter. Kenyatta is everything to her, and you really need to respect that.*

Yet, I remember my father's own attitude toward his in-laws. For most of my childhood my maternal grandmother's relationship with my dad was polite and cold. I never saw them fight, but I also never saw them have a conversation that extended beyond the level of "How's the weather?"

And my dad seemed unwilling to do much to repair it. He would not ingratiate himself in the slightest, and never believed he had to prove that he was worthy enough to be with my mother.

But like Kenyatta's father, my maternal grandfather abandoned the family when my mom was young, leaving three daughters in the care of her mother. They lived in the projects in Baltimore, and, like Camille, my grandmother obsessed over protecting her daughters. When my mother met my father, his rap sheet read exactly like the sort of guy my grandmother didn't want her daughter to end up with. He was a book-peddling college dropout with an estranged wife, who, while polite, had little tolerance for the sort of niceties and effects that my grandmother believed in. He wasn't a church man, and he'd already sired five kids by three women.

My résumé reads better than my father's did, and I am more willing to bend, but I can't escape the thought that it isn't just the daughter revisiting the sins of the mother, it's the son doing the same.

Camille walks in with my parents at about ten a.m. By then Kenyatta's hard labor is approaching the five-hour mark. The hospital regulations allow only two people in the room. Since I insist on always being present, that means that each visitor has to file in one at a time. Camille understandably comes in first. She offers me a hug and then stands over her daughter, leaning down so she can speak to her as tenderly as possible.

I've never doubted that Camille loves her Kenyatta. Now she talks to her in a really low voice, and Kenyatta responds in a similar tone, mostly because of the drugs. After a few brief moments, Camille walks out. After she leaves, Kenyatta says that she's told her mother that I had been speaking for both of us and wasn't trying to shut her out. I am impressed that Camille elects not to wage war over the issue.

My mother, and then my father file slowly in. Across the way, I can still hear that lady's besieged wails.

Soon, it is time. Kenyatta hasn't dilated enough to deliver, but the doctors don't want a protracted labor. They decide that it's best to send Kenyatta into surgery for a C-section. As it turns out, the hospital rules for surgery allow only the father to be present, so my near-confrontation with Camille seems silly—I could have just let the doctors take the heat for me.

I stand outside of the operating room while they prep Kenyatta for surgery. The waiting is agonizing, but I am happy that we are nearing the end. A nurse escorts me inside and I stand near Kenyatta's head, not just because I'm squeamish, but because I want her to know that I am here.

No more than ten minutes later, a nurse says the baby has arrived. And I see her walk away with Samori, who is bluish-red. I am babbling every detail I can think of to Kenyatta. Finally, they bring me over and let me hold him. I realize then how inexorably I am now tied to Kenyatta. Samori's birth feels as binding as a wedding ring.

Then the nurse swaddles him in a blanket. Kenyatta is lying on a gurney. The nurse places him in her arms and wheels them both out, to where our old family awaits our new family. When Camille holds Samori, I realize how bonded I am to her, too. Samori's presence is a bridge extending between both of our families. I like to think of myself as the ultimate modernist and my relationship with Kenyatta as the ultimate modern romance. And yet except for the absence of titles—husband, wife—there is very little different about what I am ultimately charged with as Kenyatta's partner.

I think back to a conversation I had with Camille on the last day of her first visit after Kenyatta got pregnant. At the time I thought she was being old-fashioned, but now I understand what she was getting at. On the day Camille was going home, I drove her up I-95 to catch her flight. We were pulling up to the airport. She looked at me and began talking. *Kenyatta didn't have a father. She was raised by me alone. I really appreciate your willingness to be a father. I want you to take care of my baby.*

SARAH JENKINS

My In-laws Made Me Do It

●●●

I have a friend who's been married five times, who's experienced just about every equation of romantic misery available in the age of no-contest divorce. Clara's left a husband who refused to stay out of the bars and get a job, and has been left by another husband with the same M.O. She nursed her most companionable husband through a decade-long disease, and lost the follow-up husband, whom she met on the Internet, to a freak sailing accident off Baja. Clara's had more than her share of in-laws, and once said that while a good set would never jump-start a dead marriage, a bad set would be one of the first things on your tearstained list of Why I Should Go.

At the time of our conversation, I had been married just over a year to Carl, and still labored under the influence of several of Western culture's most popular romantic myths: that heaving, Category 5 arguments which left me swollen-eyed and emotionally hung over the next morning were a sign of passion; that opposites attract (I was a writer, by vocation and avocation; Carl's idea of reading was cuddling up in front of the computer with the most recent strategy guide for his favorite video game); and that "Love Will Keep Us Together," to quote the Captain and Tennille, who apparently still *are* together, despite the skipper's cap.

But this is not the story of the Jerry! Jerry! Springer–like collapse of my marriage to Carl, a warm and sneaky working-class guy whose personal life was rife with red flags, but rather the evolution of my strange and doomed attachment to his parents, my in-laws, whom I will call Roberta and Russ.

As is the case so many times with love, I'd unwittingly turned Roberta and Russ into the people I needed them to be, rather than seeing them for who they were. I'd made the same foolish mistake with their son, but failing to see the true nature of your beloved is a common problem (some people argue it's a necessary precondition to tumbling into love in the first place). But failing to see the true nature of your beloved's parents is mystifying and complicated; it underscores the strange romantic desire for family, and for belonging to a tribe.

I met my future in-laws at the same time I met their son, at gun camp. An outdoor magazine had sent me on a story assignment to the high desert of northern Arizona for a weeklong handgun shooting course. I was intrigued. I have a curious proclivity for subjecting myself to unpleasant, embarrassing, and sometimes dangerous situations, which I then turn into self-deprecating tales of bumbling triumph.

The course involved standing in the brain-sautéing desert sun for eight hours a day shooting hundreds of rounds at human-shaped targets while getting hollered at by the instructors, an ex–Navy Seal, an ex–Army Ranger, and a SWAT-team trainer from Chicago. Roberta and Russ along with Carl were bunking in the trailer they'd towed from their home in California. This alone rendered them exotic. My own parents, Joan and Richard, were rabid non-campers. Roughing it in Joan's eyes was a hotel without a mini-bar. Once, when I was a child, in response to one of my routine pleas to go to a KOA (I had no idea what a KOA was), she announced that she would sooner stick a hot poker in her eye than cook anything over a campfire.

Roberta and Russ had little in common with Joan and Richard. I found this desperately attractive. My father was educated, erudite, and although he possessed the social graces of Middle European royalty (his parents were born into the property-owning Polish upper middle class), he was a cowboy hero at heart, silent and phlegmatic. That was okay, because my mother talked enough for both of them. She was a devotee of the cocktail party, and could make hosting a dinner party for twenty look no more difficult than calling out for pizza. She was a fiend for good manners, the importance of developing the knack for "general conversation," and knowing how to set a table with three forks.

All this she instilled in me with the ferocity and devotion of a stage mother stuck with the least talented child at the audition. I resented it. Then, when I was seventeen and she was forty-five, and I was away at my first semester at college, she swiftly and inelegantly died of brain cancer. I sometimes wonder if the fact of her death hasn't been the plutonium that's powered every lousy decision I've ever made since.

Unlike my coquettish redheaded mother, with her dry wit, and loathing of sport and nature, Roberta was earnest and tomboyish. She lived in jeans and plaid shirts, loved to hike and whittle (whittle!), and was such a stupendously lousy cook I mistook her ineptitude for feminism.

Roberta couldn't have cared less about how to set a table—Carl and his older brother, Russ, Jr., grew up eating in front of the TV. I fell in love with their rough and ready natures, their undiscerning vim. Joan and Richard had had so many unwritten expectations about behavior and taste; being with Roberta and Russ was like repairing to the ladies' room during some torturously dressy function, kicking off your too-tight shoes, and having an illicit smoke.

Of course, I didn't marry Roberta and Russ, I married Carl. I told my mystified friends that he looked like Kevin Costner, only losing his hair. I said he made me laugh. The truth was Carl was only average-looking, and had pretty much made a mess of his life; at thirty-one he lived at home and had already blown through two marriages (when we first met he'd lied and told me he'd only been married once). I saw him as a diamond-in-the-rough, a fixer-upper, the sweet, three-legged dog you rescue from the pound. The men I'd been involved with prior to Carl were all aspiring writers or directors, introspective artist-types sour with failed ambition. Carl seemed like a straightforward working-class guy, an optimist who had no mixed feelings about Christmas.

A year after I shacked up with Carl and his two kids (Nicole was ten and Scotty four) but a year before we married, Roberta and Russ moved to a nearby suburb. Even though they were thirty merciful minutes away, they began dropping in twice a week, unannounced, to sit in my living room. I'd stop whatever I was doing—usually writing or trying to write or preparing to try to sit down and write—and offer them a glass of wine. Russ would commandeer the most comfortable chair, where he would nap, then vigorously clean his ear with his car key while ranting about the crimes perpetrated against humanity by Bill Clinton, whom he despised with a zeal so personal and vigorous, I began to suspect that this was the only thing that gave emotional meaning to his life. Roberta would blather on about the series of gnomes she was carving. I viewed this as eccentric, but in-law-ish, the stuff of stand-up comedy routines.

If Carl was home, he'd wander in and say hi, then wander back to the basement to play MechWarrior or EverQuest, waiting for them to leave. Roberta and Russ seemed to view this as normal, their adult son hiding out with his video games until they went away. When Roberta had questions about Nicole and Scotty's schedules, their clothing needs or Christmas lists, she contacted me, not Carl, even though I was just getting to know his children, and probably rushing into my stepmothering obligations with the typical enthusiasm born of insecurity.

Carl drove part-time for UPS, where he worked Saturday mornings for pocket change and health insurance for all of us. He enjoyed this job, so we decided to adopt the mantle of the Cutting Edge Couple. I would make the money, and Carl would be the househusband. This would give him a chance to be there for Nicole and Scotty, to help them with their homework, drive them to lessons and practices and play dates, and in general offer them the sense of stability they'd lacked in their earlier lives. He'd also shop, clean, and cook. (I know, I know.)

A recent study about the division of labor in the average American household revealed that even in a two-wage-earner household, women do more housework than men. What gave me pause was a tidbit at the end of the report, that women who made more money than their husbands did far more housework than women who made less or the same amount, as if to make amends for their competence.

It will come as no surprise, then, that the more I worked, the more I made, the more I wound up helping Nicole and Scotty with their homework, the more I chauffeured them around, shopped, cooked, and either cleaned, or hired cleaners, depending on how overwhelmed I felt. I hosted the sleepovers, oversaw the baking of Christmas cookies. I paid for the attorney who helped us win full custody of Scotty from Carl's second ex-wife.

Except for Saturdays, when Carl donned his UPS browns as if he were a superhero, he lived, unshaven, in his Mickey Mouse sweatpants. In all fairness, he did sweep the kitchen floor once in a while.

Roberta and Russ—it was always a united front; never in the time I knew them did Roberta have one opinion and Russ another—stayed mum on the subject of Carl's meager contribution to our household. They did, however, approve of my domesticity. I was the woman and the wife. Even though Nicole and Scotty weren't mine, they were children, and thus fell under my jurisdiction. In some unexplored trench of my brain where light never reaches, I found their attitude unsettling, but mostly I was happy to be Nicole and Scotty's mom. Nicole was bright—she could memorize a poem after one reading—and observant; Scotty was one of those sweet boys who risk being trounced by the world.

What Roberta and Russ couldn't figure out, and therefore couldn't trust, were my career and my income. I didn't make an enormous amount as a freelance writer, but I did make enough to support us, and to send Nicole and Scotty to private school. Because I worked from home, Roberta and Russ pretended I was a housewife, behaving as if a Brinks truck swung by in the night and tossed a bank bag on the porch.

Sometimes if they dropped by when I was writing, Russ

would stroll into my study, hands in his pockets, and say, "Here's a word for you—the." Or he'd say, "Those idiots still paying you by the word? How about, 'It was a very very very hot day'?" It never mattered whether I was crashing some impossible deadline, messy hair stuffed up into a stained scrunchie, glancing at the clock every forty-five seconds to see how much time I had, or biting my lips lost in thought, caressing a small sentence no one cared about but me; he barged in, derision in his voice. Like a lot of working-class guys, Russ mistrusted the chattering classes, of which I was one.

A friend who attended my wedding still remembers the kiss at the altar. It was unlike any she'd seen. "You closed your eyes and almost lunged at Carl, as if you were leaping into something against your better judgment."

My marriage to Carl failed for reasons I will never fully sort out; this is the flip side of the mystery of love and attachment. In the end, it winds up being anyone's call. Perhaps it was simply a colossal mismatch. Perhaps, like any dumb guy who falls for a pair of long legs and a sultry voice, I fell unwisely for a nice set of shoulders while at the same time indulging my rescuer's complex.

A wise woman once told me, "If you want to be loved, don't help." Unfortunately, I was a Girl Scout, and helping too much is my default setting. In my marriage to Carl, all I did was "help." I didn't always like doing everything. I saw the imbalance. The alternative was asking for Carl's help, re-liable tinder for our exhausting arguments.

I would ask Carl to go to the grocery store. He would be playing a computer game. He was always playing a computer game. He rarely watched television. He never read. He would say sure. An hour would pass, in which he wouldn't move. I would ask again. He would say, "I'm *going*. I said I would *go*." At which point the true nature of our union was revealed: I was the mother, and he was the fourteen-year-old who refused to get off the computer.

It should have been alarming to me that Carl's behavior was not alarming to Roberta and Russ. They seemed comfortable treating him like a wayward fourteen-year-old, whose lack of maturity was normal and therefore should be indulged. Russ would say to me a little too frequently, "You're the answer to our prayers!" I thought at first that he meant that they were relieved that Carl's children now had someone responsible to care for them, but it dawned on me that they were relieved there was finally someone responsible and reliable to care for Carl, too.

Once, near the end, Roberta presented me with a check for $3,000 for Nicole's college fund. The check was made out to my name, not Carl's, and given to me on the sly, as if she didn't dare let Carl know there was this sort of money floating around, or else he'd race out and lose it on the ponies. An impossibility, since Carl never left the computer, much less the house. I gave the check to Carl, told him that this was between him and his parents, that I wasn't his caretaker or his financial manager or his mother. He said he understood, said he would talk to his parents, then stuck the check to the bulletin board in the kitchen, where it hung untouched for months.

I often wonder if I'd still be married to Carl had my father not died. Eighteen months into our marriage, my dad, a two-pack-a-day man for sixty years, was told by his doctor to get his affairs in order. He had lung cancer; the ropy tumor had wound its way around his aorta, making it inoperable. For the next ten months I hopped on the plane bimonthly for the two-and-a-half-hour commute to my father's house to care for him. In my absence Carl fed Nicole and Scotty pizza and Taco Bell almost exclusively, but their clothes were clean, and their grades didn't suffer too badly. When Carl couldn't cope, Roberta and Russ took the children for the weekend.

After my father died, and he was cremated, his ashes scattered over the desert, I allowed myself to be exhausted, self-pitying, and sad. For the first time since Carl and I had known each other, I was in genuine need. I don't like being in genuine need; I don't know *how* to be in genuine need. My father was a first-class stoic, and I inherited his compulsion to suck it up. He was proud that during my numerous shoulder and knee dislocations during childhood (we are a loose-jointed family) I never cried, and that on the evening of the day we buried my mother, I drove back to college, where I aced an oceanography midterm.

But now my father was dead. I was an orphan, and if you

think that doesn't freak you out, at whatever age it befalls you, think again. I begged Carl for help; his response was to log more hours on the computer. A perverse dynamic revealed itself: Carl asserted his control by refusing to give me the exact thing I told him I needed. One night around midnight I stood in my underwear crying at his shoulder, as he refused to look away from the cartoon monsters he was blasting on the computer screen. I wanted him to come to bed with me. I told him that when the day came that I could go to bed by myself and not miss him, our marriage was over. He didn't believe me.

When Carl and I attempted a trial separation six months later, during the summer of 2001, I had certain assumptions about the way Russ and Roberta would take it, based, undoubtedly, on how I thought Joan and Richard would have responded. Gracious Richard would have kept his mouth shut out of respect for what he would have viewed as my personal business; Joan would have wept with me, saying "I know, I know," then suggested a shopping trip. They wouldn't say anything bad about Carl, because if we wound up reconciling, they wouldn't have wanted to go on record saying he was a loser, or an ass. They would have foreseen decades of holidays tense with the spoken fact that they didn't like him. They would have stayed out of it.

Even though Roberta and Russ were different from my own parents, I thought there were basic tenets of the Parent Credo they would never violate. I assumed they would be circumspect, mature, and fair. I imagined that even though they'd be angry with me for hurting their child, they would realize that it takes two to make a marriage fail, and that, sadly, sometimes these things just happen.

Carl drove to their house alone to break the news of our separation. Their response was to order him to get me back, the way you might tell a kid who's tired of scouring the neighborhood for the lost family dog to get back out there and keep calling.

Russ's advice, barked impatiently at poor Carl, was: "Romance her, damn it!" Roberta interrupted, tried to talk about the value of listening and cherishing, to which (according to Carl, during one of the last companionable conversations), Russ said, "Shut up, woman, you don't know what you're talking about!"

When romancing me (two dozen roses, an expensive dinner, and a night at the same fancy hotel where we spent our wedding night—all of which I wound up paying for) didn't have the desired effect, Roberta and Russ advised their son to take harsher measures, to let me know that they were behind him 100 percent, and would happily exhaust their retirement funds securing a husband's rights attorney for him who could make my life a living hell. Carl threatened me with this more times than I can count, then hunkered down to wait me out. He refused to move out of the house; he told me he wanted to stay married, and I was just going to have to accept it.

The house was actually *my* house; the title was in my name, my name alone was on the mortgage, which I alone paid. Apparently, Carl and his parents missed all those movies where the husband, out of a sense of personal pride and male honor, moves to a hotel or his old college roommate's house when the marriage dissolves.

Instead, for the next three months, I lived with *my* old graduate school roommate out of a single suitcase. Rather than being the punitive experience for which Carl was hoping, it ended up being the best collection of months I'd had in years; my friend and I sat on her back porch all summer long, barbecuing chicken and peppers on her battered hibachi, getting plastered on cheap Chardonnay, and making endless dumb jokes about how Carl had become The Husband That Wouldn't Leave.

At no time did Carl, or his parents—somehow they'd become an entire team I was divorcing—want to have an actual conversation about what might have gone wrong in the marriage, or what Carl and I might do to fix things.

Then, the Saturday after 9/11, Carl and I met for a drink in the small bar of a Mexican restaurant where we used to take Scotty and Nicole for dinner. Before our drinks even arrived, Carl made the my-parents-have-the-resources-to-make-your-life-a-living-hell threat. I stomped out; he followed me to my car, where, in full view of passersby, he put his hand around my throat, pinning me to the headrest. He stuck his face in mine. There was spittle in the corners of his mouth.

"It's your fault this is happening to you, Sarah."

He stopped himself after ten long seconds, strode back to his truck, and roared away. The whole sordid mess resulted in my filing for a restraining order first thing Monday morning.

Over the years my father used to say, "Sometimes, you just need your mother." His own mother, a Polish dressmaker, died when he was in his mid-thirties, and it's the only time I remember seeing him cry. I could have used a mother about then. Or a father. Someone, somewhere, who could advise me on what to do. I called Roberta. She was the closest thing to a mother I had.

She listened. When I'd finished, she said, "Tell me, do you still love him?"

I said, "I can't be married to someone who chokes me."

She said, "Carl may have inherited Russ's bad temper, but you're a writer. Your job is to make things up."

No matter my intentions or purity of heart, it made no difference. Roberta wouldn't believe me. There were only two available spots open for the women Carl went through like dress shirts: like-a-daughter or sworn enemy.

The following Sunday, while I was out for the day, Carl came to pick up Nicole and Scotty, who had been living with me during our seperation. They were to be home by six p.m. for dinner. Nicole was sixteen at the time, Scotty ten; I'd been their mother for six years. In the evening, I made their favorite enchiladas and spicy refried beans. At seven they still weren't home. They weren't home by nine. The terms of the restraining order forbade my calling Carl, so I called Roberta and Russ, thinking they would at least be able to tell me the kids were safe.

Russ answered the phone.

I said, "Hi, Russ, it's Sarah. I'm sure you're pretty upset with me, with everything that's been going on, but the kids were supposed to be home by six and now they're three hours late. Do you know what's going on?"

His response was the nail on the coffin lid of my marriage to his son. It sounds melodramatic and it is. I think I'm entitled. There are so few times in life when you can point to a moment and say this, *this* was the deciding factor.

My father-in-law drawled, "Sorry, can't help ya." I could tell by his smug tone of triumph that the kids were perfectly safe and he knew exactly where they were. (In fact, Carl had taken them and they never lived in my house again.) Then he hung up on me. It was at that moment that I realized that Russ and Roberta were not simply eccentric, but bred-in-the-bone cruel.

I spent close to a year agonizing about returning to Carl. We tried to get together for coffee, during which he would dutifully pay. We celebrated Nicole and Scotty's birthdays, and I gave the kids presents for Christmas. It was futile, like when a new resident on *ER* keeps trying to revive a patient long after she should have called the time of death. Still, sadly and ineffectually, we tried.

Carl would occasionally mention his parents. He told me that they told him he was being stupid; that I was good-for-nothing; that he should cut his losses and start dating the waitress daughter of one of Russ's navy pals who lived somewhere in the Midwest (now, there was a good woman! Not

254 • SARAH JENKINS

one of those artist types with dead parents and *issues*); that Carl just had to say the word and they'd hire him that husband's rights attorney who would see that he got the house and a shitload of alimony, plus child support. Some of what he told me was probably true and some of it smelled like stuff Carl made up to try to intimidate me into coming back.

But the sobering thing was, it all sounded as if it *could* be true. Russ and Roberta were capable of saying or doing all of it, and that fact coupled with my friend Clara's observations about the role of in-laws in ending a marriage helped make my choice clear. I would never go back to Carl, or his family. If I let Roberta and Russ down in my unwillingness to be the keeper of their son, they let me down by revealing their mean little hearts, putting them firmly, and sadly, at the top of my list of Why I Should Go.

BARBARA JONES

Rough Dad, Redeployed

● ● ●

One morning, soon after I met my future father-in-law, Verle Rinehart, I was sent (or I casually volunteered; I can't remember which) to pick up a car that he had left at a local tune-up shop. When I arrived and stated my business, the checkout clerk became noticeably agitated as soon as he saw the name on my receipt. "It's the Rinehart car! The Rinehart car!" he said, and at this declaration the two other young men behind the shop counter became visibly anxious, too. All three peered out into the customer area, past me, as if Verle might be hiding behind the plastic plant.

"He's not here," I said.

"He's not with you?" one of them said.

"No," I insisted. But the auto-shop clerks snapped to business anyway. Just in case.

"We have the car, ma'am. It's been ready since nine a.m. Everything is all set, ma'am."

As I soon learned, those three young men reacted to the mere idea of my father-in-law's presence as many did—with panic, hustle, and, often, a desire to get the transaction over as quickly as possible. Verle, a former Marine who had spent his career managing recreational facilities for the Air Force, had a "Do it, do it right, do it now" credo, which he imposed on pretty much everyone, on shop clerks as well as on waitresses, receptionists, grocery shelf stockers, tollbooth operators, firefighters, pharmacists, doctors, church committee members, neighbors, friends, and anyone else he encountered, including, of course, immediate family.

Verle was tall, lean, and fit, with a good head of silvering brown hair and skin that had freckled to a golden honey color. He had large, forward-leaning ears shaped like teacup handles and a big bent nose that looked as though it must have been broken across its bridge though it had not ever been broken, but his features came together favorably. He carried himself youthfully, powerfully. He strode. Still, most people took his vigor as something less than a complete blessing.

Living in New York City, nine hundred miles north of the Atlanta suburbs where Verle and my future mother-in-law, Charlene, had settled after Verle retired, their son Steve and I were spared active Rinehart duty. Down south, Steve's older brother, Randy, and younger sister, Carrie, and their respective spouses, Linda and Mark, lived in a sort of never-ending exurban boot camp.

Verle set all family garage-door openers to the same code as his. Randy and Linda and Carrie and Mark woke any day of the week to the sound of him in their garages, jacking up their cars. Or on their roof cleaning their gutters. Or to the sound of him in their kitchens, calling them to wake up and start on their chores. He had once read that you must get a good night's sleep every night because it's scientifically impossible to catch up on sleep later, so he'd shout, "You can't catch up on sleep. Get up." Both couples took to locking their bedroom doors before having sex. But any thoughts they might have had of sleeping in were only fantasies. There were tires to rotate, oil to change, storm windows to put in, leaves to rake, tile to grout, wood to chop, leaks to stop, pumps to fix, tulips to plant, lawns to mow. And cholesterol levels to monitor.

Verle's father had suffered from heart trouble starting at a young age and it had eventually killed him, so Verle rose each morning at dawn, ran five miles, returned for a small low-fat bran muffin and a banana, and spent much of the rest of the day gauging his fat and caloric intake—and yours.

He brooked no butter on bread or potatoes. And no mayonnaise ever. He might appear in any Rinehart kitchen at any time and stand around, watching. If he saw his daughter-in-law Linda, say, start to spread mayonnaise on her sandwich roll, he'd yell, "That's just plain fat!" When the family gathered for holiday meals, he'd rip the skin off his turkey

almost before the platter hit the table, and if anyone fool-
ishly asked aloud for the gravy, he'd make a cutting remark
about "grease."

One summer soon after I met Verle and Charlene, they
were signed up to go on an Alaskan cruise with friends, and
weeks before they left for the trip a small social crisis arose
when the travelers were required to submit dinner companion requests in advance of departure. None of their friends
wanted to dine with Verle. "And why would they?" Charlene
said. "Why should they volunteer to sit there and have him
pick on everything they eat?"

Verle bitingly referred to his son-in-law, Mark, a New
Zealand native who'd gotten his green card after marrying
Carrie, as "that wetback." He decided that Linda, whose
grandparents had emigrated from France, was "the frog."
Linda had been in the Air Force and later, as a reservist, had
been called up in the first Gulf War; she told everyone that
Verle was exactly like her basic training drill sergeant, and
she volunteered that she cried often because of things that
Verle said to her.

Steve has never been forthcoming about growing up as
Verle's son. He's suggested that Verle kept up a relentless list
of tasks for his offspring even as children, and that he
pressed the boys into athletic endeavors that were beyond
their abilities, let alone their interests. He threw them into
hotel pools and demanded that they swim laps, which they
could only struggle to do, flailing and crying. He laid out
marathonlike courses that they were supposed to spend
their Saturdays running, though at least once they hid in

some bushes, ashamed, rather than attempt a particularly challenging route. There were loud fights between Verle and Charlene that left her in tears. In front of dinner guests, he would say that she was fat.

I know that Verle himself had a rough childhood. His grandfather was a drunk in their small town, and Verle's father was not only ill but mean and poor; Verle grew up moving from one run-down rental house to another. He somehow put himself through college and graduate school and he married Charlene, a great woman—steady, caring, smart, independent, forgiving, and beautiful.

But I don't have much more information about Verle's childhood or Steve's. Steve has tended to rebuff inquiries into the Verle part of his boyhood with phrases that pretend to say it all but actually pull a curtain across the details. "Just a lot of humiliation," he's said, and, "You know, like the Great Santini."

Verle and I should not have gotten along.

Not only did he pester and frighten people, but he kept guns (five rifles and a .22) in his home. He hated cities and prized living in the suburbs amid built-from-a-kit Mc-Mansions and ribbons of asphalt golf-cart paths. He rose at six every morning and ate his dinner at six-thirty every night, preferably on a tray in front of the TV. His friends were ex-military, golfing buddies, and a barbershop quartet (which he managed with a strict rehearsal schedule). He did not read for pleasure.

Right up until the moment Steve and I became romantically involved, and, in most ways, even after that, my life was pretty much the opposite of Verle's. I regularly gave a portion of my meager freelance-writer income to Handgun Control, Inc. During the first war in Iraq, I marched down Broadway in protest. I was in love with cities in general and with New York City in particular; "I love Manhattan more than any man" was my secret motto in the time before I met Steve, while I fell in and out with half a dozen boyfriends and, even, one husband. I did not keep regular hours—spending a long Tuesday afternoon, say, at the movies with writer friends, then working round the clock on a weekend to get my assignments done on time. My friends were painters, photographers, novelists, poets, composers, an opera singer; married and unmarried, straight and gay, employed and unemployed. Reading was our common passion.

Before I met Steve, I had started the process of adopting a baby from China, a pursuit I had no intention of stopping. Once Steve and I moved in together, his parents began to visit us from time to time, and at the end of each visit, we'd drive them to La Guardia Airport east along 125th Street, through Harlem. Each swell of sidewalk vendors along the traffic-jammed boulevard relaxed me. Every surge of the swarming customers in front of and around our car sang "Home, home, home" to me. And, every time we drove that way, Verle would growl with disapproval, "It's just like a furr-eign country here. Just like a furr-eign country."

But I liked Verle immediately. His aggressive grunting—

upsetting to others—to me came across as an act, as a role that he played with relish, but a role. In his "furr-eign coun-try" comment, I could hear, along with real annoyance at our slowed passage to the airport, an appreciation of the teeming street market, and a boyish pleasure in teasing me about a place I so obviously loved. From the first, Verle made me laugh.

"He's not funny," Steve would say, in Verle's presence and mine, whenever we visited his parents in Georgia. Then, finding me and his father insufficient audience for this opin-ion, Steve would circulate from kitchen to living room, from living room to screened porch, looking to his mother or sis-ter or brother or to his in-laws for support. "She thinks he's funny. He's not funny."

As we boarded our plane or pulled out of a Rinehart driveway after one of these holidays, Steve would say, "He was on his best behavior. You know that, right?"

My point of view regarding me and Steve and his father was that Steve's deepest difficulties were something he would need to work out on his own. My first husband's father had separated from his young wife when my first husband was two years old. That father had come around intermittently but always narcissistically. Lack of Father, Needy Father, and How to Grow Up and Be a Man When You Don't Have a Person in Your Life to Show You What a Man Is: those problems had endured for my first husband, misshaping his life for a time, and reaching right into our tender marriage, ending it. Steve, on the other hand, had

Pushy Father, Macho Father, Nasty Father: Steve had Too Much Father. Which is a true trouble but not, by my lights, among the more unsolvable kinds.

In any case, I'd come away from my first marriage knowing that I couldn't change any man's relationship with his parents, and that I should not even try.

The week after I brought my five-month-old baby daughter, Maria, home from China, Steve and I flew with her to Iowa for a weekend of festivities to celebrate Steve's maternal grandfather's ninetieth birthday. Steve and I had recently decided to marry, and on this trip, Maria and I had the opportunity to meet both sides of Steve's extended family. On Friday evening, everyone gathered in the vast barnlike back room of a buffet restaurant in Story City, Iowa. (The place was called, to Steve's mocking glee, The Valhalla.) Steve strode in ahead of me, and I noticed that two people were signaling vigorously to me from the bar. They were the frog and the wetback. The in-laws, Linda and Mark. "Come. Sit with us," they urged. They were smoking and drinking enthusiastically. I climbed onto a barstool next to them. Mark bought me a beer. "We want to welcome you to the support group for in-laws of Verle," they said.

A few minutes later, they hailed Charlene to the bar, too. After all, she wasn't originally a Rinehart either, they said. She'd married in. "We're outlaws," the three of them said, knocking back their drinks like stockbrokers at the end of an especially rough day, all the strain apparently caused by a single market factor: Verle.

But when I finally made my way into the airport-hangar-sized dining room for some baked chicken and overcooked green beans, Verle, not Steve, was holding Maria, and when I retrieved her and started through the buffet line, Verle quickly reappeared at my side. "Let me just take her, so you can get your food," he said.

After I'd filled my plate, found myself a place at one of the long tables, collected Maria, and settled her onto my lap, Verle showed up again. "Let me take her, so you can eat," he said.

And so it went throughout the weekend.

"Let me take her for you, so you can have a few minutes to rest," he'd say.

"Let me take her for you, so you can talk."

And sometimes, just, "Let me take her."

Before Maria came along, Verle was already a notoriously involved grandfather with Randy and Linda's two boys. When Randy and Linda were both called up during the first Gulf War, Charlene was still employed as a nurse, so Verle took care of the toddler and the nine-month-old. After the war, he continued to spend time with them. He fixed up tricycles and kid-sized jeeps for them. He played ball with them. He took them fishing. He built a tree house for them in the woods behind his house. He gave each of them an axe, a bow and arrow, and a BB gun, and showed them how to use them. He signed them up for swimming lessons and music lessons, then he took them to those lessons.

On Sunday of that long family-reunion weekend in Iowa, the whole family was sitting around as Verle was gently bouncing Maria on his knees, goo-gooing at her. Suddenly, he noticed that his children and their spouses and their cousins had all paused mid-conversation and were staring at him with the baby.

He scanned the faces of the younger generation.

"I guess I'm a better grandfather than I was a father," he said.

And for what seemed to me an extraordinarily long moment, no one said a word.

When Maria was seven months old, Verle was dandling her on his thighs when he noticed something amiss with her legs. "Look at that," he said wonderingly. "She can't stand."

I hadn't known a baby's legs were supposed to be anything different than hers were. And the pediatrician hadn't said anything. But Verle was right. Maria had almost certainly spent too much time lying unattended in the orphanage in China. When Verle bounced her gently, she didn't push out with her legs. He tried repeatedly. No pushing out. So he stood her up over and over. He coached her. He cooed to her. He kept it up until, by his lights, she'd reclaimed whatever developmental moment she'd missed. She learned to push out. She caught up in strength with her peers.

In pictures of Maria's babyhood, she is in Verle's lap, or on her toes planting a smooch on his cheek, or squinting happily in the swing he has hung for her on the porch of a rented oceanside cottage. Or she is clutched to his chest on the day Steve adopted her and her granddaughter-grandfather connection to Verle became law.

Verle built a beautiful wooden high chair for her and an exquisitely simple step stool inspired by a picture in a Shaker furniture catalogue. And one weekend, after Steve and I had bought an old house in upstate New York, Verle drove from Atlanta in his Ford pickup, built a wooden swing set in our backyard, watched Maria swing and slide on it, then drove back to Atlanta in time to take care of the boys on Monday morning.

By the time Maria was four, and Carrie and Mark had a son who was two, and Randy and Linda's sons were nine and eleven, and there were two more grandkids on the way because Steve and I were expecting twins, a kind of truce had come over the Rinehart family. All of us were busy with the children and with working to shelter and feed and clothe and educate the children, and Verle was physically with us every step of the way, taking some of the load off.

Verle was his old self in many ways—yelling at Linda when he caught her smoking behind her own garage; picking on family members who were struggling with their weight. But what more could any sleep-deprived working parent want than a U.S. Marine on call? He took our car for oil changes, split and stacked our firewood, carried in our grocery bags, ran our children to exhaustion in the fresh air, and, above all, made them happy. He called our unborn twins Verle and Verla, then laughed wickedly, because who would ever name their children that? He wouldn't. But I thought he was also saying that, you know, with time anything could be overcome, even such a name.

That idea—that any trouble might be remedied if you kept trying—was what had connected Verle and me from the first, I think. When we were each offered a second chance in our private lives, we took it. I'd been married before. He'd had children to care for before. We had each behaved badly toward the people we loved most and had each seen domestic dreams die. But we were willing to pick ourselves up, forgive ourselves for what we'd done and surely would do again, and try our best to make another go.

And into the overlapping territories of our second tries, some resolution seemed to be coming for Steve, some salve for the pains of a boy's upbringing at the hands of a rough father. Steve had become a father himself (and was soon to be the father of three, just like Verle) and was bound to gain a bit of insight into his father's situation in years past. And Verle was steadfast in his resolve to be with us all: the father who had once-upon-a-time stomped off to be alone rather than stick around for the froufrou of birthday cake and gifts on Steve's thirteenth birthday was now present not only for the larger celebrations but for an astounding number of the small, meaningful moments of life with children. I believe that Verle had somehow, miraculously, woken up from the worst nightmares of his own bad behavior to discover that his life, in every important way, was exactly as he would have wanted it to be if he'd behaved differently. Charlene was still his loving wife, and though there had been rough times, particularly when his children were teenagers, his kids were in his life, with their own spouses and their own children. Verle was grateful. He let his children see a softer side of himself, even if it confused them. One day, after Maria sang long distance to Verle over the phone, then handed the receiver to her father, Steve hung it up with a bewildered expression. "My dad had to get off the phone fast," he said quizzically. "I think he was choked up."

Verle's children rightly understood that he might still pounce on them at any moment, but they came to address him with a wry good humor that he could appreciate. The grandchildren were a bridge that Verle, Charlene, their daughters-in-law and son-in-law, and their children were building together, and it seemed to me that Verle and Steve inched across the bridge from opposite sides from time to time, met in the middle, and had a pleasant look around.

When our twins, Charlie and Josephine, were nine days old, Charlene was with us in New York, having come for the birth and to help out afterward. Verle was in Georgia, where he had stayed to take care of Randy and Linda's boys and Carrie and Mark's son. It was December. Charlene was decorating holiday cookies with Maria. I was in an armchair nursing the newborns. When the telephone rang, Steve answered it. He pressed a palm against one side of his head and the phone to the other, and fell to his knees in the living room in front of me in a gesture so dramatically absurd-looking that I could hardly believe it. Randy and Linda's boys, ages eight and ten, had been watching a video; Verle had felt a sudden tiredness and had gone into another room to lie down for a nap. The boys found him there—unconscious, blue, foaming from the mouth. "Don't die on us, Grandpa," the younger one said, before running to the neighbor's house for help. It was the neighbor who was calling. He had found our phone number on a list on the kitchen wall. He said an EMS crew was working hard, very hard, on Verle.

At the funeral, on the day the twins were two weeks old, Charlene and her children must have been in shock; they were astonishingly organized and gracious. The outlaws, on the other hand—the frog, the wetback, and the hippie (me, because, as I learned that week, "that hippie" was how Verle had referred to me behind my back)—sobbed so continuously throughout the service that the minister paused twice, hoping that we might be able to collect ourselves and quiet down.

About a month before Verle died, he and I had our first disagreement. He would talk about taking his grandchildren flying, and I told him he could never take Maria flying in his little airplane. For twenty years, Verle had had a small-aircraft pilot's license. On a beautiful day, he'd go up in a rented plane, always circling back over his own house. We'd be in the backyard—barbecuing, chatting, playing with all the toys he'd set up in his yard for the kids—then he'd drive off, and the next thing we knew he was in a plane overhead, watching us.

The summer before the twins were born, he built an ultralight. You couldn't really see anything from a Piper or a Cessna, he'd muttered; but from an open cockpit, flying at just 3,000 or 4,000 feet, so close to the land you'd be able to see. He took $20,000 out of his retirement savings, bought a kit, and built the plane.

On its maiden flight, the aircraft bounced hard off the ground several times before Verle managed a takeoff. Half of one wing was gone by the time he landed. Charlene left the field, drove herself home, and vowed never to watch him go up in that thing again.

The plane became reason for much family eye-rolling. And fear. We thought it was a crazy stunt. Somehow he'd really gone and done it this time. Even while taking care of all the grandkids, he had too much time on his hands, wasn't that it? And he'd had to go and find a big project, and now someone might get hurt because of it. He might get hurt. Or one of the children might.

Toward the end of my pregnancy, I was as huge as the front of a ship with those twins inside me, and stuck indoors for two months on bed rest. Verle and Charlene had stopped into New York City to visit me. "Don't you take my daughter up in that plane," I said. Those may have been my last words to him.

But when Verle died, everyone suddenly understood that we'd had it wrong about the plane. He did see the beautiful constellations of ordinary life looking down from it. He would practice and repair and work out the aeronautical kinks. He was not a quitting man, after all. When the craft was safe, he planned to take each of us up. One by one. He would let us know the true speed of flight. We would buzz that familiar backyard. And from a suitable distance, he could show us what we had.

TOM JUNOD

Keep It Simple, Stupid

● ● ●

I did not know what to do when my father-in-law died of cancer ten years ago. I do not mean that I was at wit's end, or overcome by grief; I mean that I did not know how to act.

I knew how I wanted to act, certainly; I wanted to act as my brother had acted, when his own father-in-law had died suddenly a few years earlier. He had come apart. He didn't have to worry about how to act, because he didn't have to worry about how to grieve—grief had been loosed upon him, and he could only succumb to its ransacking force. Grief even strained his marriage, because his wife had to console her husband instead of mourning her father. I do not remember how the rest of her family regarded the extravagance of his emotion; I do, however, remember that my own parents were impressed, until they grew concerned. In the ethos of my family, self-possession is a suspect commodity in times of crisis or loss. A person who keeps control of himself is simply one who does not care enough—does not love enough—to lose control. By the lights of my family, my brother's precariously public display of his private agony was proof of the legitimacy not only of his feelings, but also of his character. There was no doubting my brother's essential goodness. Nor was there any doubting his love for his father-in-law; there was only concern, after a while, that his love was misspent. A father-in-law is not a father; a mother-in-law is not a mother. My father and mother worried less that my brother had come apart than that he had come apart for the wrong cause, the wrong person— that he had come apart for someone other than them. Or as my father said, "If he acts like this for his father-in-law, what's he going to do when *I* go?"

I wanted to grieve as my brother had grieved, because I wanted everyone to know how much I had loved my father-in-law—because I wanted everyone to know that love was what he deserved. My father-in-law, George Folk, was in some ways a difficult man. (Okay, I'm pussyfooting: "In what ways was he *not* difficult?" my wife, Janet, just asked.) He was closer to six-five than he was to six-four, and he was one of those tall men whose height conveyed not only distinction but also apartness. He slept in a bed designed to accommodate him, and he never stooped. His vanity was purely physical, expressed in his grace as a tennis player and his power as a golfer, but he was also of the generation for whom vanity itself was a secret indulgence. He was intimidating, but not confident. He had eyes of unclear coloration, with the sad, soft expression of a giraffe. He was an insurance man, who wore the same meticulously preserved brogans to work for nearly forty years, his thin hair slicked with arrowroot he bought at an odd-lot store. He cultivated a small, neatly trimmed mustache—white when I knew him—and a whole raft of eccentricities to go with it: he behaved as if his dearest aspiration was to become a British character actor. He was a harrumpher. Both finicky and maddeningly imprecise in his speech, he sounded, even in the most casual conversation, as though he were reading from an instruction manual—if he'd had to describe his own style of speaking, he'd have called it "highly irregular." He was extremely sensitive, in the sense of being highly strung, rather than poetical; as a result, he did not like most music, especially music played on piano, and sometimes made a public show of putting his fingers in his ears at loud restaurants. The only song I knew him to like was "Fernando," by Abba, because his despised middle name was Ferdinand, and the song made it sound heroic. He found it easy to speak to strangers, hard to speak to his family. He was cheap—unabashedly and extravagantly cheap—and sometimes seemed to buy his off-brand cars (a Rambler, an AMC Hornet, and a German Taunus) for the purpose of embarrassing his three children. Because he was all too willing to admit de-

feat in emotional matters, he came across as emotionally
withholding, and what he gave his children to deal with—
the difficulty of his legacy—was what they called his "nega-
tivity." Although he admired those for whom the glass was
half full, he did not trouble himself with fine distinctions:
for him, the glass was not only half empty, but, as he might
say, "well on its way toward complete evaporation." He was
predisposed to seeing the worst in everything (though not
everyone). His family hoped he was happy, but was forced to
wonder if he was. As possible compensation to his saturnine
temper, he liked to smoke, and he liked to drink. He quit
both, but the former he quit not soon enough, and in August of 1995 he caused the wedding of his son Jon (whom
he called "son Jon") to be postponed when he turned
around on his way from Florida to New York because he
was not feeling well. "I'm just not feeling well!" he said when
pressed by his children to elaborate, but in this case his difficulty with ordinary communication did not obscure his
point. He had lung cancer, inoperable and untreatable, and
in three months this impeccably flawed near-giant was dead.

Did I love him? I did. I did not tell him then, when he
was sick, nor did I think to. I simply tried to do my
duty. I went down to Florida as often as I could, and raised a
stink when I saw his bare feet hanging off the end of the
short bed at the nursing home to which his HMO consigned
him once he was classified a terminal case. I stayed by his

bedside when Janet needed a rest, and one afternoon I was employed as amanuensis when he dictated a last letter to his friends, a letter that ended with the words "I wouldn't have changed a thing. I wouldn't have missed it—any of it—for the world."

I had never seen death at such close hand before. It had never touched my immediate family. And although my parents were older than either of my in-laws, I had never even been able to intimate that one day they *might* die, without fear of giving grave offense. They were committed—and committed everyone else in my family—to a policy of ignoring death's prospect, as a way of insisting on their immortality; if what they owed the dead was their tears, what they owed death itself was their denial. I was so indoctrinated to their way of thinking that George's insistence on preparing for death as soon as he found out that he was sick struck me as something close to a betrayal, or at least a last concession to his overall gloominess. It turned out to be anything but. In the end, he told each of his children that he loved them. He told his friends he loved them, and he told life that he loved *it*. In the last words he ever spoke to me, he told me to take care of his daughter. When he died, at home, in the care of a hospice nurse, with son Jon asleep by his side, his family was able to refer to a letter he had written long before his illness, instructing them to "employ the KISS method," when it came to remanding him to his final rest. The KISS method, as his wife and children well knew, meant, "Keep it simple, stupid." There would be no wake, no funeral, no coffin, no extravagance. There would be a short memorial service, and after that George Folk was gone.

I wanted more. I wanted more of everyone, and more of myself. I wanted the family I married into to be more than briskly efficient, more than functional, more than dutiful; I wanted it to be *wounded,* by irrevocable loss. I wanted to know that maybe my own family—where love was not necessarily consistent with functionality—was not so strange after all, and so, when I flew to Florida the night before the memorial service, I did so intending to be an emissary for my family's way of doing things. It was a confusing effort. I did my best to be strong when Janet picked me up at West Palm Beach International, and then, when we reached her parents' home in the disorienting whitewashed sprawl of the retirement community called Boynton Beach Leisureville, I did my best to be weak. My mother-in-law, Helen, happened to be standing in the middle of the living room floor when I arrived. Upon seeing her, I dramatically ditched my luggage by the front door and stumbled toward her, with my arms spread wide open. I navigated the five or six steps that separated us by sort of falling forward, like a toddler, and when I reached her I simultaneously engulfed her in a bear hug and released most of my weight against her. I wasn't acting; I was waiting for a cue. If she'd so much as sniffled, I was ready to let go with the full complement of tears. She didn't sniffle. She didn't move. Where I expected to settle into an embrace softened by the acknowledgment of shared loss, I encountered only spine, steely and straight. She was holding *me,* and when I rested my head against her shoulder, she patted my back, and said, in sympathy, "Aw, Tom." I responded by tightening my bear hug, and it was then that I felt a conclusive stiffening: "Okay," she said, as in, "Let go"; as in, "That's enough"; as in, "I know what you're up to, and we don't go in for that sort of thing here." I let go, and gained a fresh look at my mother-in-law Helen, my brother-in-law Jon, my sister-in-law Lee Ann, and my wife Janet. There wasn't a wet eye in the house, and I, for the first time in my life, knew exactly how I felt in the face of death: right at home.

My wife Janet is not an unemotional woman. On the contrary, she is ardent, and easily moved. In our relationship, she was the first to declare her affection—"I like you, I like you a lot"—and then her love. Over the years, I have too many times experienced the pain of seeing her cry from sadness, and, less frequently, the privilege—the blessing—of seeing her cry from joy. She is capable of being overwhelmed by tears, suddenly, from stories she reads in the newspapers, from movies, from the misfortunes of friends, and from criticism she regards not simply as unfair but as unjust. Her sobbing, when it spills forth, tends to be seismic: a breaking of the mask of her composure. It starts almost as if she's been stung, radiating out from some smarting spot on the bridge of her nose, until it involves— and transforms—her entire face. Her skin turns pink, her hair goes back to being blond, and her eyes, listed "hazel" on her license, turn a desolate and almost stonewashed shade of blue. We've been married twenty years, and together twenty-seven, and I've never been less than amazed by the way her tears restore the shock of meeting her, when I was still a boy.

I had never met anyone like Janet Folk, when I first started dating her my freshman year in college. I had gone to Catholic school in Long Island. In my mind, human beings were Irish or Italian, unless they were Jews. Janet was Protestant. Half Scandinavian—Finnish, yet—she was very blond, and five feet, ten inches tall. She wore no makeup, and did not pierce her ears. Although when I first went to college I'd never even had a close Jewish friend, Janet made me understand the forbidden thrill of dating a shiksa. She was my idea of unobtainable, because she was my idea of all-American. She was so normal as to seem exotic, and her family was so normal as to seem downright alien. They were the Folk family, and although they were beneficiaries of an immigrant ancestor possessed of enough foresight to understand that "Fock" would create problems for his descendants, they did their best to live up to their forthrightly generic surname. They were *all* tall, with an allure that was part WASP, part Mennonite. They all prided themselves on their plainness and practicality, their thrift, and their ability to read maps. The men knew how to fix things, and the women knew how to clip coupons. The first time I called the house, I did so at six-thirty, only to be told by Mr. Folk that my phone call was "interrupting the dinner hour." He hung up. I called right back. My own family did not set aside a dinner hour. We ate dinner, and if it took about an hour, it was also open to the intrusions of the newspaper and the telephone and the hi-fi, not to mention the interruptions of my father's bookie. I was stunned when I first had dinner with the Folks, not just because of the vast white spaces that bracketed each plate's orderly assortment of meat, vegetable, and starch. What surprised me were the spaces in the conversation. In my house, there was no shortage of talk, even of debate, but it was discursive to say the least, as might be expected when the subject being debated was the possibility of the action driving the point spread of the Notre Dame game from seven to seven and a half. In Janet's house, they didn't talk as much as we did, but when they did talk, they talked to one another. More to the point, they *stopped* talking when someone else talked—they listened, even when the subject of conversation was the supermarket sale that tempted Mrs. Folk to buy slivered almonds for the rice instead of buying them whole and slivering them herself. The reasonable procedure of one person speaking while others listened—or of one person asking a question and another person volunteering an answer—rang in my ears as a disconcerting variation of silence. I had to learn how to do it when I visited the Folks, just as Janet had to learn how to keep talking over continual interruptions when visiting the Junods, and the continual effort that we had to devote to mastering each other's families charged our relationship from the start. Janet and her siblings were the second-generation spawn of immigrants, but they seemed settled, almost Middle American. I was the son of parents who never considered themselves anything *but* American—who never bothered to trace the family tree one branch beyond their own parents—and yet wound up comporting themselves with hectic immigrant energy. We each found in one another an inkling of some other America, a taste of what our own families had withheld. Janet was drawn to my family because she wanted to find out if human beings could watch three television sets showing three different football games during the dinner hour and still survive; I was drawn to Janet's family because I wasn't sure if I *could* survive the three televisions and the three football games, and the Folks offered the refuge of sanity.

Even among people as sane as the Folks, however, sanity had its degrees and distinctions, like snow among the Eskimos. Janet, Jon, and Lee Ann boasted a *relative* sanity—that is, they were pretty sane, for Long Islanders. As it turned out, George pursued sanity to the point of eccentricity and beyond. Helen Folk was another story. Her sanity was an absolute. She was, without a doubt, the least eccentric human being I have ever known, which is not to say that she was lacking in human qualities. It is to say that the human qualities she possessed, she embodied, so that, say, "fairness" was not an abstraction, but something as ordinary in her hands as soap. She was, above all, a Finn and a nurse. Or a nurse and a Finn. I could never be sure which was the defining pole of Helen's identity, after motherhood. Her parents, the Mannistos, had immigrated from Finland, part of the generation of Finns who had come to the United States to work as domestics in rich people's houses. She hadn't spoken English until she went to elementary school, and still spoke Finnish when in the company of her mother, Hilma. Her children were able to ape the incomprehensibility of that isolated and isolating language—its inelegant tongue-wagging vowels and its skittery, tongue-tying consonants—but could neither comprehend nor speak it, except for two words: *bempoo,* for rear end, and *nookooma,* for sleep.

The Finnish race was notoriously dour, notoriously contradictory, notoriously fatalistic, notoriously proud of its capacity for self-effacement, notoriously suspicious of the dirty trick of joy, notoriously willing to pursue the ideal of silence until silence itself seemed an empty vanity. True Finns weren't silent, for silence attracts attention; true Finns, being partial to anonymity, were simply noiseless, especially as they went about their labors, which they preferred to think of as their ceaseless toil. Helen, of course, was a true Finn, not only for the traits she inherited and the language she tried to discard, but also because of the labor she chose. That she was smart enough to have done anything, or been anybody, was an article of deep faith with her children. Instead, toward the end of the Second World War—and just about ten years after American schools taught her how to speak a completely unaccented English—she went to Adelphi University on a full nursing scholarship, and was still working at a local hospital when I met her. Two days during the week, and then on Sundays, she cooked a dinner that George could reheat for the kids, then changed into her whites and worked from three to eleven, waiting till she came home to eat her dinner, cold, while listening to Jean Shepherd or Larry King on the radio. Janet and the rest of them were always ambivalent about their mother's nursing career, because it took her away from them, and because it spoke of economic necessity. The Folk children grew up learning to hate Sundays, and to deemphasize the significance of Christmas Day, which was the holiday Helen owed to the hospital. It was only later that Janet came to realize that nursing was the language Helen tried to bequeath her. It was not Finnish, but it was a demonstration of Finnishness in action. And it left Janet irrevocably prejudiced toward deeds, rather than words, even when dealing with my family, which trafficked in a language wholly alien to her ears: the language of good intentions, where the prevailing tense was the subjunctive, and the subjunctive was never meant to be binding.

I was trying on a second language for myself when I first met Helen. I was trying to become a writer, which meant that I was looking for a language that I could call my own— a language that was singular, instead of tribal; a language that I didn't have to answer for, except as an expression of myself. Of course, I didn't know what I was doing; indeed, because my family had no aesthetic ideals or pretensions beyond the possibility of perpetual health, I probably knew less than many other kids who hear a similar calling. But if I was born into the kind of household that produces writers without nourishing them, I gravitated to the kind of family that does precisely the opposite. Here's what I remember from my first visit to the Folks: they had *books*. And not just any books—not the crunchy beach-curled paperbacks by Sheldon and Robbins that piled up next to my mother's side of my parents' king bed. These were books of a particular kind; books purchased through Book-of-the-Month Club, by a subscriber in good standing to the *Saturday Review.* There were the massive histories and biographies; there were the multivolume editions of Shakespeare and English-language poetry; there were the dictionaries, grammars, stylebooks, puzzle books, and the inevitable Bartlett's. And they were all in *hardcover.* And Helen had read them.

I was smitten. I had never met anyone with intellectual cachet before, much less a mother whose intellectual cachet was acknowledged by her own children. Helen was not in any way a glamorous woman; tall, but not as tall as Janet—about five-eight—she, like her daughter, abjured makeup, and neglected to pierce her ears. She wore big square eye-glasses, and routinely frayed her thin hair with brave, mis-guided permanents. Her long face was already slightly puckered and pouched by her thirty-odd years of deter-minedly smoking cigarettes, and she already had a scary cough. She tended to wear big-pocketed long sweaters, and long pants, both in deferential colors that might have had the brightness boiled out of them—the mauves and greens that all seemed to aspire to the state of being brown. A vinyl handbag swung protectively from her shoulder on a short strap. She wore her nursing shoes even when she wasn't on call, and the shoes she wore when she wasn't wearing nurs-ing shoes were in the same style as her nursing shoes, though in beige instead of white: her nod to fashion. She never wore high heels, and she never wore a dress. She stood for a prac-ticality raised nearly to the level of fancy—for the intellectual upside of what used to be called household management.

She had the kind of sturdy charisma that is earned and cultivated by people who are smarter than the requirements of
their station, and know it. She had a special place in her own
household, a special place accorded to her by her own husband and children, who not only respected her judgments,
but deferred to them. She had something that I wanted—
freedom and distance, even among those who loved her, and
those she loved—and she didn't get it the way my father got
it, through physical obsession, through the exercise of absolute domestic power, and through vice. She got it by
watching *Upstairs, Downstairs* and all the rest of the shows on
Masterpiece Theatre. She got it by finishing the *New York Times*
crossword every Sunday in pen. She got it by playing bridge
every Friday night, expert and fierce. She got it by winning,
invariably, at Scrabble and, later, Trivial Pursuit. She got it
by making intelligence her one and only vanity. She got it,
above all, by reading books—by leading what seemed back
then the life of the mind.

She was not the kind of person who overtly encouraged
my own intellectual ambitions, because she did nothing
overtly, and besides, she was not in the business of promoting dreams at the expense of practical considerations. She
must have known that I was going to marry her youngest
daughter, so she wanted to be sure that I could make a living.
I'm not sure it mattered to her whether I ended up as a
writer or as a salesman, as long as I could say that I was tol-
erably happy, and Janet could say the same. (I'm confident
that she would have named tolerable happiness a tolerable
aspiration: why ask for more?) When I did in fact become a

salesman right after college—a handbag salesman, following in the footsteps of my father and brother—she evinced no disappointment, and indeed showed nothing but pride when, for my first Christmas gift as a working man, I gave her the first all-leather handbag she ever owned. What she gave me, for her part, was a subscription to a periodical and a book. The periodical was *The New York Review of Books*, which I'd asked for, and which I read, on the road, in steakhouses from Amarillo to Lake Charles to Tulsa to Little Rock—the compass of my prohibitively large territory. The book? I forget the name of the book, though I'm sure I got whatever title I requested, because that's what Helen gave me every Christmas for twenty-seven years: a subscription (first the *New York Review*, and then, until I started working there, *Esquire*) and a book. I never got anything else, and once I lost my sales job, I never gave her another handbag. I gave her books. We had discovered a mutual greed, and a system of barter meant to satisfy it, once a year, on holidays. I never gave Helen novels, because although she read them occasionally, she always seemed disappointed to find out they weren't true. She'd had to suspend her dogged accrual of *facts*, and for that insult she gave every novel she ever read the same leveling brush-off, whether it was by Philip Roth or Nelson DeMille: *"Eh,"* which, as far as I knew, was Finnish for "What's the big deal?" She was a nonfiction gal, all the way, and for most of my adult life, I didn't take a step through the sober-minded sections of bookstores without seeing some impossible tome in terms of its ultimate place on Helen's nightstand. She was a more voracious reader than

I was; once she retired she also had more time, and so she became the proxy for my own laggardly ambitions. Year after year, I gave her the books I knew I'd never slog through, and by God, she read them all. Books on the Holocaust, books on immigration, books on the Depression, books on New York City, books on trade unions, books on hurricanes and fires and disasters of all kinds: you know, the heavy lifting. Jonathan Raban's *Old Glory,* and then, twenty years later, his story of drought and misery on the Plains, *Bad Land.* E. O. Wilson's sociobiological memoir, *On Human Nature.* Karen Armstrong's *A History of God.* The three volumes of Robert Caro's biography of Lyndon Johnson. I can remember the titles of most of the books I gave her, because I gave selfishly: I gave Helen books as a way of giving them to myself. You hear of writers who keep in mind, as they write, an Ideal Reader, someone real or imagined whose needs determine the shape of their sentences. Well, that was Helen, except that I didn't write for her—she read for me. It was a relationship at once abstract and intimate, with expectations, at least on my part, of immortality, because *books* are immortal. With its firmly delineated contours, it was also one of the easiest relationships I've ever had with another human being, and when, about two years ago, Helen called and instructed me not to buy her any more fat hardcover books because she was no longer strong enough to lift them, there was a part of me that said, "Well, who am I going to give them to, then?"—a part of me that wanted to ignore the reality of Helen's health, and keep spilling books on her sickbed, as a way of keeping her alive.

My own parents never gave books as gifts. They were dogged about it. Every year, my mother asked me what I wanted for Christmas, and when I told her, she always responded with a peevish silence, a mildly disappointed sigh. A few days later, she'd call Janet, and ask the same hopeful question. "Books," Janet would insist, prompting my mother to go out and buy me a sweater. It wasn't that she was against reading; indeed, if I was an early reader as a child, it was at my mother's encouragement. My parents just felt that books were modest things, stocking stuffers at best, not suitable for placement under the Christmas tree. Books did not lend themselves to the big production, and the big production was exactly what my parents were about. Although they would never think of themselves as complicated people, they managed to complicate the simplest action or event by the mere fact of their presence. Books weren't proper gifts because they promoted self-sufficiency and required silence, substituting their own narrative for the drama unfolding inevitably in the kitchen. A sweater, on the other hand, could be incorporated into the drama in the kitchen, because it gave rise to questions—beginning with "Do you like it?"—which gave rise to answers, which gave rise to doubt, which gave rise to controversy.

Understandably, then, Janet and I were very anxious when we first introduced our parents to one another. My guess is that each of us were slightly embarrassed by them, or by how true they were to type: the Junods loud, the Folks quiet; the Junods extravagant, the Folks cheap; the Junods flashy, the Folks modest; the Junods reckless, the Folks prudent; the Junods indulgent, the Folks (lately) abstemious; the Junods dedicated to ignoring the bulwark of privacy the Folks valued above all; and on and on. To each of us, our own parents seemed so extreme that we could imagine no common ground between them. But not only did they enjoy each other's company; much to our surprise, they sought it out, without first asking permission of their children. Not long after Janet and I married, both the Folks and the Junods retired, and moved from Long Island to Florida; there, free of our meddling, and just thirty-five miles apart, they began to see each other socially. The prospect was somewhat horrifying: matter and anti-matter, united at last, through the auspices of the early-bird special. We no longer worried about the possibility of their mutual regard; now we worried about their survival. Janet, in particular, was afraid that my parents, by superior force, would overwhelm her parents' meager defenses.

As it turned out, our parents got along because they recognized one another as exotics, in a way they couldn't recognize themselves. There was something almost anthropological in their relationship: the day after their meeting, they would each call their children with a report. We couldn't imagine what they did together, but in fact their "dates" tended to follow a fairly typical course, with the Folks deferring to the logistics of the Junods' vices: that is, my father would take Janet's father to buy Lotto tickets, and my

KEEP IT SIMPLE, STUPID • 289

mother would take Janet's mother shopping at flea markets. The Folks would end up neither gambling nor buying, but my parents, in their reports, could not help but be charmed: my father by George's eccentricities—"Oh, he comes out with some stuff!"—and my mother by Helen's intelligence, practicality, and preternatural calm, not to mention her talent for silence. As for Helen and George: my parents wore them out with their relentless *doings,* which sometimes took twelve hours to accomplish. When Helen called on what was termed "the day after," Janet would always ask, "What are you doing?" to which came the inevitable and invariable reply: "Recovering."

It took two days, usually. The Folks wouldn't golf after my parents went home; they wouldn't go out to dinner. Their resources were tapped out, because their resources weren't endless. Janet's family insisted on handling things, so none of them could handle much. They were daunted by *a lot*—a lot of activity, a lot of food, a lot of noise, a lot of stimulation, a lot of everything but sleep. My parents were the opposite. They didn't handle anything, so they could handle everything. It didn't matter what tasks were set before them, because they were so endlessly resourceful in putting them off; it didn't matter what situation they found themselves in, because they never accepted the consequences. They were always hopeful, heedless, profligate; they had startling energy, startling youth, startling vigor. They were almost ten years older than Helen and George, and thought of themselves as ten years younger. They sought not to deal with trouble, but to simply outlast it, and so they have wound up outlasting *everything,* including their financial resources, and including Helen and George.

It is supposed to be inspiring, and it is in a way: My parents have not gone gentle into that good night. They have no intention of *going,* period. They have made no concessions to old age because they refuse to see old age coming. One day it will just surprise them—and *then* they will rage, rage, at the dying of the light.

The undying energy they've devoted to the simple act of *refusal* is, as such, my inheritance. I've received the blessing that Dylan Thomas asked for, and then some, to the extent that they refuse to even indicate where and how they would like to be buried, for fear that an inch's concession will dispatch them the fatal mile.

It was different with Helen, to say the least. To fight against the end, she prepared for it. She made plans, choices, decisions, firmly and decisively. The first one came right after George died: in separate phone calls to her children, she warned each of them against trying to move her from Florida. She didn't want to live with her children. She wanted, quite specifically, to live without them—to live, for the first time in her adult life, alone. She wanted to golf, as long as she could. She wanted to play bridge. She wanted to read the newspaper, and do crossword puzzles. She especially wanted to read. There were no other men, of course. There was no mention of other men, although Helen lived in a sprawling retirement community famed for the legions of widows ready to carry seductive casseroles to the latest widower's door. There was, in truth, rarely a mention of George, unless his name came up anecdotally. Helen never admitted missing him, until one time Janet came out and asked her if she did. "At night," she answered. "In my own way."

We never asked again, and I don't imagine anyone else did, either. She guarded her privacy by living in the public spirit, and took care of her neighbors, as a way of making sure they left her alone. I had always been taught "never volunteer" by a father who had gone through the Second World War and had learned that a raised hand was the surest sign of a sucker. Helen, though, used volunteerism as a basis of emotional thrift: a means of conserving some of the resources she spent, spending some of the resources she conserved. She *always* raised her hand, and found her freedom in service—as a servant. She was the distribution manager for the community newspaper, in Leisureville. She ferried little old ladies to the supermarket. She took blood pressures and took an annual accounting course so that she could do the taxes of people who could no longer figure them or pay to have them figured. She even volunteered to do my father's taxes, and so knew, long before I did, the emptiness of his accounts. She did not warn me of the reckoning to come, and I didn't expect her to. There was something inviolate about Helen, and I would no sooner have asked her to compromise the confidentiality she promised my father than asked her what she thought each night, when she drifted off to sleep in her single bed.

By all appearances, she was a liberated woman—or, rather, a woman who had liberated herself from emotional encumbrance. Does this mean that she was cold? That's a tough one. She was emotionally guarded, certainly, but even her children had trouble figuring out what she was guarding. They each had their crises, as adults, and they each could have used more from their mother. They each wanted more, especially Janet. Throughout her thirties, she—and I—faced the nullifying prospect of infertility, and it came to exist as a void inside her, a shadow whose precise black contours aped and very nearly swallowed her own. To this Helen offered: silence. She never brought it up unless Janet did first, and if Janet did bring it up, she only listened, with a sympathetic and uncomfortable and maddeningly neutral ear. Her wisdom tended toward the prescriptive, and so she was paralyzed by our paralysis. She was unable to address the crisis—any crisis—with words, and we were unable to conceive of any actions to ease our pain, beyond the actions initiated by the infertility specialist—actions that didn't work, and then didn't work for a *long time* and so eventually took the form of vigil. What Janet wanted, what I wanted, what we wanted from Helen was simply an acknowledgment that what we were facing was not mere misfortune but *tragedy,* a canceling thing, and that unless we were able to generate life our lives, as we knew them, were over. And she wouldn't give it. She didn't have it in her. To the threnodies I occasionally sang to her over the phone, she could only add a faint minor-key echo that sounded more wistful than bereaved: "Ah, Tom."

Echoes come from empty spaces, of course, but if Janet

saw it that way, she never said so to me or to her mother. She never threw herself against the unyielding mystery of Helen's emotional core, never mounted anything like an accusation. As we entered our forties, we, without ever quite saying so, dropped the dream of having a child of our own conception, and Janet dropped the dream of getting *more* from Helen. To Janet, it was a mark of growing up: realizing the limitations of a parent, and asking no more than what that parent was capable of. Helen was not capable of tears, or escalating her sympathy for us into something like grief. What she was capable of was absolute consistency. She might not have been there, for Janet's inestimable heartache, but she was always there, on the phone, when Janet called. There, on Monday mornings, to discuss the funny bits in the "Metro Diary" feature in *The New York Times;* there, to tell Janet not only how to scrape the stringy hide off a stalk of broccoli, but why it was worth the bother; there, to tell Janet nothing at all, or, even better, only what Janet asked; there, to be there. And she was there, particularly, on Sunday mornings, at precisely eleven o'clock, when she would give us her weekly call, announcing herself with the words "Florida calling," in the slightly warbly and intentionally off-key voice of a woman who seemed to have absorbed her style not from the femmes fatales of '40s movies, but from their comedic sidekicks. Once a week, week after week, year after year, for as long as she lived in Leisureville: "Florida calling" . . . so that we would know not only when she was there but also when she wasn't. It was just as Helen wanted it: silence being sufficient for unspoken understanding; unspoken understanding being sufficient for family efficiency. Without being told, without having to be told, we all knew that when the clock struck eleven on a Sunday morning and Florida *didn't* call, it was time to start calling hospitals.

About three years ago, Sunday morning came and went, and Florida didn't call. The other calls started: Lee Ann to Janet, Janet to Jon, Jon back to Lee Ann. "Have you heard from Mom?" None of them had. They called information. They called hospitals. They understood their tasks, and they went about them briskly, without panic or confusion. They finally found their mother at a hospital in Boynton Beach, weak, but cheerfully dispassionate in her account of what had happened the night before, because she accepted what happened the night before as an inevitability: She had been awakened by her inability to breathe. Over the years, the smoker's cough I'd heard when I first came courting her daughter had been as consistent as Helen herself, a track that never stopped playing—that never stopped monopolizing more and more of her time—as though in dreadful mockery of her preference for going without words. In the early '90s, she'd been diagnosed with chronic obstructive pulmonary disease, which is inclusive of emphysema, asthma, and chronic bronchitis; it was a terminal diagnosis, and now she was facing her terminus, or, more precisely, the onset of her disease's terminal phase. In the middle of the night, she couldn't stop coughing, and couldn't start breathing. She'd made it to the phone, and, as calmly as someone facing the possibility of choking to death could, summoned an ambulance. She was relieved to be in the hospital, because she was so tired—tired of coughing, tired of sipping air through the collapsed straw of her lungs. The doctor gave her massive doses of prednisone, and sent her home after a few days, quenched and temporarily relieved. Just as she did before her trip to the hospital, Helen treated her illness as no big deal, so much so that Janet was tempted to do the same, until one day—apropos a conversation about adoption, in which Janet pretended, as we both did in those days, that time wasn't also running out on *us*—Helen gently corrected her. "You know, Janet," she said, "I'm not going to live forever."

The rest of her life became an exercise in management: an orderly retreat. Thrift gave way to parsimony; she woke up every morning deciding how much to cut back her spending, against an account that was nearly depleted. I'm not talking about her money here. With her money, she became almost extravagant, buying herself a new car, sending large checks to her children every Christmas. Money she had, and so money she spent. What I'm talking about is her essence: the life force, as measured by the elemental ability to take oxygen from the air. Here, she was bankrupt; here, she was quite literally drowning in the debt accrued by her constant wet ransacking cough. So she began to relinquish that which her body could no longer support. She had given up golf long before she started frequenting the hospital; she had given up international travel after she went to Paris with friends and spent most of the time in a hotel room, her skin cold to the touch and as gray as primer. Now she gave up, in order: any kind of travel at all, including travel to the homes of her children in New York, Georgia, and New Jersey; distribution of the Leisureville newspaper; participation in the community program by which the little old ladies went to the store and got their blood pressure taken; her duties as accountant to the infirm; and then, finally, her weekly bridge game. It was not a letting go, quite: it was a strategy, reasoned and deliberate, and rather cool in its execution—an exercise in necessary fatalism. She kept grasping at more, by holding on to less, and so she eventually surrendered silence itself, to the creepily hissing pneumatic compressor that pushed oxygen into her lungs by way of a web of plastic tubing that ensnared her pristine home.

And yet, because she was a Folk, or a Finn, or a Folk and a Finn, routine asserted itself. Florida kept calling. The only difference: Occasionally, Florida called from the hospital. It was the new routine: the prednisone treatments would fill Helen with air, and then, after two months or so, the air would find a way to leak out, like the helium in a child's balloon. She was familiar to the 911 operators, on a first-name basis with the paramedics. There was even a new schedule: On the days when Florida failed to call at eleven o'clock sharp, we would wait for Florida to call at around two, after she left intensive care. The calls were sheepish in tone, as though she were in the hospital on account of her clumsiness—as a consequence of some pratfall—rather than her ongoing death by suffocation. Only when Janet asked, "Mom, do you want me to come down there?" would Helen acknowledge how dire her situation had become. Of course, she wouldn't be inclined to issue the acknowledgment in anything like *words,* any more than she'd be inclined to come right out and ask for Janet's company. No, she'd just say, "That would be nice," or "I'd like that," and to ears raised on silence those abashed sentences registered like cries for help.

She was as reliable an invalid as she'd been a mother, and so it was a shock how abruptly her new routine—instituted in the netherworld between home and hospital—ended. One night, in the middle of the night, she got up to go to the bathroom, and then didn't have the strength to lift herself off the seat. She exhausted herself on the toilet, fully aware, as a nurse, that exhaustion would be her personal toxin. I don't know exactly how long she sat there, alone. I do know that she tried to pull herself off the toilet seat by grabbing the salmon-colored bath towel hanging from the chrome rack in front of her. She succeeded in grabbing the towel, but it didn't hold; it slid off the rack, and she pitched forward onto the tile floor, to the sound of the chrome bar mercilessly spinning. Then she crawled—she had no choice but to crawl. She made it to the phone, in the dark, and then made it to the hospital, in the familiar ambulance. Even in extremis, she would not deviate from the routine that had become essential, in its familiarity—that had become her life. The hospital, though, was under no obligation to honor her steadfast effort. It did not admit her, her pulmonologist saying at last that he had done all he could. From the familiar emergency room, the familiar ambulance took her to the last, unfamiliar place: to a nursing home, to die.

Janet flew down to Florida, with our daughter, Nia, whom we had adopted from China five months earlier. We had dallied and procrastinated for years before adopting, but the drastic timeline of Helen's illness had restored our sense of urgency. Janet was terribly afraid that her mother would die without meeting our daughter, without seeing that her own daughter had finally *done something,* instead of wallowing in the pain of childlessness. It was never said, of course, but there was an aspect of leave-taking in the shy kiss Helen was able to bestow on Nia's forehead, without being able to hold her in her arms. I drove down the next day, with our dog. We were going to commit ourselves not merely to a nursing home vigil, but, rather, to a new routine. We would simply keep visiting the nursing home as long as we had to, relocating our lives to her house, until Helen was strong enough to go home with an aide. Helen, though, was having none of it. When I saw her in the nursing home, she was in many ways the same woman I'd known for the last twenty-seven years—she had, in her lap, a copy of the book I'd recently bought her, Russell Shorto's history of the Dutch settlement in New York, *The Island at the Center of the World,* and the crossword from the previous Sunday's *New York Times* was spread out on the bed. Yet the book was unfinished, and would remain so. The crossword was unfinished, and would remain so. The food on the tray was un-eaten, and Helen weighed 106 pounds. Her muscles were wasting—had wasted—away, accentuating the lankiness of her frame against an insufficient mattress; her skin was pa-pery, and mapped with scabs where it had simply given way. Mothers-in-law often expect their sons-in-law to render them services, and in this regard, anyway, Helen was typical during the two weeks she stayed in the nursing home. She expected me to be her messenger. With Janet, she was, by force of habit, a mother who extolled the forces of habit; with me, she was a dying woman who wanted it known, in no uncertain terms, that she was dying. There was very little small talk between us, very little small talk left. As soon as Janet would take her leave with Nia, Helen would train her gaze upon me, and I had a chance to register how stern it could be, how direct and frank and imploring. "You know, Tom, I'm running out of time. . . ." "You know, Tom, I don't know how much longer I have. . . ." And so, at the end of the day, I would operate on her tacit instructions, and first tell Janet what she had said, and then, on the phone, Lee Ann and son Jon.

There was no resistance from anybody. Well, anybody, that is, but my parents. I would call them from Leisureville, and when they asked how Helen was doing, I'd say rather heartlessly, "She's dying," provoking the same responses every time: "God forbid" or "Don't talk like that." No mat-ter how many times I told them that Helen was in the end stages of a terminal illness, they could not be prevailed upon to contemplate the finality, until one night, when my mother at last answered my insistent alarm in terms as innocent as a child's: "But she was such a *nice* woman." And then she began weeping, as though Helen, cursed by the act of concession, was already gone.

We still hoped that she could come home to die. We arranged for an aide. On a Wednesday, Helen had her seventy-ninth birthday. But by Thursday afternoon, her breathing had grown so labored that Helen, for the first and last time in her life, lost the self-possession most precious to her. "Janet," she asked, "what is *happening* to me?"

Very late that night Helen was admitted to hospice. Jon arrived at around the same time, Lee Ann on Friday morning, in the company of a woman named Pat, the family friend we intended to be Helen's aide when Helen returned home. Helen recognized Pat immediately, from a visit of a few years before, and said, between numbered breaths, "Pat, you're not still smoking, are you? Look at me, Pat. You don't want to wind up like this."

She was still ingrained in the habit of service, in the habit of dividing life into *tasks,* but now the tasks—even the task of her birthday—were nearly complete: she was in the company of her son, her daughters, and then Nia, her daughter's daughter. On Friday night, Jon and Lee Ann visited her after dinner, but Helen tired quickly and asked them to leave: "I want to go *nookooma.*"

Nookooma: Finnish for sleep.

Later that evening, Janet, Lee Ann, Jon, and I drank beer as Nia slept in her portable crib. At eleven o'clock the phone

rang, in a house restored, in the snap of an instant, to silence. Janet picked up. She was very polite. "Okay," she said.
"Thank you." She looked at us, and winced. "Mom's gone,"
she said, her voice twisted by its pang into something like an
apology. Helen Dagmar Folk—the racy middle name as eccentric to her legacy as the milquetoasty "Ferdinand" was to
her husband's—had been speaking to the hospice nurse, until the nurse excused herself for a moment. She died alone,
as though not to be a bother. It was May 21, 2004. She was—
just—seventy-nine years old.

Oh, Janet wept. She wept when she went along with her
brother and sister to identify her mother's body, and
realized that what she saw in front of her—what she
touched—"wasn't Mom," as she told me later. She wept
when she opened the steel file box in Helen's closet, and
found that neither she nor Jon nor Lee Ann would have to
make any decisions in her mother's stead—all the decisions
had been made, in terms as blunt and straightforward as
possible. Helen spoke from the grave as evenly and reason-
ably as she'd spoken from the kitchen table, except that
there wasn't a grave: like her husband, she instructed her
children to employ the KISS method, and so without further
ado she was cremated and deposited in a plain urn. Janet
wept at the short memorial service, too, with Nia in her
arms, as she told the crowd—assembled, mostly, from the
ranks of white-haired female survivors with whom Helen

associated—that she would consider her life a success if she were half the mother to Nia that Helen had been to her.

I didn't. Weep, that is: I didn't shed a tear for my mother-in-law. Even when I spoke at the memorial service, testifying to the degree that Helen influenced and taught me, and then promising that I'd never forget either her or her lessons, a tear advanced to one of my eyes, but went no farther. Since then, I've *never* shed a tear for Helen. I've often come upon Janet, in her grief, at the odd times and in the odd places that suggest she is always grieving; I've at times come to bed, late at night, and thought her asleep, only to hear her say, in the darkness, to the darkness, "I miss my mommy." I, on the other hand, have found myself missing Helen most exactly where I *found* her, in life—in bookstores. I have not gotten out of the habit of buying books for her, if only in my mind. I have not gotten out of the habit of coming across some impossibly capacious historical tome, and saying to myself, "This should last Helen a week," before realizing that I'll have to read it myself. Simon Sebag Montefiore's 816-page *Stalin: The Court of the Red Tsar*—that seemed like a good choice, for Helen. So did Steve Oney's *And the Dead Shall Rise,* twenty years in the making. So did Paul Hendrickson's *Sons of Mississippi.* So did Ron Chernow's biography of Alexander Hamilton, natch, as well as Joseph Ellis's of George Washington. A few of these books, I've actually gone out and bought. But I haven't read any of them, and I doubt if I ever will.

How do I feel when I quicken at the thought of sending a book to my collaborator in this great task of reading, only to realize that the collaboration died with the collaborator? I feel empty—empty and alone in the bookstore, like some-one who has tossed his voice across a canyon without hear-ing an echo in return—but never pained enough, never torched enough, to summon tears. I am, in fact, at the same place I was when I first met Janet: unsure of my capacity for grief. Oh, sure, I have grieved, rather spectacularly, rather indulgently, at the death of my dogs, and I have no doubt that I shall have to endure that vicious bite again. As for los-ing a member of my family: I watched Nia suffer a terrible fall a few months ago, and from the presentiment of grief I experienced before she landed unhurt, I knew that I could never have sustained the burden of my life had she fallen out of it.

I do not know, however, what to expect of myself, and what should be expected of me, in the event that I endure a loss that has to be endured—the loss, say, of my father and mother. Long ago, I would have considered the ability to en-dure the mark of some essential failing, a judgment upon the quality of my love for them, and theirs for me. I would have asked myself to fall apart. Now I would look askance at my own shattering, because to fulfill the expectations of my own family, I would have to violate the standards of the family I married into. Janet has always said that, unlike a lot of women, she didn't set out to marry a vestige of her father when she married me—she married her mother. I always figured she meant that she married someone who liked to read. It was not until I accepted my role in the various crises that have befallen our families over the last few years that I understood what she might be getting at. The sad, the terrible, the inexcusable fact: I am *good* at self-possession. I am good at doing my duty, and living up to my obligations. In crisis, I am determined to spend only what I have in reserve, and as such count as an oddity—albeit a calming, stable one—in my own family. I had to marry Janet Folk, to accept the DNA of a family less foreign. I had to mourn the death of my mother-in-law—without tears—to understand how diligently I went about the business of becoming something like her son.

Acknowledgments

• • •

I want to thank all the contributors to this book who embraced a dicey and tangled topic with great zeal. They allowed me to enter into their family lives by openly discussing, often at great length, their particular in-law dynamics. They were willing to work and re-work their essays until they conveyed—touchingly, humorously, honestly—the intimacy and complexity of each experience. I was deeply impressed by, and appreciative of, each writer's tenacious desire to get it right.

I also want to thank several people at Penguin who made this whole process feel easy. Jake Morrissey, my editor, who inherited this project but then took it on with all the smarts, care, and patience of an editor shepherding his own brainchild. David Moldawer, his assistant, who graciously and hyper-competently helped with all the logistics. Susan Lehman, my first editor, who came up with the excellent idea of a book about in-laws in the first place. Cindy Spiegel and Julie Grau, who showed enthusiasm and confidence throughout. Anna Jardine, Meredith Phebus, and Gary Mailman, for their hard work and fine attention to detail.

Thanks also to those whose thoughts helped me in many a pinch. Gillian Silverman, whose thoughtful reading and general excitement about this book were an ongoing source of encouragement. Maggie Jones and Vera Titunik, who helped out with needed feedback. Paul Tough, also a terrific reader, who introduced me to some of the contributors in this book. Sarah Chalfant, who also had great instincts about which writers might successfully contribute to this book. And Sam Stoloff, my husband, whose incisive editing and always calm and supportive manner helped make this project go smoothly. And also to Sam for giving me the kind of in-laws you can't live without—instead of the kind you can't live with.

About the Contributors

• • •

AMY BLOOM

Amy Bloom is the author of a novel, *Love Invents Us;* two short story collections, *Come to Me,* a National Book Award finalist, and *A Blind Man Can See How Much I Love You,* a National Book Critics Circle finalist; and a collection of essays. Her work has appeared in *The New Yorker, The New York Times,* and *The Atlantic Monthly,* and in *Best American Short Stories* and other anthologies. Bloom teaches at Yale.

MATT BAI

Matt Bai writes on national politics for *The New York Times Magazine.* He is currently at work on a book about the future of Democratic politics, which will be published by Henry Holt in 2007. He lives in Washington, D.C., with his wife and son.

MICHAEL CHABON

Michael Chabon is the author of two short story collections and four novels, including *The Mysteries of Pittsburgh, Wonder Boys, The Amazing Adventures of Kavalier & Clay,* which won the Pulitzer Prize for fiction, and the young adult novel *Summerland.* His most recent book is the novella *The Final Solution.* His novel *The Yiddish Policemen's Union* will be published by HarperCollins in spring 2006. Chabon's work has appeared in *The New Yorker, Harper's, GQ, Esquire,* and *Playboy,* and in a number of anthologies, among them the *O. Henry Prize Stories* and *Best American Short Stories.* He lives in Berkeley with his wife, the writer Ayelet Waldman, and their four children.

TA-NEHISI COATES

Ta-Nehisi Coates is a staff writer for *Time* magazine. He has written for *The Village Voice, The New York Times Magazine,* and the Washington *City Paper.* He is now working on a memoir. Coates lives in New York City with his partner, Kenyatta, and their son, Samori.

ANTHONY GIARDINA

Anthony Giardina is the author of the novels *Men with Debts, A Boy's Pretensions, Recent History,* and a story collection, *The Country of Marriage.* His stories and essays have appeared in *Harper's, Esquire, GQ,* and *The New York Times Magazine,* and in the recent anthology *The Bastard on the Couch.* He is also a playwright whose plays have been staged in New York at Playwrights Horizons and the Manhattan Theatre Club, and at Seattle Rep and the Long Wharf in New Haven. His novel *White Guys* will be published by Farrar, Straus & Giroux in 2006. Giardina lives in Northampton, Massachusetts, with his family.

JONATHAN GOLDSTEIN

Jonathan Goldstein lives in Montreal, where he is the host and producer of CBC Radio One's *Wire Tap,* a show that features his monologues and phone conversations. A frequent contributor to the radio program *This American Life,* he is the author of the novel *Lenny Bruce Is Dead,* which will be published in the United States in the winter of 2006.

COLIN HARRISON

Colin Harrison is a senior editor at Scribner's and the author of five novels: *The Havana Room, Afterburn, Manhattan Nocturne, Bodies Electric,* and *Break and Enter.* He lives in Brooklyn with his wife, the writer Kathryn Harrison, and their three children.

KATHRYN HARRISON

Kathryn Harrison is the author of the novels *Envy, The Seal Wife, The Binding Chair, Poison, Exposure,* and *Thicker Than Water.* She has also written the memoirs *The Kiss* and *The Mother Knot;* a travel memoir, *The Road to Santiago;* a biography, *Saint Thérèse of Lisieux;* and a collection of personal essays, *Seeking Rapture.* She lives in Brooklyn with her husband, the writer Colin Harrison, and their three children.

SARAH JENKINS

Sarah Jenkins is a pseudonym for a writer who lives in the Pacific Northwest.

BARBARA JONES

Barbara Jones has been an editor at *Grand Street, Vogue,* and *Harper's.* She was one of the founding editors of *Real Simple* and is an editor at *More.* Her essays, short stories, and criticism have appeared in numerous magazines, newspapers, and anthologies. Jones lives in New York City with her husband, the writer Steven Rinehart, and their three children.

TOM JUNOD

Tom Junod is a writer-at-large for *Esquire,* and has written for *GQ, Sports Illustrated,* and *Life.* He has been a finalist for the National Magazine Award nine times, winning twice. He and his wife, Janet, and their daughter, Nia, split their time between Marietta, Georgia, and Shelter Island, New York.

MARTHA McPHEE

Martha McPhee is the author of the novels *Bright Angel Time,* a *New York Times* Notable Book, and *Gorgeous Lies,* a National Book Award finalist. She has received fellowships from the National

Endowment for the Arts and from the John Simon Guggenheim Memorial Foundation. Her third novel, *L'America,* will be published by Harcourt in April 2006. McPhee received her MFA from Columbia University and teaches at Hofstra. She lives in New York City with her husband, the poet and writer Mark Svenvold, and their children.

PETER RICHMOND

Peter Richmond is a contributing writer for *GQ* magazine. His work has appeared in *The New Yorker, The New York Times Magazine, Vanity Fair, Rolling Stone,* and several anthologies, including *Best American Sportswriting of the Twentieth Century.* His third book, a biography of the late singer Peggy Lee, will be published by Henry Holt in 2006. He lives in Dutchess County, New York, with his wife, Melissa Davis.

DANI SHAPIRO

Dani Shapiro is the author of four novels: *Family History, Picturing the Wreck, Fugitive Blue,* and *Playing with Fire.* She is also the author of the bestselling memoir *Slow Motion.* Her work has appeared in *The New Yorker, Granta, The New York Times Magazine, Elle, O: The Oprah Magazine, House & Garden, Tin House, Ploughshares,* and *Bookforum,* among others. She has taught at Columbia, Bread Loaf, Bennington, and NYU, and currently teaches in the MFA program at New School University. Shapiro's work has been widely anthologized, and has been translated into seven languages. She is at work on a new novel.

DARCEY STEINKE

Darcey Steinke is the author of four novels, *Milk* being the most recent. *Up Through Water* and *Jesus Saves* were her *New York Times* Notable Books of the Year; *Suicide Blonde* has been translated into eight languages. Steinke's short fiction has appeared in *The Heretic's Bible, Story,* and *Bomb,* and her nonfiction has been featured in the *Washington Post,* the *Chicago Tribune, The Village Voice, Spin,* and *The New York Times Magazine.* Her Web project, Blindspot, was included in the Whitney Museum's 2000 Biennial. Steinke teaches at New School University and lives in Brooklyn with her daughter.

SUSAN STRAIGHT

Susan Straight is the author of five novels: *Aquaboogie, I Been in Sorrow's Kitchen and Licked Out All the Pots, Blacker Than a Thousand Midnights, The Gettin Place,* and *Highwire Moon,* which was a National Book Award finalist. Her novel *A Million Nightingales* will be published by Pantheon in 2006. Her essays have appeared in *The New York Times Magazine,* the *Los Angeles Times Magazine, Harper's, Real Simple, Family Circle,* and *Salon.* Straight was born in Riverside, California, where she still lives with her family.

AYELET WALDMAN

Ayelet Waldman is the author of the novels *Love and Other Impossible Pursuits* and *Daughter's Keeper.* A columnist for *Salon,* she lives in Berkeley with her husband, the writer Michael Chabon, and their four children.